SAINT THOMAS AQUINAS

SUMMA CONTRA GENTILES

BOOK THREE: PROVIDENCE
Part I

University
of
Notre Dame Press
Notre Dame
London

Translated,
with an Introduction
and Notes,
by
VERNON J. BOURKE

University of Notre Dame Press edition 1975

Copyright © 1956 by Doubleday & Company, Inc.

First published in 1956 by Hanover House as

On the Truth of the Catholic Faith

First paperback edition 1956 by Image Books

Published by arrangement with Doubleday & Company, Inc.

Printed in the United States of America

Library of Congress Cataloging in Publication Data

Thomas Aquinas, Saint, 1225?–1274.
    Summa contra gentiles.

    Reprint of the ed. published by Hanover House,
Garden City, N.Y., under title: On the truth of
the Catholic faith.
    Includes bibliographies.
    CONTENTS: book 1. God, translated, with an
introd. and notes, by A. C. Pegis. —book 2. Crea-
tion, translated, with an introd. and notes, by
J. F. Anderson. [etc.]
    1. Apologetics—Middle Ages, 600–1500. I. Ti-
tle.
[BX1749.T4 1975]   239   75-19883
ISBN 0-268-01675-5
ISBN 0-268-01676-3 pbk.

FOR JANET

Between
man and wife
there seems to be
the greatest
friendship

—SAINT THOMAS AQUINAS

Contents

Introduction

Book Three of St. Thomas' *Summa Contra Gentiles* contains a great deal of his practical thought. It is most important for the study of his moral, political, and social views. Moreover, since St. Thomas always keeps his practical science firmly grounded in his speculative views, the central teachings of his general theory of reality are continually summarized in this Book. While the subjects treated are all related to the general or particular functions of divine providence, they will be found to range over the whole area of ancient and mediaeval learning.

As in Books One and Two, St. Thomas is here expounding the teachings of his Catholic faith, and judging the errors of competing world views, by the use of natural reason and experience. However, two enlargements of his original purpose seem to occur in this Book. First, the use of Scripture grows quantitatively, and in importance, as the Book progresses. Toward the end, the reader is almost prepared for the shift to the more definitely Scriptural argument of Book Four. Secondly, the "Gentiles" seem to grow in number and in historical extent. A glance at the Bibliography of source works indicates this: if the Gentiles were originally a few Greek and Arabian and Jewish thinkers, they now include scientists, historians, Roman essayists, heretics of many brands, and the followers of strange religious cults. St. Thomas' canvas is much broader than many interpreters have realized.

If we consider, with necessary brevity, the situation in which he completed Book Three, we may better understand St. Thomas' purpose. When he left the University of Paris, in May 1259, Aquinas went to Valenciennes, where an important meeting of Dominican officials was held on

the first of June. It was decided there that study in the
liberal arts be required on the part of the younger monks
in all the provinces of the Order. This regulation meant
that more work in philosophy was henceforth to be done in
the Order of Preachers.[1] At about the same time, the Mas-
ter General, Humbert de Romans, wrote his explanation
of the Rule, in the course of which he stressed the value
of philosophical studies for the monks who could do them
well.[2] Later in the summer, Thomas went on to Italy,
presumably bringing a copy of the partly completed SCG
with him. We know that he spent the years 1261–1264
at the Dominican monastery in Orvieto, in which city
Pope Urban IV was in residence. This Pope was much
interested in philosophy and he appears to have encouraged
Thomas Aquinas, and others, to attempt to settle the problem which had annoyed scholars and ecclesiastical officials
for several decades. This was the question of the place to
be given Aristotle and the other philosophers in the program of Church studies.[3] William of Moerbeke, O.P.,
was apparently assigned to Orvieto, to make and revise
translations of Greek philosophical works. Moreover, St.
Albert the Great seems to have spent a good part of the year
1262 in Orvieto.[4] This was quite a gathering of talent and
it must have had some purpose. It is possible that the Pope
and the key men in the Dominican Order now realized
the need for a full-scale study of non-Catholic science and
learning. In any case, St. Thomas Aquinas was given the
opportunity and facilities to devote a great deal of his time,

1. See A. Walz, O.P., *Thomas von Aquin* (Basel: Thomas-
   Morus-Verlag, 1953), p. 67.
2. The pertinent passage from Humbert's *Expositio regulae B.
   Augustini*, on philosophical studies, is printed in C. Douais,
   Essai sur l'organisation des études chez les Frères Prêcheurs
   (Paris: 1884), pp. 175–177.
3. See F. Van Steenberghen, *Aristotle in the West*, trans. L. John-
   ston (Louvain: Nauwelaerts, 1955); and M. Grabmann, *I
   divieti ecclesiastici di Aristotele sotto Innocenzo III e Gregorio
   IX* (Roma: Università Gregoriana, 1941).
4. M. Grabmann, *Guglielmo di Moerbeke* (Roma: 1946), p. 46.

from 1260 to 1270, to commenting on Aristotle and other philosophers.

Apparently, Thomas had written a good part of the SCG before leaving Paris. Some think that he had completed it to Book Three, ch. 45, for that is the termination of a group of manuscripts in circulation at Paris.[5] There is little question that the rest of this Book, at least, was written in Italy. Among other reasons, it is clear that Thomas was now using translations of Aristotle's *Magna Moralia* (by Bartholomew of Messina) and *De animalibus* (by William of Moerbeke), which could not have been available to him in the first Paris period.[6] Hence, Book Three of SCG may have been begun as early as 1258–1259, in Paris, and it may not have been completed before 1263, at Orvieto. As a result of these circumstances, and of the evident personal interest of St. Thomas in the philosophical implications of his basically theological subject matter, it may be suggested that the SCG has now, in Book Three, become a most important product of the effort of Christian scholarship to confront the learning and science of the non-Catholic world, at a period when such confrontation had become almost inevitable.

The structure of Book Three is clearly indicated by St. Thomas in its first chapter.[7] It has three main divisions. The following analysis shows these divisions and their component treatises:

A. God as the end and good of all things (ch. 1–63)
   1. the end as good, contrasted with evil (ch. 1–16)
   2. God as the end of physical and intellectual things (ch. 17–25)
   3. man's ultimate happiness: what it is not (ch. 26–48)
   4. the vision of God and ultimate happiness (ch. 49–63)

5. M. D. Chenu, *Introduction à l'étude de saint Thomas d'Aquin* (Montréal-Paris: 1950), p. 251, note 1.
6. M. Grabmann, *Die Werke des hl. Thomas von Aquin*, Aufl. 3 (Münster: 1949), p. 293; *Guglielmo di Moerbeke*, p. 66.
7. SCG, III, ch. 1, ¶10; see Pegis, SCG, I, Introd., p. 38.

B. God's general government of things (ch. 64–110)

1. what providence does, and does not, do (ch. 64–74)
2. providence in relation to singulars, secondary causes, and choice (ch. 75–97)
3. God and actions apart from the providential order (ch. 75–110)

C. Providence and rational creatures (ch. 111–163)

1. divine law and the governing of rational beings (ch. 111–118)
2. man's obligations under divine law (ch. 119–129)
3. counsels of perfection and divine law (ch. 130–138)
4. merit, sins, and punishments (ch. 139–146)
5. grace and predestination (ch. 147–163)

Attention may be directed to three sections of primary importance in this Book. The first is the famous discussion of the end of man, in ch. 26–63. Two things are interesting in connection with this topic: its background and its foreground. St. Thomas drew extensively on a series of earlier works dealing with human happiness and the purpose of man's life. These included Book Ten of Aristotle's *Nicomachean Ethics*, Varro's lost work on ancient theories of the good life for man, which St. Thomas knew, as we do, through Book Nineteen of St. Augustine's *City of God*, and, finally, Book Three of Boethius' famous *Consolations of Philosophy*. Much of the technique and content of Thomas' treatment of the "goods of fortune, of the body, and of the soul" comes from this historical background. Even the view that man's final happiness consists in a continued act of intellectual contemplation is not new with St. Thomas.

Equally interesting, perhaps, have been the twentieth-century controversies arising out of this topic. One much-discussed problem in our day has centered in the relation of the natural and the supernatural aspects of man's last end. Such discussions can make valuable contributions to the understanding of St. Thomas' views on human nature and action, and to the development of a moral science contemporary in its applications, yet rooted in the wisdom of St. Thomas.

Closely related is the second topic, that of man's desire for the vision of God. In fact, this question is handled by St. Thomas in the later chapters (49–63) of the same section. He speaks of this desire as natural to man, yet he ends with a description of a vision which is supernatural in character. Much of the difficulty lies in the precise determination of the meaning of the term "natural." There has been much difference of scholarly opinion on this point, from the fourteenth century onward. On both these problems, for which SCG III is a central text in St. Thomas, it is only possible to refer the reader to a few modern studies as an introduction to the extensive literature of these discussions.[8]

A third quite important section of this Book is that in which St. Thomas treats moral problems under the precepts and counsels of divine law (ch. 114–138). Here, his moral teachings are arranged, not according to the virtues as in the Summa Theologiae, but under the Ten Commandments. Moreover, the treatment of several moral questions, notably those connected with matrimony, that is found in this Book is not surpassed by anything done later by Thomas Aquinas, since the questions in the Supplement to the Summa Theologiae dealing with such matters were compiled from Thomas' earlier Commentary on the Sentences.[9] Indeed, no student of the moral teaching of St. Thomas can afford to neglect SCG III.

A word about the natural science which runs through this Book may not be amiss. The astronomy, physics, biology, and other scientific information was the best that was available in his time. This is very largely material from Aristotle and his Greek and Arabian commentators.

8. See the accompanying Bibliography, sect. IV.

9. M. Grabmann, Die Werke, pp. 296–301.

St. Thomas was not a natural scientist; he was a theologian. Some of the scientific information that he used is surprisingly good; he knew that the moon shines with reflected light, that astronomers treated their own eye-level as mathematically equivalent to the center of the earth, and other such things. However, it is also clear that St. Thomas accepted the current views on celestial bodies as constituted of a different matter from terrestrial bodies, and that he thought these bodies in the heavens, such as the sun and moon, exercise considerable influence on physical and biological events on this earth—much more influence than scientists today would admit. It is difficult to determine to what extent he was misled by this science of his century. The histories of mediaeval science by L. Thorndike and A. C. Crombie do not suggest that it was a useless study.

The translation of this Book matches as closely as possible the style adopted by Dr. Pegis for Book One. It is a literal translation and no attempt has been made to "improve" the literary style of St. Thomas. Certain words presented a special problem, either because of their polyvalent meaning, or because modern English cognate terms have shifted their significance. The term esse has been translated as "being," "act of being," "existing being," and, in a few cases, "to be." Similarly, ratio is translated as "rational character," "formal character," "intelligible meaning," "rational plan," and even as "reason." Simpliciter, when contrasted with some relative expression such as secundum quid, is translated by the phrase "in an unqualified sense"; in a few cases, it is rendered as "absolutely" or "simply." An attempt has been made to avoid using "patient" for patiens, but it is sometimes so translated and the modern reader should be warned that a "patient" is not simply a person in a physician's waiting room. Though now the last meaning in Webster, it still signifies "the object or recipient of an action." Finally, operatio is usually translated as "operation," another term which is broader than its restricted surgical meaning.

In compliance with uniform editorial policy for the four Books of SCG, texts of Scripture are from the Douay-

Rheims version.[10] Some changes in punctuation and capitalization of divine names have been made without special note. In some cases, the Latin Bible quotations given in the text of St. Thomas differ somewhat from the Douay reading. In these cases, the Latin has been followed and such changes are indicated by the insertion of the words, "Douay modified." This does not imply any criticism of the Douay version; doubtless, St. Thomas frequently quoted Scripture from memory, or left blanks in his autograph manuscript to be filled by copyists.[11]

It is a pleasant duty to express my gratitude to some of those who have assisted with this translation: to my graduate class of 1952, to Mr. and Mrs. John S. Johnson for help in typing, to my wife, Janet, and my daughters, Jane and Nancy, for reading and checking the typescript.

VERNON J. BOURKE

Saint Louis University
1 August, 1955

---

10. *The Holy Bible*, New York, The Douay Bible House, 1941.

11. See the late Father Mackey's brief English study of this manuscript, which is listed in the Bibliography. He was one of the few men who could read it.

Bibliography

I. ST. THOMAS AQUINAS

The same standard editions of the Latin text of St. Thomas have been used in translating and annotating Book Three as are listed by Dr. Pegis in his bibliography for SCG I, p. 53. In addition, the following translations are cited in the footnotes:

Summa contra Gentiles, 5 vols., trans. by the English Dominican Fathers, London, Burns & Oates, and New York, Benziger, 1928–1929.

Contra Gentiles, Livre troisième, trans. M. F. Gerlaud, Paris, Lethielleux, 1951.

Of God and His Creatures, trans. J. Rickaby, S. J., St. Louis, Herder, and London, Burns & Oates, 1905. (An annotated translation of SCG, with some abridgement.)

Truth, Vol. III, trans. R. W. Schmidt, S. J., Chicago, Regnery, 1954. (De veritate, qq. XXI–XXIX.)

Basic Writings of St. Thomas Aquinas, 2 vols., edited by Anton C. Pegis, New York, Random House, 1945. (Vol. II, pp. 3–224, contains a revision of SCG III, ch. 1–113.)

II. THE SOURCES

In addition to the Berlin Academy printing of Aristotle, and the Venice printings of the Latin Averroes and Avicenna, as listed in SCG I, pp. 55–56, the following sources are cited in the footnotes:

Albumasar, Introductorium ad artem astronomiae, Augsburg, 1489.

Algazel, *Metaphysics* (Latin text), ed. J. T. Muckle, C. S. B., Toronto, Institute of Mediaeval Studies, 1933.

Avicebron, *Fons vitae*, ed. Cl. Baeumker (Beiträge, I, 2–4), Münster i. W., 1892–1895.

Bardenhewer, O., ed., *Die pseudo-aristotelischen Schrift über das reine Gute, bekannt unter dem Namen, Liber de Causis*, Freiburg i. B., 1882.

Bonaventure, St., *Opera Omnia*, 10 vols., Quaracchi, Typographia Collegii S. Bonaventurae, 1882–1902.

Cicero, *De inventione rhetorica*, Leipzig, Teubner, 1915.

Homer, *Odyssea*, Leipzig, Teubner, 1889.

Josephus, *Josephus*, ed. and trans. H. Thackeray and R. Marcus, Cambridge, Mass., Harvard University Press, 1926.

Maimonides, *Guide for the Perplexed*, trans. M. Friedländer, London, Routledge, 1936.

Ptolemaeus, *Liber quattuor tractuum (Quadripartitum) cum Centiloquio*, Venetiis, 1484.

Plato, *Opera Omnia*, ed. J. Burnet, Oxford, Clarendon Press, 1905–1913.

Sallust, *Bellum Catilinae*, Leipzig, Teubner, 1919.

Valerius Maximus, *Factorum et Dictorum Memorabilium libri novem*, Paris, Didot, 1841.

Christian writers in Latin (St. Augustine, Boethius, St. Gregory the Great, St. Jerome, Peter Lombard, Pelagius) are quoted from J. P. Migne, *Patrologia Latina*, 221 vols., Paris, 1844–1864 (abbreviated as *PL*).

Christian writers in Greek (Dionysius the Pseudo-Areopagite, St. John Damascene, Nemesius, whom St. Thomas cites as Gregory of Nyssa, and Origen) are quoted from J. P. Migne, *Patrologia Graeca*, 162 vols., Paris, 1857–1866 (abbreviated as *PG*).

III. SECONDARY STUDIES

Indices auctoritatum et rerum occurrentium in Summa Theologiae et in Summa contra Gentiles, in S. Thomae Aquinatis, *Opera Omnia,* t. XVI, ed. Leonina, Roma, apud Sedem Commissionis Leoninae, 1948.

Franciscus de Sylvestris Ferrariensis, *Commentaria in Summam contra Gentiles,* in ed. Leonina, tt. XIII–XV, Roma, 1918–1930.

Bourke, V. J., *Ethics,* New York, Macmillan, 1951.

Chenu, M. D., *Introduction à l'étude de saint Thomas d'Aquin,* Montréal-Paris, Vrin, 1950.

Crombie, A. C., *Augustine to Galileo. The History of Science, A. D. 400–1650,* Cambridge, Mass., Harvard University Press, 1953.

———, *Grosseteste and Experimental Science,* Oxford, Clarendon Press, 1953.

Denomy, A. J., C. S. B., "An Enquiry into the Origins of Courtly Love," *Mediaeval Studies,* 6 (1944), 221–228.

Douais, C., *Essai sur l'organisation des études dans l'Ordre des Frères Prêcheurs,* Paris, Picard, 1884.

Duhem, P., *Le système du monde,* 6 vols., Paris, Hermann, 1913–1917.

Duns Scotus, *De primo principio,* ed. and trans. E. Roche, O. F. M., St. Bonaventure, N.Y., Franciscan Institute, 1949.

Eschmann, I. Th., O. P., "Bonum commune melius est quam bonum unius: Eine Studie ueber den Wertvorrang des Personalen bei Thomas von Aquin," *Mediaeval Studies,* 6 (1944), 62–120.

———, "In Defense of J. Maritain," *Modern Schoolman,* 22 (1945), 183–208.

Garrigou-Lagrange, R., *Reality, A Synthesis of Thomistic Thought*, St. Louis, Herder, 1950.

Giles of Rome, *Errores Philosophorum*, ed. J. Koch, trans. J. Riedl, Milwaukee, Marquette University Press, 1944.

Gilson, E., *History of Christian Philosophy in the Middle Ages*, New York, Random House, 1955.

————, "Pourquoi s. Thomas a critiqué s. Augustin," *Archives d'Histoire doctrinale et littéraire du Moyen Age*, 1 (1926–1927), 8–35.

Grabmann, M. *Guglielmo di Moerbeke, O. P., il traduttore delle opere di Aristotele*, Roma, Università Gregoriana, 1946.

————, *Die Werke des hl. Thomas von Aquin*, Aufl. 3 (Beiträge, XXII, 1–2), Münster i. W., 1949.

Laurent, M. H., O. P., ed., *Fontes Vitae S. Thomae Aquinatis*, t. VI, Saint Maximin, Revue Thomiste, 1937.

Mackey, P., O. P., "The Autograph of St. Thomas," in *Papers from the Summer School*, Cambridge, London, Sheed & Ward, 1925, pp. 35–44.

Mandonnet, P., O. P., "Thomas d'Aquin, novice prêcheur," *Revue Thomiste*, n.s. 8 (1925), 222–249.

Maritain, J., *Approaches to God*, New York, Harper, 1954.

Martinez, Mother M. L., R. S. C. J., "Distributive Justice according to St. Thomas," *Modern Schoolman*, 24 (1947), 208–223.

McAllister, J. B., "Chance in Aristotle and Aquinas," in *Philosophical Studies in Honor of Ignatius Smith, O. P.*, Westminster, Md., Newman Press, 1952, pp. 76–91.

Peghaire, J., C. S. Sp., "L'Axiome *Bonum* est diffusivum sui dans le néo-platonisme et le thomisme," *Revue de l'Université d'Ottawa*, 2 (1932), 5–32.

Thorndike, L., A *History of Magic and Experimental Science*, 6 vols., New York, Macmillan, 1923–1943.

IV. STUDIES ON THE END OF MAN AND THE VISION OF GOD

Bastable, P. K., *Desire for God*, London, Burns, Oates & Washbourne, 1947.

Brisebois, E., S. J., "Human Desire and the Vision of God," *Modern Schoolman*, 16 (1938), 9–14; (1939), 29–38.

Buckley, J., *Man's Last End*, St. Louis, Herder, 1949.

Lubac, H. de, *Surnaturel*, Paris, Aubier, 1946.

O'Connor, W. R., *The Eternal Quest*, New York, Longmans, Green, 1947.

————, *The Natural Desire for God* (Aquinas Lecture), Milwaukee, Marquette University Press, 1949.

————, "Some Historical Factors in the Development of the Concept of Human Finality," *Proceedings of the American Catholic Philosophical Association*, 23 (1949), 15–35.

O'Mahony, J., *The Desire of God*, Dublin-Cork, Cork University Press, 1929.

Pegis, A. C., "Nature and Spirit: Some Reflections on the Problem of the End of Man," *Proceedings of the American Catholic Philosophical Association*, 23 (1949), 62–79.

Smith, G., S. J., "The Natural End of Man," *Ibid.*, 47–61.

(Numerous other foreign language studies are listed in the above works, and in the Bibliographies compiled by Mandonnet-Destrez, Bourke, and the *Bulletin Thomiste*.)

Saint Thomas Aquinas

ON THE TRUTH OF THE CATHOLIC FAITH

BOOK THREE: PROVIDENCE

PART I

Chapter 1.

PROLOGUE

"The Lord is a great God and a great King above all gods" (Ps. 94:3). "For the Lord will not cast off His people" (Ps. 93:14). "For in His hand are all the ends of the earth, and the heights of the mountains are His. For the sea is His and He made it, and His hands formed dry land" (Ps. 94:4–5).

[1]　That there is one First Being, possessing the full perfection of the whole of being, and that we call Him God, has been shown in the preceding Books.[1] From the abundance of His perfection, He endows all existing things with being, so that He is fully established not only as the First Being but also as the original source of all existing things. Moreover, He has granted being to other things, not by a necessity of His nature but according to the choice of His will, as has been made clear in our earlier explanations.[2] From this it follows that He is the Lord of the things that He has made, for we are masters of the things that are subject to our will. In fact, He holds perfect dominion over things produced by Himself, since to produce them He is in need neither of the assistance of an external agent nor of the underlying presence of matter, for He is the universal maker of the whole of being.

[2]　Now, each of the things produced through the will of an agent is directed to an end by the agent. For the

---

1. St. Thomas Aquinas, *On the Truth of the Catholic Faith, Book One: God,* trans. Anton C. Pegis, Hanover House, Garden City, N. Y., 1955; *Book Two: Creation,* trans. James Anderson, Hanover House, Garden City, N. Y., 1956.
2. SCG, II, ch. 23.

proper object of the will is the good and the end. As a result, things which proceed from will must be directed to some end. Moreover, each thing achieves its ultimate end through its own action which must be directed to the end by Him Who gives things the principles through which they act.

[3]   So, it must be that God, Who is in all ways perfect in Himself, and Who endows all things with being from His own power, exists as the Ruler of all beings, and is ruled by none other. Nor is there anything that escapes His rule, just as there is nothing that does not receive its being from Him. As He is perfect in being and causing, so also is He perfect in ruling.

[4]   Of course, the result of this rule is manifested differently in different beings, depending on the diversity of their natures. For some beings so exist as God's products that, possessing understanding, they bear His likeness and reflect His image. Consequently, they are not only ruled but are also rulers of themselves, inasmuch as their own actions are directed to a fitting end. If these beings submit to the divine rule in their own ruling, then by virtue of the divine rule they are admitted to the achievement of their ultimate end; but, if they proceed otherwise in their own ruling, they are rejected.

[5]   Still other beings, devoid of understanding, do not direct themselves to their end, but are directed by another being. Some of these are incorruptible and, as they can suffer no defect in their natural being, so in their own actions they never fail to follow the order to the end which is prearranged for them. They are unfailingly subject to the rule of the First Ruler. Such are the celestial bodies whose motions occur in ever the same way.

[6]   Other beings, however, are corruptible. They can suffer a defect in their natural being, yet such a defect works to the advantage of another being. For, when one thing is corrupted, another comes into being. Likewise, in their proper actions they may fall short of the natural

order, yet such a failure is balanced by the good which comes from it. Thus, it is evident that not even those things which appear to depart from the order of the primary rule do actually escape the power of the First Ruler. Even these corruptible bodies are perfectly subject to His power, just as they are created by God Himself.

[7] Contemplating this fact, the Psalmist, being filled with the Holy Spirit, first describes for us the perfection of the First Ruler, in order to point out the divine rule to us: as a perfection of nature, by the use of the term "God"; as a perfection of power, by the use of the words, "great Lord" (suggesting that He has need of no other being for His power to produce His effect); and as a perfection of authority, by the use of the phrase, "a great King above all gods" (for even if there be many rulers, they are all nonetheless subject to His rule).

[8] In the second place, he describes for us the manner of this rule. First, as regards those intellectual beings who are led by Him to their ultimate end, which is Himself, he uses this expression: "For the Lord will not cast off His people." Next, in regard to corruptible beings which are not removed from the power of the First Ruler, even if they go astray sometimes in their own actions, he says: "For in His hands are all the ends of the earth." Then, in regard to celestial bodies which exist above all the highest parts of the earth (that is, of corruptible bodies) and which always observe the right order of the divine rule, he says: "and the heights of the mountains are His."

[9] In the third place, he indicates the reason for this universal rule: the things created by God must also be ruled by Him. Thus it is that he says: "For the sea is His," and so on.

[10] Therefore, since we have treated of the perfection of the divine nature in Book One, and of the perfection of His power inasmuch as He is the Maker and Lord of all things in Book Two, there remains to be treated in this third Book His perfect authority or dignity, inasmuch as

He is the End and Ruler of all things. So, this will be our order of procedure: first, we shall treat of Himself, according as He is the end of all things; second, of His universal rule, according as He governs every creature;[3] third, of His particular rule, according as He governs creatures possessed of understanding.[4]

Chapter 2.

HOW EVERY AGENT ACTS FOR AN END

[1]   The first thing that we must show, then, is that in acting every agent intends an end.

[2]   In the case of things which obviously act for an end, we call that toward which the inclination of the agent tends the end. For, if it attain this, it is said to attain its end; but, if it fail in regard to this, it fails in regard to the end intended, as is evident in the case of the physician working for the sake of health, and of the man who is running toward a set objective. As far as this point is concerned, it makes no difference whether the being tending to an end is a knowing being or not. For, just as the target is the end for the archer, so is it the end for the motion of the arrow. Now, every inclination of an agent tends toward something definite. A given action does not stem from merely any power, but heating comes from heat, cooling from cold. Thus it is that actions are specifically distinguished by virtue of a diversity of active powers. In fact, an action may sometimes terminate in something which is made, as building does in a house, and as healing does in health. Sometimes, however, it does not, as in the cases of understanding and sensing. Now, if an action does in fact terminate in something that is made, the inclination of the agent tends through the action toward the thing that is produced. But,

3. See below, ch. 64–110.
4. See below, ch. 111–163.

if it does not terminate in a product, then the inclination of the agent tends toward the action itself. So, it must be that every agent in acting intends an end, sometimes the action itself, sometimes a thing produced by the action.[1]

[3] Again, with reference to all things that act for an end, we say that the ultimate end is that beyond which the agent seeks nothing else; thus, the action of a physician goes as far as health, but when it is attained there is no desire for anything further. Now, in the action of all agents, one may find something beyond which the agent seeks nothing further. Otherwise, actions would tend to infinity, which is impossible. Since "it is impossible to proceed to infinity,"[2] the agent could not begin to act, because nothing is moved toward what cannot be reached. Therefore, every agent acts for an end.

[4] Besides, if the actions of an agent are supposed to proceed to infinity, then there must be as a consequence to these actions either something that is produced, or nothing. Supposing that there is something that results, then the existence of this thing would come about after an infinite number of actions. But that which presupposes an infinite number of things cannot come into existence, since it is impossible to proceed to infinity. Now, that which is impossible in regard to being is impossible in regard to coming into being. And it is impossible to produce that which cannot come into being. Therefore, it is impossible for an agent to begin to produce something that presupposes an infinite number of actions.

Supposing, on the other hand, that nothing follows as a product of these actions, then the order of such actions must either depend on the ordering of the active powers (as in the case of a man who senses so that he may imagine, imagines so that he may understand, and then understands

1. This is the passage to which Duns Scotus (*De primo principio*, ed. and trans. E. Roche [St. Bonaventure, N. Y.: 1949], ch. 2, concl. 5, p. 18) took definite exception, calling St. Thomas' view of the end as action or product *falsa imaginatio*.
2. Aristotle, *Posterior Analytics*, I, 22 (82b 38).

so that he may will); or it depends on the ordering of objects (thus, I think of body so that I may be able to think of soul, which latter I think so that I may be able to think of immaterial substance, which in turn I think so that I may be able to think about God). Indeed, it is impossible to proceed to infinity, either through a series of active powers (for instance, through the forms of things, as is proved in *Metaphysics* II,[3] for the form is the principle of action) or through a series of objects (for there is not an infinite number of beings, because there is one First Being, as we demonstrated earlier).[4] So, it is not possible for actions to proceed to infinity. There must, then, be something which satisfies the agent's desire when it is attained. Therefore, every agent acts for an end.

[5]   Moreover, for things which act for an end, all things intermediate between the first agent and the ultimate end are as ends in regard to things prior, and as active principles with regard to things consequent. So, if the agent's desire is not directed to some definite thing, but, rather, the actions are multiplied to infinity, as was said, then the active principles must be multiplied to infinity. This is impossible, as we showed above. Therefore, the agent's desire must be directed to some definite thing.

[6]   Furthermore, for every agent the principle of its action is either its nature or its intellect. Now, there is no question that intellectual agents act for the sake of an end, because they think ahead of time in their intellects of the things which they achieve through action; and their action stems from such preconception. This is what it means for intellect to be the principle of action. Just as the entire likeness of the result achieved by the actions of an intelligent agent exists in the intellect that preconceives it, so, too, does the likeness of a natural resultant pre-exist in the natural agent; and as a consequence of this, the action is determined to a definite result. For fire gives rise to fire,

3. Aristotle, *Metaphysics*, I*a*, 2 (994a 1–b 6).
4. SCG, I, ch. 42.

and an olive to an olive. Therefore, the agent that acts with nature as its principle is just as much directed to a definite end, in its action, as is the agent that acts through intellect as its principle. Therefore, every agent acts for an end.

[7]   Again, there is no fault to be found, except in the case of things that are for the sake of an end. A fault is never attributed to an agent, if the failure is related to something that is not the agent's end. Thus, the fault of failing to heal is imputed to the physician, but not to the builder or the grammarian. We do find fault with things done according to art, for instance, when the grammarian does not speak correctly, and also in things done according to nature, as is evident in the case of the birth of monsters. Therefore, it is just as true of the agent that acts in accord with nature as of the agent who acts in accord with art and as a result of previous planning that action is for the sake of an end.

[8]   Besides, if an agent did not incline toward some definite effect, all results would be a matter of indifference for him. Now, he who looks upon a manifold number of things with indifference no more succeeds in doing one of them than another. Hence, from an agent contingently indifferent to alternatives no effect follows, unless he be determined to one effect by something. So, it would be impossible for him to act. Therefore, every agent tends toward some determinate effect, and this is called his end.

[9]   Of course, there are some actions that do not seem to be for an end. Examples are playful and contemplative actions, and those that are done without attention, like rubbing one's beard and the like. These examples could make a person think that there are some cases of acting without an end. However, we must understand that contemplative actions are not for another end, but are themselves ends. On the other hand, acts of play are sometimes ends, as in the case of a man who plays solely for the pleasure attaching to play; at other times they are for an end, for instance, when we play so that we can study better after-

ward. Actions that are done without attention do not stem from the intellect but from some sudden act of imagination or from a natural source. Thus, a disorder of the humors produces an itch and is the cause of rubbing the beard, and this is done without intellectual attention. So, these actions do tend to some end, though quite apart from the order of the intellect.

[10] Through this consideration the error of the ancient natural philosophers is refuted; they claimed that all things come about as a result of material necessity, for they completely excluded final cause from things.[5]

Chapter 3.

THAT EVERY AGENT ACTS FOR A GOOD

[1] Next after this we must show that every agent acts for a good.

[2] That every agent acts for an end has been made clear from the fact that every agent tends toward something definite. Now, that toward which an agent tends in a definite way must be appropriate to it, because the agent would not be inclined to it except by virtue of some agreement with it. But, what is appropriate to something is good for it. So, every agent acts for a good.

[3] Again, the end is that in which the appetitive inclination of an agent or mover, and of the thing moved, finds its rest. Now, the essential meaning of the good is that it provides a terminus for appetite, since "the good is that which all desire."[1] Therefore, every action and motion are for the sake of a good.

[4] Besides, every action and movement are seen to be ordered in some way toward being, either that it may be

5. See Aristotle, Physics, II, 8 (198b 12).
1. Aristotle, Nicomachean Ethics, I, 1 (1094a 1).

preserved in the species or in the individual, or that it may be newly acquired. Now, the very fact of being is a good, and so all things desire to be. Therefore, every action and movement are for the sake of a good.

[5]   Moreover, every action and movement are for the sake of some perfection. Even if the action itself be the end, it is clear that it is a secondary perfection of the agent. But, if the action be a changing of external matter, it is obvious that the mover intends to bring about some perfection in the thing that is moved. Even the thing that is moved also tends toward this, if it be a case of natural movement. Now, we call what is perfect a good. So, every action and movement are for the sake of a good.

[6]   Furthermore, every agent acts in so far as it is in act, and in acting it tends to produce something like itself. So, it tends toward some act. But every act has something of good in its essential character, for there is no evil thing that is not in a condition of potency falling short of its act. Therefore, every action is for the sake of a good.

[7]   Again, an intelligent agent acts for the sake of an end, in the sense that it determines the end for itself. On the other hand, an agent that acts from a natural impulse, though acting for an end, as we showed in the preceding chapter, does not determine the end for itself, since it does not know the meaning of an end, but, rather, is moved toward an end determined for it by another being. Now, the intelligent agent does not determine the end for itself, unless it do so by considering the rational character of the good, for an object of the intellect is only motivating by virtue of the rational meaning of the good, which is the object of the will. Therefore, even the natural agent is neither moved, nor does it move, for the sake of an end, except in so far as the end is a good; for the end is determined for the natural agent by some appetite. Therefore, every agent acts for the sake of a good.

[8]   Besides, there is the same general reason for avoiding evil that there is for seeking the good, just as there is the

same general reason for moving downward and for moving upward. But all things are known to flee from evil; in fact, intelligent agents avoid a thing for this reason: they recognize it as an evil thing. Now, all natural agents resist corruption, which is an evil for each individual, to the full extent of their power. Therefore, all things act for the sake of a good.

[9] Moreover, that which results from the action of an agent, but apart from the intention of the agent, is said to happen by chance or by luck. But we observe that what happens in the workings of nature is either always, or mostly, for the better. Thus, in the plant world leaves are arranged so as to protect the fruit, and among animals the bodily organs are disposed in such a way that the animal can be protected. So, if this came about apart from the intention of the natural agent, it would be by chance or by luck. But this is impossible, for things which occur always, or for the most part, are neither chance nor fortuitous events, but only those which occur in few instances.[2] Therefore, the natural agent tends toward what is better, and it is much more evident that the intelligent agent does so. Hence, every agent intends the good when it acts.

[10] Furthermore, everything that is moved is brought to the terminus of the movement by the mover and agent. So, the mover and the object moved must tend toward the same thing. Now, the object moved, since it is in potency, tends toward act, and so toward the perfect and the good, for it goes from potency to act through movement. Therefore, both the mover and the agent always intend the good in their movement and action.

[11] This is the reason why the philosophers, in defining the good, have said: "the good is what all desire."[3] And Dionysius states that "all crave the good and the best."[4]

2. See Aristotle, *Physics*, II, 5 (196b 11).
3. Aristotle, *Nicomachean Ethics*, I, 1 (1094a 1).
4. Pseudo-Dionysius, *De divinis nominibus*, IV, 4 (PG, 3, col. 699).

Chapter 4.

THAT EVIL IN THINGS IS NOT INTENDED

[1]   From this it is clear that evil occurs in things apart from the intention of the agents.

[2]   For that which follows from an action, as a different result from that intended by the agent, clearly happens apart from intention. Now, evil is different from the good which every agent intends. Therefore, evil is a result apart from intention.

[3]   Again, a defect in an effect and in an action results from some defect in the principles of the action; for instance, the birth of a monstrosity results from some corruption of the semen, and lameness results from a bending of the leg bone. Now, an agent acts in keeping with the active power that it has, not in accord with the defect of power to which it is subject. According as it acts, so does it intend the end. Therefore, it intends an end corresponding to its power. So, that which results as an effect of the defect of power will be apart from the intention of the agent. Now, this is evil. Hence, evil occurs apart from intention.

[4]   Besides, the movement of a mobile thing and the motion of its mover tend toward the same objective. Of itself, the mobile thing tends toward the good, but it may tend toward evil accidentally and apart from intention. This is best seen in generation and corruption. When it is under one form, matter is in potency to another form and to the privation of the form it already has. Thus, when it is under the form of air, it is in potency to the form of fire and to the privation of the form of air. Change in the matter terminates in both at the same time; in the form of fire, in so far as fire is generated; in the privation of the form of air, inasmuch as air is corrupted. Now, the intention and

appetite of matter are not toward privation but toward form, for it does not tend toward the impossible. Now, it is impossible for matter to exist under privation alone, but for it to exist under a form is possible. Therefore, that which terminates in a privation is apart from intention. It terminates in a privation inasmuch as it attains the form which it intends, and the privation of another form is a necessary result of this attainment. So, the changing of matter in generation and corruption is essentially ordered to the form, but the privation is a consequence apart from the intention. The same should be true for all cases of change. Therefore, in every change there is a generation and a corruption, in some sense; for instance, when a thing changes from white to black, the white is corrupted and the black comes into being. Now, it is a good thing for matter to be perfected through form, and for potency to be perfected through its proper act, but it is a bad thing for it to be deprived of its due act. So, everything that is moved tends in its movement to reach a good, but it reaches an evil apart from such a tendency. Therefore, since every agent and mover tends to the good, evil arises apart from the intention of the agent.

[5]   Moreover, in the case of beings that act as a result of understanding or of some sort of sense judgment, intention is a consequence of apprehension, for the intention tends to what is apprehended as an end. If it actually attains something which does not possess the specific nature of what was apprehended, then this will be apart from the intention. For example, if someone intends to eat honey, but he eats poison, in the belief that it is honey, then this will be apart from the intention. But every intelligent agent tends toward something in so far as he considers the object under the rational character of a good, as was evident in the preceding chapter. So, if this object is not good but bad, this will be apart from his intention. Therefore, an intelligent agent does not produce an evil result, unless it be apart from his intention. Since to tend to the good is common to the intelligent agent and to the agent that acts by natural

instinct, evil does not result from the intention of any agent, except apart from the intention.

[6] Hence, Dionysius says, in the fourth chapter of *On the Divine Names:* "Evil is apart from intention and will."[1]

Chapter 5.

ARGUMENTS WHICH SEEM TO PROVE THAT EVIL IS NOT APART FROM INTENTION

[1] Now, there are certain points which seem to run counter to this view.

[2] That which happens apart from the intention of the agent is called fortuitous, a matter of chance, something which rarely happens.[1] But the occurrence of evil is not called fortuitous, a matter of chance, nor does it happen rarely, but always or in most cases. For corruption always accompanies generation in the things of nature. Even in the case of volitional agents sin occurs in most cases, since "it is as difficult to act in accord with virtue as to find the center of a circle," as Aristotle says in the *Nicomachean Ethics.*[2] So, evil does not seem to happen apart from intention.

[3] Again, in *Ethics* III[3] Aristotle expressly states that "wickedness is voluntary." He proves this by the fact that a person voluntarily performs unjust acts: "now it is unreasonable for the agent of voluntarily unjust actions not to will

1. Pseudo-Dionysius, *De divinis nominibus*, IV, 32, 35 (*PG*, 3, col. 732, 736).
1. Aristotle, *Physics*, II, 4–6 (195b 30–198a 12) discusses the event of luck (τὸ ἀπὸ τύχης) which is *fortuitum* in St. Thomas' text, the event of chance (τὸ ἀπὸ τοῦ αὐτομάτου) which is *casuale*, and the rare event (τὸ μὴ ὡς ἐπὶ τὸ πολύ) which is *in paucioribus accidens*. See J. B. McAllister, "Chance in Aristotle and Aquinas," in *Philosophical Studies in Honor of Ignatius Smith* (Westminster, Md.: 1952), pp. 76–91.
2. *Op. cit.*, II, 9 (1109a 24).
3. *Op. cit.*, III, 5 (1113b 16).

to be unjust, and for the self-indulgent man not to wish to be incontinent";[4] and he proves it also by the fact that legislators punish evil men as doers of evil in a voluntary way.[5] So, it does not seem that evil occurs apart from the will or the intention.

[4]   Besides, every natural change has an end intended by nature. Now, corruption is a natural change, just as generation is. Therefore, its end, which is a privation having the rational character of evil, is intended by nature: just as are form and the good, which are the ends of generation.

Chapter 6.

ANSWERS TO THESE ARGUMENTS

[1]   So that the solution of these alleged arguments may be made more evident we should notice that evil may be considered either in a substance or in its action. Now, evil is in a substance because something which it was originally to have, and which it ought to have, is lacking in it. Thus, if a man has no wings, that is not an evil for him, because he was not born to have them; even if a man does not have blond hair, that is not an evil, for, though he may have such hair, it is not something that is necessarily due him. But it is an evil if he has no hands, for these he is born to, and should, have—if he is to be perfect. Yet this defect is not an evil for a bird. Every privation, if taken properly and strictly, is of that which one is born to have, and should have. So, in this strict meaning of privation, there is always the rational character of evil.

[2]   Now, since it is in potency toward all forms, matter is indeed originated to have all of them; however, a certain one of them is not necessarily due it, since without this certain one it can be actually perfect. Of course, to each

4. *Ibid.* (1114a 11).
5. *Ibid.* (1113b 22).

thing composed of matter some sort of form is due, for water cannot exist unless it have the form of water, nor can fire be unless it possess the form of fire. So, the privation of such forms in relation to matter is not an evil for the matter, but in relation to the thing whose form it is, it is an evil for it; just as the privation of the form of fire is an evil for fire. And since privations, just as much as habits and forms, are not said to exist, except in the sense that they are in a subject, then if a privation be an evil in relation to the subject in which it is, this will be evil in the unqualified sense. But, otherwise, it will be an evil relative to something, and not in the unqualified sense. Thus, for a man to be deprived of a hand is an unqualified evil, but for matter to be deprived of the form of air is not an unqualified evil, though it is an evil for the air.

[3] Now, a privation of order, or due harmony, in action is an evil for action. And because there is some due order and harmony for every action, such privation in an action must stand as evil in the unqualified sense.

[4] Having observed these points, we should understand that not everything that is apart from intention is necessarily fortuitous or a matter of chance, as the first argument claimed. For, if that which is apart from intention be either an invariable or a frequent consequence of what is intended, then it does not occur fortuitously or by chance. Take, for example, a man who directs his intention to the enjoyment of the sweetness of wine: if intoxication is the result of drinking the wine, this is neither fortuitous nor a matter of chance. Of course, it would be a matter of chance if this result followed in but few cases.

[5] So the evil of natural corruption, though a result which is apart from the intention of the agent of generation, is nevertheless an invariable consequence, for the acquisition of one form is always accompanied by the privation of another form. Hence, corruption does not occur by chance, nor as something that happens in few cases; even though privation at times is not an unqualified evil, but is only so

in relation to some definite thing, as has been said. However, if it be the kind of privation which takes away what is due to the thing generated, this will be by chance and unqualifiedly evil, as in the case of the birth of monsters. For, such a thing is not the necessary result of what is intended; rather, it is repugnant to what is intended, since the agent intends a perfect product of generation.

[6]   Now, evil in relation to action occurs in the case of natural agents as a result of the defect of an active power. Hence, if the agent has a defective power, the evil is a result apart from the intention, but it will not be a chance result because it follows necessarily from this kind of agent, provided this kind of agent is subject to this defect of power, either always or frequently. However, it will be a matter of chance if this defect is rarely associated with this kind of agent.

[7]   In the case of voluntary agents, the intention is directed to some particular good, if action is to result, for universals cause no movement, but particular things do, since actions go on in their area. Therefore, if a particular good that is intended has attached to it, either always or frequently, a privation of good according to reason, then the result is a moral evil; and not by chance, but either invariably or for the most part. This is clearly the case with a man who wills to enjoy a woman for the sake of pleasure, to which pleasure there is attached the disorder of adultery. Hence, the evil of adultery is not something which results by chance. However, it would be an instance of chance evil if some wrong resulted in a few cases from the object intended: for example, in the case of a person who kills a man while shooting at a bird.

[8]   That a person may frequently direct his intention to goods of this kind, to which privations of good according to reason are consequent, results from the fact that most men live on the sense level, because sensory objects are better known to us, and they are more effective motives in the domain of particular things where action goes on. Now,

the privation of good according to reason is the consequence of most goods of this kind.

[9] From this it is evident that, though evil be apart from intention, it is nonetheless voluntary, as the *second* argument suggests, though not essentially but accidentally so. For intention is directed to an ultimate end which a person wills for its own sake, but the will may also be directed to that which a person wills for the sake of something else, even if he would not will it simply for itself. In the example of the man who throws his merchandise into the sea in order to save himself,[1] he does not intend the throwing away of the merchandise but his own safety; yet he wills the throwing not for itself but for the sake of safety. Likewise, a person wills to do a disorderly action for the sake of some sensory good to be attained; he does not intend the disorder, nor does he will it simply for itself, but for the sake of this result. And so, evil consequences and sins are called voluntary in this way, just as is the casting of merchandise into the sea.

[10] The answer to the *third* difficulty is similarly evident. Indeed, the change of corruption is never found without the change of generation; neither, as a consequence, is the end of corruption found without the end of generation. So, nature does not intend the end of corruption as separated from the end of generation, but both at once. It is not the unqualified intention of nature that water should not exist, but that there should be air, and while a thing is so existing it is not water. So, nature directly intends that this existing thing be air; it does not intend that this thing should not exist as water, except as a concomitant of the fact that it is to be air. Thus, privations are not intended by nature in themselves, but only accidentally; forms, however, are intended in themselves.

1. For the source of the famous example see Aristotle, *Nicomachean Ethics*, III, 1 (1110a 8–29). For other texts in which St. Thomas discusses the relation of involuntariness and voluntariness, see V. J. Bourke, *Ethics* (New York: 1951), pp. 100–106.

[11] It is clear, then, from the foregoing that what is evil in an unqualified sense is completely apart from intention in the workings of nature, as in the birth of monsters; on the other hand, that which is not evil in the unqualified sense, but evil in relation to some definite thing, is not directly intended by nature but only accidentally.

Chapter 7.

THAT EVIL IS NOT AN ESSENCE

[1] From these considerations[1] it becomes evident that no essence is evil in itself.

[2] In fact, evil is simply a privation of something which a subject is entitled by its origin to possess and which it ought to have, as we have said. Such is the meaning of the word "evil" among all men. Now, privation is not an essence; it is, rather, a negation in a substance.[2] Therefore, evil is not an essence in things.

[3] Again, each thing has actual being in accord with its essence. To the extent that it possesses being, it has something good; for, if good is that which all desire, then being itself must be called a good, because all desire to be. As a consequence, then, each thing is good because it possesses actual being. Now, good and evil are contraries. So, nothing is evil by virtue of the fact that it has essence. Therefore, no essence is evil.

[4] Besides, everything is either an agent or a thing that is made. Now, evil cannot be an agent, because whatever acts does so inasmuch as it is actually existent and perfect. Similarly, it cannot be a thing that is made, for the termination of every process of generation is a form, and a good thing. Therefore, nothing is evil by virtue of its essence.

1. See above, ch. 6.
2. Aristotle, *Metaphysics*, IV, 2 (1004a 16).

[5] Moreover, nothing tends toward its contrary, for each thing inclines to what is like and suitable to itself. Now, every being intends a good, when it is acting, as has been proved.[3] Therefore, no being, as being, is evil.

[6] Furthermore, every essence belongs to some definite thing in nature. Indeed, if it falls in the genus of substance, it is the very nature of the thing. However, if it is in the genus of accident, it must be caused by the principles of some substance, and thus it will be natural to this substance, though perhaps it may not be natural to another substance. For example, heat is natural to fire, though it may not be natural to water. Now, what is evil in itself cannot be natural to anything. For it is of the very definition of evil that it be a privation of that which is to be in a subject by virtue of its natural origin, and which should be in it. So, evil cannot be natural to any subject, since it is a privation of what is natural. Consequently, whatever is present naturally in something is a good for it, and it is evil if the thing lacks it. Therefore, no essence is evil in itself.

[7] Again, whatever possesses an essence is either a form itself, or has a form. In fact, every being is placed in a genus or species through a form. Now, a form, as such, has the essential character of goodness, because a form is a principle of action; so, too, does the end to which every agent looks; and so also does the action whereby each thing having a form is perfected. Hence, everything that has an essence is, by virtue of that fact, a good thing. Therefore, evil has no essence.

[8] Besides, being is divided by act and potency. Now, act, as such, is good, for something is perfect to the extent that it is in act. Potency, too, is a good thing, for potency tends toward act, as appears in every instance of change. Moreover, potency is also proportionate to act and not contrary to it. It belongs in the same genus with act; privation does not belong to it, except accidentally. So, everything that exists, whatever the mode of its existence, is a good thing

3. See above, ch. 3.

to the extent that it is a being. Therefore, evil does not possess any essence.

[9] Moreover, we have proved in Book Two of this work[4] that every act of being, whatever its type may be, comes from God. And we have shown in Book One[5] that God is perfect goodness. Now, since evil could not be the product of a good thing, it is impossible for any being, as a being, to be evil.

[10] This is why Genesis (1:31) states: "God saw all the things that He had made, and they were very good"; and Ecclesiastes (3:11): "He hath made all things good in their time"; and also I Timothy (4:4): "Every creature of God is good."

[11] And Dionysius, in chapter four of *On the Divine Names*,[6] says that "evil is not an existing thing," that is, in itself; "nor is it something among things that have existence," but it is a sort of accident, something like whiteness or blackness.

[12] Through this consideration, the error of the Manicheans[7] is refuted, for they claimed that some things are evil in their very natures.

Chapter 8.

ARGUMENTS WHICH SEEM TO PROVE THAT EVIL IS A NATURE OR SOME REAL THING

[1] Now, it appears that the preceding view may be opposed by certain arguments.

[2] Each thing is specified by its own specific difference. But evil is a specific difference in some genera; for instance,

4. *SCG*, II, ch. 15.
5. *SCG*, I, ch. 28 and 41.
6. Pseudo-Dionysius, *De divinis nominibus*, IV, 20–21 (*PG*, 3, col. 721).
7. St. Augustine, *De haeresibus*, 46 (*PL*, 42, 34).

among habits and acts in the moral order. Just as virtue is specifically a good habit, so is the contrary vice specifically a bad habit. The same may be said of virtuous and vicious acts. Therefore, evil is that which gives specificity to some things, and thus it is an essence and is natural to certain things.

[3] Again, of two contraries, each is a definite nature, for, if one contrary were supposed to be nothing, then it would be either a privation or a pure negation. But good and evil are said to be contraries. Therefore, evil is a nature of some sort.

[4] Besides, good and evil are spoken of by Aristotle in the *Categories*[1] as "genera of contraries." Now, there is an essence and a definite nature for each kind of genus. There are no species or differences for non-being; so, that which does not exist cannot be a genus. Therefore, evil is a definite essence and nature.

[5] Moreover, everything that acts is a real thing. Now, evil does act precisely as evil, for it attacks the good and corrupts it. So, evil precisely as evil is a real thing.

[6] Furthermore, wherever the distinction of more or less is found, there must be certain things arranged in hierarchic order, since neither negations nor privations admit of more or less. But among evils, one may be worse than another. It would seem, then, that evil must be a real thing.

[7] Again, thing and being are convertible. There is evil in the world. Therefore, it is a real thing and a nature.

Chapter 9.

ANSWERS TO THESE ARGUMENTS

[1] It is not difficult to answer these arguments. Evil and good are assigned as specific differences in moral matters,

1. Aristotle, *Categories*, 8 (14a 24).

as the first argument asserted, because moral matters depend on the will. For this reason, anything that is voluntary belongs in the class of moral matters. Now, the object of the will is the end and the good. Hence, moral matters get their species from the end, just as natural actions are specified by the form of the active principle; for instance, the act of heating is specified by heat. Hence, because good and evil are so termed by virtue of a universal order, or privation of order, to the end, it is necessary in moral matters for the primary distinction to be between good and evil. Now, there must be but one primary standard in any one genus. The standard in moral matters is reason. Therefore, it must be from a rational end that things in the moral area are termed good or evil. So, in moral matters, that which is specified by an end that is in accord with reason is called good specifically; and that which is specified by an end contrary to the rational end is termed evil specifically. Yet that contrary end, even though it runs counter to the rational end, is nevertheless some sort of good: for instance, something that delights on the sense level, or anything like that. Thus, these are goods for certain animals, and even for man, when they are moderated by reason. It also happens that what is evil for one being is good for another. So, evil, as a specific difference in the genus of moral matters, does not imply something that is evil in its own essence, but something that is good in itself, though evil for man, inasmuch as it takes away the order of reason which is the good for man.

[2]   From this it is also clear that evil and good are contraries according to the way they are understood in the area of moral matters, but they are not when taken without qualification, as the second argument suggested. Rather, in so far as it is evil, evil is the privation of good.

[3]   In the same way, too, one may understand the statement that evil and good, as found in the moral area, are "genera of contraries"—from which phrase the third argument begins. Indeed, in all moral contraries, either both contraries are evil, as in the case of prodigality and illiberal-

ity, or one is good and the other evil, as in the case of liberality and illiberality. Therefore, moral evil is both a genus and a difference, not by the fact that it is a privation of the rational good whence it is termed evil, but by the nature of the action or habit ordered to some end that is opposed to the proper rational end. Thus, a blind man is an individual man, not inasmuch as he is blind but in so far as he is this man. So, also, irrational is an animal difference, not because of the privation of reason but by virtue of a certain kind of nature, to which the absence of reason follows as a consequence.

One can also say that Aristotle calls good and evil *genera*, not according to his own opinion (for he does not number them among the primary ten genera in which every kind of contrariety is found[1]) but according to the opinion of Pythagoras, who supposed that good and evil are the first genera and first principles, and who placed ten prime contraries under each of them: *under the good* were, "limit, even, one, right, male, rest, straight, light, square, and finally good"; and *under evil* were, "the unlimited, *odd*, multitude, left, female, motion, curved, darkness, oblong, and finally evil."[2] Thus, here and in several places in the treatises on logic, he uses examples in accord with the views of other philosophers, as if they were more acceptable in his time.

In fact, this statement has some truth, since it is impossible for a probable statement to be entirely false. In the case of all contraries, one is perfect and the other is a

1. Aristotle, *Categories*, 4 (1b 25).

2. The source of this list of Pythagorean opposites is doubtless Aristotle, *Metaphysics*, I, 5 (986a 24-27). However, as St. Thomas lists them here, odd and even (*impar* and *par*) have been interchanged, possibly due to an error in the Latin version of the *Metaphysics* used by St. Thomas. Compare his commentary (*In Metaph.*, ad loc., lect. 8) where Thomas first (correctly in view of modern texts of Aristotle) makes *par* the *principium infinitatis*; then giving his summary list, he reverses them and puts *par* in the same column with *finitum*. The present translation italicizes *even* and *odd* to indicate the discrepancy, but keeps the list as given in the Leonine text of St. Thomas.

diminished perfection, having, as it were, some privation mixed with it. For instance, white and hot are perfect conditions, but cold and black are imperfect, connoting something of privation. Therefore, since every diminution and privation pertains to the formal character of evil, and every perfection and fulfillment to the formal character of good, it appears to be always so between contraries, that one is included under the good and the other approaches the notion of evil. From this point of view, good and evil seem to be genera of all contraries.

[4]   In this way it also becomes apparent how evil is opposed to the good, which is the starting point of the *fourth* argument. According as there is added a privation of a contrary form, and a contrary end, to a form and an end (which have the rational character of good and are true principles of action) the action that results from such a form and end is attributed to the privation and the evil. Yet, this attribution is accidental, for privation, as such, is not the principle of any action. Hence, Dionysius says, quite properly, in the fourth chapter of On the Divine Names,[3] that "evil does not fight against good, except through the power of the good; in itself, indeed, it is powerless and weak," the principle of no action, as it were. However, we say that evil corrupts the good, not only when it acts in virtue of the good, as has been explained, but also formally of itself. Thus, blindness is said to corrupt sight, for it is itself the corruption of sight; similarly, whiteness is said to color a wall, when it is the actual color of the wall.

[5]   We do indeed say that something is more or less evil than another thing, in reference to the good that it lacks. Thus, things which imply a privation admit of increase or decrease in degree, as do the unequal and the dissimilar. For we say that something is more unequal when it is more removed from equality and, likewise, that something is more dissimilar when it is farther away from similitude. Consequently, a thing that is more deprived of goodness is

3. Pseudo-Dionysius, *De divinis nominibus*, IV, 29 (PG, 3, col. 729).

said to be more evil, as it were, more distant from the good. However, privations do not increase as do things that have an essence, such as qualities and forms, as the *fifth* argument assumes, but through increase of the depriving cause. Thus, just as the air is darker when more obstacles have been placed before the light, so does a thing become farther removed from participation in the light.

[6] We also say that evil is in the world, not as possessing some essence, nor as a definitely existing thing, as the *sixth* argument suggested, but for the same reason that we may call something evil by virtue of its evil. For instance, blindness, or any other sort of privation, is said to exist because an animal is blinded by its blindness. Indeed, there are two ways of talking about being, as the Philosopher teaches in his *Metaphysics*.[4] In one way, being means the essence of a thing, and thus it falls into the ten categories; so taken, no privation can be called a being. In another way, being means the truth in a judgment; in this meaning, privation is called a being, inasmuch as something is said *to be* deprived by virtue of a privation.

Chapter 10.

THAT GOOD IS THE CAUSE OF EVIL

[1] The foregoing arguments enable us to conclude that evil is caused only by the good.

[2] For, if an evil thing were the cause of a certain evil, then the evil thing would not act, except by virtue of the good, as has been proved.[1] So, this good must be the primary cause of the evil.

[3] Again, what does not exist is not the cause of anything. So, every cause must be a definite thing. But evil is not a

4. Aristotle, *op. cit.*, IV, 7 (1017a 8); see St. Thomas, *In Metaph.*, V, lect. 9.
1. See above, ch. 9.

definite being, as has been proved.[2] Therefore, evil cannot
be the cause of anything. If, then, evil be caused by anything, this cause must be the good.

[4]   Besides, whatever is properly and of itself the cause of
something tends toward a proper effect. So, if evil were of
itself the cause of anything, it would tend toward an effect
proper to it; namely, evil. But this is false, for it has been
shown that every agent tends toward the good.[3] Therefore,
evil is not the cause of anything through evil itself, but only
accidentally. Now, every accidental cause reduces to a cause
that works through itself. And only the good can be a cause
through itself, for evil cannot be a cause through itself.
Therefore, evil is caused by the good.

[5]   Moreover, every cause is either matter, or form, or
agent, or end. Now, evil cannot be either matter or form,
for it has been shown that both being in act and being in
potency are good.[4] Similarly, evil cannot be the agent, since
anything that acts does so according as it is in act and has
form. Nor, indeed, can it be an end, for it is apart from intention, as we have proved.[5] So, evil cannot be the cause of
anything. Therefore, if anything is the cause of evil, it must
be caused by the good.

[6]   In fact, since evil and good are contraries, one of these
contraries cannot be the cause of the other unless it be accidentally; as the cold heats, as is said in *Physics* viii.[6]
Consequently, the good could not be the active cause of
evil, except accidentally.

[7]   Now, in the order of nature, this accidental aspect
can be found either on the side of the agent or of the
effect. It will be on the side of the agent when the agent
suffers a defect in its power, the consequence of which is a

2. See above, ch. 7.
3. See above, ch. 3.
4. See above, ch. 7.
5. See above, ch. 4.
6. Aristotle, *Physics*, VIII, 1 (251a 33).

defective action and a defective effect. Thus, when the power of an organ of digestion is weak, imperfect digestive functioning and undigested humor result; these are evils of nature. Now, it is accidental to the agent, as agent, for it to suffer a defect in its power; for it is not an agent by virtue of the fact that its power is deficient, but because it possesses some power. If it were completely lacking in power, it would not act at all. Thus, evil is caused accidentally on the part of the agent in so far as the agent is defective in its power. This is why we say that "evil has no efficient, but only a deficient, cause,"[7] for evil does not result from an agent cause, unless because it is deficient in power, and to that extent it is not efficient.—And it reduces to the same thing if the defect in the action and in the effect arise from a defect of the instrument or of anything else required for the agent's action; for example, when the motor capacity produces lameness because of a curvature of the tibia. For the agent acts both by means of its power and of its instrument.

[8] On the side of the effect, evil is accidentally caused by the good, either by virtue of the matter of the effect, or by virtue of its form. For, if the matter is not well disposed to the reception of the agent's action on it, there must result a defect in the product. Thus, the births of monsters are the result of lack of assimilation on the part of the matter. Nor may this be attributed to some defect in the agent, if it fail to convert poorly disposed matter into perfect act. There is a determinate power for each natural agent, in accord with its type of nature, and failure to go beyond this power will not be a deficiency in power; such deficiency is found only when it falls short of the measure of power naturally due it.

[9] From the point of view of the form of the effect, evil occurs accidentally because the privation of another form is the necessary concomitant of the presence of a given form. Thus, simultaneously with the generation of one thing

7. St. Augustine, *De civitate Dei*, XII, 7 (PL, 41, col. 355).

there necessarily results the corruption of another thing. But this evil is not an evil of the product intended by the agent, but of another thing, as was apparent in the preceding discussion.[8]

[10]   Thus it is clear that, in the natural order, evil is only accidentally caused by the good. Now, it works in the same way in the realm of artifacts. "For art in its working imitates nature,"[9] and bad results occur in both in the same way.

[11]   However, in the moral order, the situation seems to be different. It does not appear that moral vice results from a defect of power, since weakness either completely removes moral fault, or at least diminishes it. Indeed, weakness does not merit moral punishment that is proper to guilt, but, rather, mercy and forgiveness. A moral fault must be voluntary, not necessitated. Yet, if we consider the matter carefully, we shall find the two orders similar from one point of view, and dissimilar from another. There is dissimilarity on this point: moral fault is noticed in action only, and not in any effect that is produced; for the moral virtues are not concerned with making but with doing. The arts are concerned with making, and so it has been said that in their sphere a bad result happens just as it does in nature. Therefore, moral evil is not considered in relation to the matter or form of the effect, but only as a resultant from the agent.

[12]   Now, in moral actions we find four principles arranged in a definite order. One of these is the *executive power*, the moving force, whereby the parts of the body are moved to carry out the command of the will. Then this power is moved by the *will*, which is a second principle. Next, the will is moved by the *judgment* of the apprehensive power which judges that this object is good or bad, for the objects of the will are such that one moves toward at-

8. See above, ch. 6.
9. Aristotle, *Physics*, II, 2 (194a 21).

tainment, another moves toward avoidance. This apprehensive power is moved, in turn, by the *thing apprehended.* So, the first active principle in moral actions is the thing that is cognitively apprehended, the second is the apprehensive power, the third is the will, and the fourth is the motive power which carries out the command of reason.

[13] Now, the act of the power that carries out the action already presupposes the distinction of moral good or evil. For external acts of this kind do not belong in the moral area, unless they are voluntary. Hence, if the act of the will be good, then the external act is also deemed good, but if it be bad, the external act is bad. It would have nothing to do with moral evil if the external act were defective by virtue of a defect having no reference to the will. Lameness, for instance, is not a fault in the moral order, but in the natural order. Therefore, a defect of this type in the executive power either completely excludes moral fault, or diminishes it. So, too, the act whereby a thing moves the apprehensive power is free from moral fault, for the visible thing moves the power of sight in the natural order, and so, also, does any object move a passive potency. Then, too, this act of the apprehensive power, considered in itself, is without moral fault, for a defect in it either removes or diminishes moral fault, as is the case in a defect of the executive power. Likewise, weakness and ignorance excuse wrongdoing, or diminish it. The conclusion follows, then, that moral fault is found primarily and principally in the act of the will only, and so it is quite reasonable to say, as a result, that an act is moral because it is voluntary. Therefore, the root and source of moral wrongdoing is to be sought in the act of will.

[14] However, a difficulty seems to result from this investigation. Since a defective act stems from a defect in the active principle, we must understand that there is a defect in the will preceding the moral fault. Of course, if this defect be natural, then it is always attached to the will, and so the will would always commit a morally bad action when it acts. But virtuous acts show that this conclusion is false.

On the other hand, if the defect be voluntary, it is already a morally bad act, and we will have to look in turn for its cause. Thus, our rational investigation will never come to an end. Therefore, we must say that the defect pre-existing in the will is not natural, to avoid the conclusion that the will sins in everyone of its acts. Nor can we attribute the defect to chance or accident, for then there would be no moral fault in us, since chance events are not premeditated and are beyond the control of reason. So, the defect is voluntary. Yet, it is not a moral fault; otherwise, we should go on to infinity. How this is possible we must now explain.

[15] As a matter of fact, the perfection of the power of every active principle depends on a higher active principle, since a secondary agent acts through the power of a primary agent. While, therefore, a secondary agent remains in a position of subordination to the first agent, it acts without any defect, but it becomes defective in its action if it happens to turn away from its subordination to the primary agent, as is illustrated in the case of an instrument, when it falls short of the motion of the agent. Now, it has been said that two principles precede the will in the order of moral actions: namely, the apprehensive power, and the object apprehended, which is the end. Since to each movable there corresponds a proper motive power, not merely any apprehensive power is the suitable motive power for any and every appetite; rather, one pertains to this appetite and another to a second appetite. Thus, just as the proper motive power for the sensory appetite is the sensory apprehensive power, so the reason itself is the proper motivator for the will.

[16] Again, since reason is able to apprehend many goods and a multiplicity of ends, and since for each thing there is a proper end, there will be, then, for the will an end and a first motivating object which is not merely any good, but some determinate good. Hence, when the will inclines to act as moved by the apprehension of reason, presenting a proper good to it, the result is a fitting action. But when the will breaks forth into action, at the apprehension of

sense cognition, or of reason itself presenting some other good at variance with its proper good, the result in the action of the will is a moral fault.

[17] Hence, a defect of ordering to reason and to a proper end precedes a fault of action in the will: in regard to reason, in the case of the will inclining, on the occasion of a sudden sense apprehension, toward a good that is on the level of sensory pleasure; and in regard to a proper end, in the case when reason encounters in its deliberation some good which is not, at this time or under these conditions, really good, and yet the will inclines toward it, as if it were a proper good. Now, this defect in ordering is voluntary, for to will and not to will lie within the power of the will itself. And it is also within its power for reason to make an actual consideration, or to abstain from such a consideration, or further to consider this or that alternative. Yet, such a defect of ordering is not a moral evil, for, if reason considers nothing, or considers any good whatever, that is still not a sin until the will inclines to an unsuitable end. At this point, the act of will occurs.

[18] Thus, it is clear, both in the natural order and in the moral order, that evil is only caused by good accidentally.

Chapter 11.

THAT EVIL IS BASED ON THE GOOD

[1] It can also be shown from the preceding considerations that every evil is based on some good.

[2] Indeed, evil cannot exist by itself, since it has no essence, as we have demonstrated.[1] Therefore, evil must be in some subject. Now, every subject, because it is some sort of substance, is a good of some kind, as is clear from the foregoing. So, every evil is in a good thing.

1. See above, ch. 7.

[3]   Again, evil is a certain privation, as is evident from the foregoing.[2] Now, privation and the form that is deprived are in the same subject. But the subject of form is being in potency to form, and such being is good, because potency and act belong in the same genus. Therefore, the privation which is evil is present in a good thing, as in a subject.

[4]   Besides, something is called evil due to the fact that it causes injury.[3] But this is only so because it injures the good, for to injure the evil is a good thing, since the corruption of evil is good. Now, formally speaking, it would not injure the good unless it were in the good; thus, blindness injures a man to the extent that it is in him. So, evil must be in the good.

[5]   Moreover, evil is not caused, except by the good, and then only accidentally.[4] But everything that occurs accidentally is reducible to that which is by itself. So, with a caused evil which is the accidental effect of the good, there must always be some good which is the direct effect of the good as such, and thus this good effect is the foundation of the evil. For what exists accidentally is based on that which exists by itself.

[6]   However, since good and evil are contraries, one of these contraries cannot be the subject for the other; rather, it excludes the other. It will seem to someone, at first glance, that it is improper to say that good is the subject of evil.

[7]   Yet it is not improper, provided the truth be investigated to its limit. Good is spoken of in just as general a way as being, since every being, as such, is good, as we have proved.[5] Now, it is not improper for non-being to be present in being, as in a subject. Indeed, any instance of

2. See above, ch. 9.
3. Compare St. Augustine, *Enchiridion*, 12 (*PL*, 40, col. 237).
4. See above, ch. 10.
5. See above, ch. 7.

privation is a non-being, yet its subject is a substance which is a being. However, non-being is not present in a being contrary to it, as in a subject. For blindness is not universal non-being, but, rather, this particular non-being whereby sight is taken away. So, it is not present in the power of sight as its subject, but, rather, in the animal. Likewise, evil is not present in a good contrary to it, as in its subject; rather, this contrary good is taken away by the evil. For instance, moral evil is present in a natural good, while a natural evil, which is a privation of form, is present in matter which is a good, in the sense of a being in potency.

Chapter 12.

THAT EVIL DOES NOT WHOLLY DESTROY GOOD

[1] It is evident from the foregoing explanation that, no matter how much evil be multiplied, it can never destroy the good wholly.

[2] In fact, there must always continue to be a subject for evil, if evil is to endure. Of course, the subject of evil is the good,[1] and so the good will always endure.

[3] Yet, because it is possible for evil to increase without limit, and because good is always decreased as evil increases, it appears that the good may be infinitely decreased by evil. Now, the good that can be decreased by evil must be finite, for the infinite good does not admit of evil, as we showed in Book One.[2] So, it seems that eventually the good would be wholly destroyed by evil, for, if something be subtracted an infinite number of times from a finite thing, the latter must be destroyed eventually by the subtraction.

1. See above, ch. 11.
2. *SCG*, I, ch. 39.

[4]   Now, it cannot be answered, as some people say,[3] that if the subsequent subtraction be made in the same proportion as the preceding one, going on to infinity, it is not possible to destroy the good, as happens in the division of a continuum. For, if you subtract half of a line two cubits long, and then half of the remainder, and if you go on in this way to infinity, something will always remain to be divided. But, in this process of division, that which is subtracted later must always be quantitatively diminished. In fact, the half of the whole is quantitatively greater than half of the half, though the same proportion continues. This, however, cannot in any sense happen in the decreasing of good by evil, for the more the good would be decreased by evil the weaker would it become, and so, more open to diminution by subsequent evil. On the contrary, the later evil could be equal to, or greater than, the earlier evil; hence a proportionately smaller quantity of good would not always be subtracted by evil from the good in subsequent cases.

[5]   So, another sort of answer must be given. It is evident from what has been said[4] that evil does take away completely the good which is its contrary, as blindness does with sight. Yet there must remain the good which is the subject of evil. This, in fact, inasmuch as it is a subject, has the essential character of goodness, in the sense that it is in potency to the act of goodness which is lacking due to the evil. So, the less it is in potency to this good, the less will it be a good. Now, a subject becomes less potential to a form, not simply by the subtraction of any of its parts, nor by the fact that any part of the potency is subtracted, but by the fact that the potency is impeded by a contrary act from being able to proceed to the actuality of the form. For example, a subject is less potential in regard to cold to the extent that heat is increased in it. Therefore, the good is diminshed by evil more as a result of the addition of its con-

3. For Zeno of Elea and this argument, see Aristotle, De genera-
    tione et corruptione, I, 8 (325a 20–35); Physics, VI, 1 (231b
    15–232a 17); VI, 8–9 (239b 4–240a 19).
4. See above, ch. 11.

trary than by the subtraction of some of its goodness. This is also in agreement with the things that have been said about evil. Indeed, we said[5] that evil occurs apart from the intention of the agent, and that he always intends a definite good, and that it consequently implies the exclusion of another good which is contrary to it. So, the more this intended good (which apart from the agent's intention results in evil) is multiplied, the more is the potency to the contrary good diminished. And this is rather the way in which the good is said to be diminished by evil.

[6] Now, in the natural order, this diminution of the good by evil cannot proceed to infinity. All natural forms and powers are limited, and they reach some limit beyond which they cannot extend. So, it is not possible for any contrary form, or any power of a contrary agent, to be increased to infinity, in such a way that the result would be an infinite diminution of good by evil.

[7] However, in the moral order, this diminution can proceed to infinity. For the intellect and the will have no limits to their acts. The intellect is able to go on to infinity in its act of understanding; this is why the mathematical species of numbers and figures are called infinite. Likewise, the will proceeds to infinity in its act of willing: a man who wills to commit a theft can will again to commit it, and so on to infinity. Indeed, the more the will tends toward unworthy ends, the greater is its difficulty in returning to a proper and worthy end. This is evident in the case of people in whom vicious habits have developed already, as a result of their growing accustomed to sinning. Therefore, the good of natural aptitude can be infinitely decreased by moral evil. Yet, it will never be wholly destroyed; rather, it will always accompany the nature that endures.

5. See above, ch. 4.

Chapter 13.

THAT EVIL HAS A CAUSE OF SOME SORT

[1]   From what has been said above it can be shown that, though evil has no direct cause of itself, still there must be an accidental cause for every evil.

[2]   Whatever exists in another thing as in its subject must have some cause, for it is caused either by the principles of the subject or by some extrinsic cause. Now, evil is in the good as in a subject, as has been indicated,[1] and so it is necessary for evil to have a cause.

[3]   Again, that which is in potency to either of two contraries is not advanced to actuality under one of them unless through some cause, for no potency makes itself be in act. Now, evil is a privation of something that is natural to a man, and which he ought to have. This is why anything whatever is called evil. So, evil is present in a subject that is in potency to evil and to its contrary. Therefore, it is necessary for evil to have some cause.

[4]   Besides, whatever is present in something and is not due to it from its nature comes to it from some other cause, for all things present in existing beings as natural components remain there unless something else prevents them. Thus, a stone is not moved upward unless by something else that impels it, nor is water heated unless by some heating agent. Now, evil is always present as something foreign to the nature of that in which it is, since it is a privation of what a thing has from its natural origin, and ought to have. Therefore, evil must always have some cause, either directly of itself, or accidentally.

[5]   Moreover, every evil is the consequence of a good,[2] as corruption is the result of an act of generation. But every

1. See above, ch. 11.
2. See above, ch. 10.

good has a cause, other than the first good in which there is no evil, as has been shown in Book One.[3] Therefore, every evil has a cause, in regard to which it is an accidental result.

Chapter 14.

THAT EVIL IS AN ACCIDENTAL CAUSE

[1]   It is plain, from the same consideration, that evil, though not a direct cause of anything by itself, is, however, an accidental cause.

[2]   For, if a thing is the direct cause of something, then that which is an accidental concomitant of this direct cause is the accidental cause of the resultant. Take, for instance, the fact that a builder happens to be white, then whiteness is the accidental cause of the house. Now, every evil is present in something good.[1] And every good thing is the cause of something in some way, for matter is in one way the cause of form; in another way the converse is so. The same is true of the agent and the end. Hence, the result is not a process to infinity in causes if each thing is the cause of another thing, for there is a circle involved in causes and effects, depending on the different types of cause. So, evil is an accidental cause.

[3]   Again, evil is a privation, as we have seen before.[2] Now, privation is an accidental principle in beings subject to motion, just as matter and form are essential principles.[3] Therefore, evil is the accidental cause of something else.

[4]   Besides, from a defect in a cause there follows a defect in the effect. Now a defect in a cause is an evil. Yet, it cannot be a direct cause in itself, for a thing is not a cause by

3. *SCG*, I, ch. 39.
1. See above, ch. 11.
2. See above, ch. 7.
3. Aristotle, *Physics*, I, 7 (191a 20).

the fact that it is defective but rather by the fact that it is a being. Indeed, if it were entirely defective, it would not cause anything. So, evil is the cause of something, not as a direct cause by itself, but accidentally.

[5] Moreover, evil is found to be an accidental cause in a discursive examination of all types of cause. This is so, in the kind of cause which is efficient, since a defect in the effect and in action results from a deficiency of power in the acting cause. Then, in the type of cause that is material, a defect in the effect is caused by the unsuitable character of the matter. Again, in the kind of cause which is formal, there is the fact that a privation of another form is always the adjunct of the presence of a given form. And, in the type of cause that is final, evil is connected with an improper end, inasmuch as the proper end is hindered by it.

[6] Therefore, it is clear that evil is an accidental cause and cannot be a direct cause by itself.

Chapter 15.

THAT THERE IS NO HIGHEST EVIL

[1] As a consequence, it is evident that there cannot be any highest evil which would be the first source of all evils.

[2] The highest evil ought to be quite dissociated from any good; just as the highest good is that which is completely separate from evil. Now, no evil can exist in complete separation from the good, for we have shown that evil is based upon the good.[1] Therefore, the highest evil is nothing.

[3] Again, if the highest evil be anything, it must be evil in its own essence, just as the highest good is what is good in its own essence. Now, this is impossible, because evil has

1. See above, ch. 11.

no essence, as we proved above.[2] So, it is impossible to posit a highest evil which would be the source of evils.

[4] Besides, that which is a first principle is not caused by anything. But every evil is caused by a good, as we have shown.[3] Therefore, evil is not a first principle.

[5] Moreover, evil acts only through the power of the good, as is clear from what has been established previously.[4] But a first principle acts through its own power. Therefore, evil cannot be a first principle.

[6] Furthermore, since "that which is accidental is posterior to that which is per se,"[5] it is impossible for that which is first to be accidental. Now, evil arises only accidentally, and apart from intention, as has been demonstrated.[6] So, it is impossible for evil to be a first principle.

[7] Again, every evil has an accidental cause, as we have proved.[7] Now, a first principle has no cause, whether direct or accidental. Therefore, evil cannot be a first principle in any genus.

[8] Besides, a per se cause is prior to one which is accidental.[8] But evil is not a cause, except in the accidental sense, as we have shown.[9] So, evil cannot be a first principle.

[9] By means of this conclusion, the error of the Manicheans is refuted, for they claimed that there is a highest evil which is the first principle of all evils.[10]

2. See above, ch. 7.
3. See above, ch. 10.
4. See above, ch. 9.
5. Aristotle, *Physics*, II, 6 (198a 7).
6. See above, ch. 4.
7. See above, ch. 13.
8. See Aristotle, *Physics*, loc. cit.
9. See above, ch. 14.
10. St. Augustine, *De haeres.*, 46 (PL, 42, 34).

Chapter 16.

THAT THE END OF EVERYTHING IS A GOOD

[1] If every agent acts for the sake of a good, as was proved above,[1] it follows further that the end of every being is a good. For every being is ordered to its end through its action. It must be, then, that the action itself is the end, or that the end of the action is also the end of the agent. And this is its good.

[2] Again, the end of anything is that in which its appetite terminates. Now, the appetite of anything terminates in a good; this is how the philosophers define the good: "that which all things desire."[2] Therefore, the end for everything is a good.

[3] Besides, that toward which a thing tends, while it is beyond the thing, and in which it rests, when it is possessed, is the end for the thing. Now, if anything lacks a proper perfection, it is moved toward it, in so far as lies within its capacity, but if it possess it the thing rests in it. Therefore, the end of each thing is its perfection. Now, the perfection of anything is its good. So, each thing is ordered to a good as an end.

[4] Moreover, things that know their end are ordered to the end in the same way as things which do not know it, though the ones that do know their end are moved toward it through themselves, while those that do not know it incline to their end, as directed by another being. The example of the archer and the arrow shows this clearly. However, things that know their end are always ordered to the good as an end, for the will, which is the appetite for a foreknown end, inclines toward something only if it has the rational character of a good, which is its object. So, also, the

1. See above, ch. 3.
2. Aristotle, *Nicomachean Ethics*, I, 1 (1094a 2).

things which do not know their end are ordered to a good as an end. Therefore, the end of all things is a good.

Chapter 17.

THAT ALL THINGS ARE ORDERED TO ONE END WHO IS GOD

[1] It is, consequently, apparent that all things are ordered to one good, as to their ultimate end.

[2] If, in fact, nothing tends toward a thing as an end, unless this thing is a good, it is therefore necessary that the good, as good, be the end. Therefore, that which is the highest good is, from the highest point of view, the end of all things. But there is only one highest good, and this is God, as has been demonstrated in Book One.[1] So, all things are ordered to one good, as their end, and this is God.

[3] Again, that which is supreme in any genus is the cause of all the members that belong in that genus;[2] thus, fire, which is the hottest of corporeal things, is the cause of the heat of other things. Therefore, the highest good which is God is the cause of the goodness in all good things. So, also, is He the cause of every end that is an end, since whatever is an end is such because it is a good. Now, "the cause of an attribute's inherence in a subject always itself inheres in the subject more firmly than does the attribute."[3] Therefore, God is obviously the end of all things.

[4] Besides, in any kind of causes, the first cause is more a cause than is the secondary cause, for a secondary cause is only a cause through the primary cause. Therefore, that which is the first cause in the order of final causes must be more the final cause of anything than is its proximate final

1. SCG, I, ch. 42.
2. Aristotle, *Metaphysics*, Iα, 1 (993b 22–25).
3. Aristotle, *Posterior Analytics*, I, 2 (72a 28).

cause. But God is the first cause in the order of final causes, since He is the highest in the order of goods. Therefore, He is more the end of everything than is any proximate end.

[5]   Moreover, in every ordered series of ends the ultimate end must be the end of all preceding ends. For instance, if a potion is mixed to be given a sick man, and it is given in order to purge him, and he is purged in order to make him thinner, and he is thinned down so that he may become healthy—then health must be the end of the thinning process, and of the purging, and of the other actions which precede it. But all things are found, in their various degrees of goodness, to be subordinated to one highest good which is the cause of all goodness. Consequently, since the good has the essential character of an end, all things are subordinated to God, as preceding ends under an ultimate end. Therefore, God must be the end of all things.

[6]   Furthermore, a particular good is ordered to the common good as to an end;[4] indeed, the being of a part depends on the being of the whole.[5] So, also, the good of a nation is more godlike than the good of one man.[6] Now, the highest good which is God is the common good, since the good of all things taken together depends on Him; and the good whereby each thing is good is its own particular good, and also is the good of the other things that depend on this thing. Therefore, all things are ordered to one good as their end, and that is God.

[7]   Again, order among ends is a consequence of order among agents, for, just as the supreme agent moves all secondary agents, so must all the ends of secondary agents

4. On this famous axiom, see: I. Th. Eschmann, O. P., "Bonum commune melius est quam bonum unius," *Mediaeval Studies*, 6 (1944), 62–120; and the same writer's shorter article: "In Defense of J. Maritain," *Modern Schoolman*, 22 (1945), 183–208.

5. Aristotle, *Politics*, I, 2 (1254a 9).

6. Aristotle, *Nicomachean Ethics*, I, 2 (1094b 8–9).

be ordered to the end of the supreme agent, since whatever the supreme agent does, He does for the sake of His end. Now, the supreme agent does the actions of all inferior agents by moving them all to their actions and, consequently, to their ends. Hence, it follows that all the ends of secondary agents are ordered by the first agent to His own proper end. Of course, the first agent of all things is God, as we proved in Book Two.[7] There is no other end for His will than His goodness, which is Himself, as we proved in Book One.[8] Therefore, all things, whether made by Him immediately, or by means of secondary causes, are ordered to God as to their end. Now, all things are of this kind, for, as we proved in Book Two,[9] there can be nothing that does not take its being from Him. So, all things are ordered to God as an end.

[8] Besides, the ultimate end of any maker, as a maker, is himself; we use things made by us for our own sakes, and, if sometimes a man makes a thing for some other purpose, this has reference to his own good, either as useful, delectable, or as a good for its own sake. Now, God is the productive cause of all things, of some immediately, of others by means of other causes, as is shown in the foregoing.[10] Therefore, He Himself is the end of all things.

[9] Moreover, the end holds first place over other types of cause, and to it all other causes owe the fact that they are causes in act: for the agent acts only for the sake of the end, as was pointed out.[11] Matter is brought to formal act by the agent, and thus matter actually becomes the matter of this particular thing, as form becomes the form of this thing: through the action of the agent, and consequently through the end. So, too, the posterior end is the cause of the preceding end being intended as an end, for a thing is not

7. *SCG*, II, ch. 15.
8. *SCG*, I, ch. 74.
9. *SCG*, II, ch. 15.
10. *Ibid.*
11. See above, ch. 2.

moved toward a proximate end unless for the sake of a last
end. Therefore, the ultimate end is the first cause of all.
Now, to be the first cause of all must be appropriate to the
first being, that is, to God, as was shown above.[12] So, God
is the ultimate end of all things.

[10]   Thus it is said in Proverbs (16:4): "God[13] hath
made all things for Himself"; and in the Apocalypse
(22:13): "I am Alpha and Omega, the First and the Last."

Chapter 18.

HOW GOD IS THE END OF ALL THINGS

[1]   We must further investigate how God is the end of
all. This will be made clear from the foregoing.

[2]   The ultimate end of all is such that He is, nonetheless, prior to all things in existing being.[1] Now, there is a
sort of end which, though it holds first place causally in the
order of intention, is posterior in existing. This is the situation with an end which the agent sets up by his own action,
as a physician sets up health in a sick man by his own
action; this is, of course, the physician's end. And then
there is an end which takes precedence in existing being,
just as it precedes in the causal order. For instance, we call
that an end which one intends to obtain by his action or
motion, as fire inclines upward by its motion, and a king
intends to establish a city by fighting. Therefore, God is not
the end of things in the sense of being something set up as
an ideal, but as a pre-existing being Who is to be attained.

[3]   Again, God is at once the ultimate end of things and
the first agent, as we have shown.[2] But the end that is produced by the action of the agent cannot be the first agent;

12. SCG, II, 15.
13. Douay has "the Lord."
1. SCG, I, ch. 13.
2. See above, ch. 17.

it is, rather, the effect of the agent. Therefore, God cannot be the end of things in this way, as something produced, but only as something pre-existing that is to be attained.

[4] Besides, if something act for the sake of an already existing thing, and should then set up something by its action, then this something must be added by the action of the agent to the thing for the sake of which the action is done: thus, if soldiers fight for the sake of their leader, victory will come to the leader, and this is what the soldiers cause by their actions. Now, something cannot be added to God by the action of a thing, for His goodness is completely perfect, as we showed in Book One.[3] The conclusion stands, then, that God is the end of things, not in the sense of something set up, or produced, by things, nor in the sense that something is added to Him by things, but in this sense only, that He is attained by things.

[5] Moreover, the effect must tend toward the end in the same way that the agent works for the end. Now, God, Who is the first agent of all things, does not act in such a way that something is attained by His action, but in such a way that something is enriched by His action. For He is not in potency to the possibility of obtaining something; rather, He is in perfect act simply, and as a result He is a source of enrichment. So, things are not ordered to God as to an end *for which* something may be obtained, but rather so that they may attain Himself from Himself, according to their measure, since He is their end.

Chapter 19.

THAT ALL THINGS TEND TO BECOME LIKE GOD

[1] Created things are made like unto God by the fact that they attain to divine goodness. If then, all things tend

3. *SCG*, I, ch. 37ff.

toward God as an ultimate end, so that they may attain His goodness,[1] it follows that the ultimate end of things is to become like God.

[2]   Again, the agent is said to be the end of the effect because the effect tends to become like the agent; hence, "the form of the generator is the end of the generating action."[2] But God is the end of things in such a way that He is also their first agent. Therefore, all things tend to become like God as to their ultimate end.

[3]   Besides, it is quite evident that things "naturally desire to be,"[3] and if they can be corrupted by anything they naturally resist corrupting agents and tend toward a place where they may be preserved, as fire inclines upward and earth downward. Now, all things get their being from the fact that they are made like unto God, Who is subsisting being itself, for all things exist merely as participants in existing being. Therefore, all things desire as their ultimate end to be made like unto God.

[4]   Moreover, all created things are, in a sense, images of the first agent, that is, of God, "for the agent makes a product to his own likeness."[4] Now, the function of a perfect image is to represent its prototype by likeness to it; this is why an image is made. Therefore, all things exist in order to attain to the divine likeness, as to their ultimate end.

[5]   Furthermore, everything tends through its motion or action toward a good, as its end, which we showed above.[5] Now, a thing participates in the good precisely to the same extent that it becomes like the first goodness, which is God. So, all things tend through their movements and actions toward the divine likeness, as toward their ultimate end.

1. See above, ch. 18.
2. Aristotle, *Physics*, II, 7 (198b 2).
3. Aristotle, *Nicomachean Ethics*, IX, 7 (1168a 5).
4. Aristotle, *De generatione et corruptione*, I, 7 (324a 1).
5. See above, ch. 16.

Chapter 20.

HOW THINGS IMITATE DIVINE GOODNESS

[1] From what has been said, then, it is clear that to become like God is the ultimate end of all. Now, that which possesses the formal character of an end, in the proper sense, is the good. Therefore, things tend toward this objective, of becoming like God, inasmuch as He is good.

[2] Creatures do not attain goodness in the same measure that it is in God, though each thing imitates divine goodness according to its measure. For, divine goodness is simple, entirely gathered together, as it were, into one being. Indeed, this divine existing being includes the entire fullness of perfection, as we proved in Book One.[1] As a result, since anything is perfect to the extent that it is good, this divine being is His perfect goodness. In fact, for God it is the same thing to be, to live, to be wise, to be blessed, and to be whatever else seems to belong to perfection and goodness; the whole divine goodness is, as it were, His divine existing being. Again, this divine being is the substance of the existing God.[2] Now, this cannot obtain in the case of other things. We have pointed out in Book Two[3] that no created substance is its own act of being. Hence, if anything is good by virtue of the fact that it exists, none of them is its own act of being; none of them is its own goodness. Rather, each of them is good by participation in goodness, just as it is being by participation in existing being itself.

[3] Again, not all creatures are established on one level of goodness. For some of them, substance is their form and their act: this is so for the creature to whom, because of

1. *SCG*, I, ch. 28.
2. *SCG*, I, 21ff.
3. *SCG*, II, ch. 15.

what it is essentially, it is appropriate to be, and to be good. For others, indeed, substance is composed of matter and form: to such a being it is appropriate to be, and to be good—but by virtue of some part of it, that is to say, by virtue of its form. Therefore, divine substance is its own goodness, but a simple substance participates goodness by virtue of what it is essentially, while composite substance does so by virtue of something that belongs to it as a part.

[4]   In this third grade of substance, in turn, there is found a diversity in regard to being itself. For some of them that are composed of matter and form, the form fulfills the entire potentiality of the matter, so that there remains in their matter no potentiality for another form. And consequently, there is no potentiality in other matter for the form of this type of substance. Beings of this type are celestial bodies, which actuate their entire matter when they exist. For other substances, the form does not exhaust the entire potentiality of their matter; consequently, there still remains a potentiality for another form, and in some other portion of matter there remains a potentiality for this sort of form, as is the case in the elements and in things composed of the elements. In fact, since privation is the negation in a substance of something which can be present in that substance, it is clear that the privation of a form is found combined with the type of form that does not exhaust the entire potentiality of matter. Indeed, privation cannot be associated with a substance whose form exhausts the entire potentiality of its matter; nor with one which is a form in its essence; still less with one whose essence is its very act of being. Now, since it is obvious that change cannot take place where there is no potentiality to something else, for motion is the "act of that which exists potentially,"[4] and since it is also clear that evil is the very privation of the good, it is plain that, in this lowest order of substances, the good is mutable and mixed with its contrary evil. This cannot occur in the higher orders of substances. Therefore, this substance which we have said is on

4. Aristotle, *Physics*, III, 1 (201a 10).

the lowest level holds the lowest rank in goodness, just as it has the lowest grade in being.

[5] Still, among the parts of this sort of substance composed of matter and form, an order of goodness is found. In fact, since matter, considered in itself, is potential being and form is its act, and since composite substance is actually existent through form, the form will be good in itself; while the composite substance is so in so far as it actually possesses form; and the matter is good inasmuch as it is in potentiality to form. Besides, though anything is good in so far as it is a being, it is not, however, necessary for matter which is merely potential being to be good only in potency. For being is a term used absolutely, while good also includes a relation. In fact, a thing is not called good simply because it is an end, or because it has achieved the end; provided it be ordered to the end, it may be called good because of this relation. So, matter cannot be called a being without qualification, because it is potential being, in which a relation to existing being is implied, but it can be called good, without qualification, precisely because of this relation. It is apparent in this conclusion that good is, in a way, of wider scope than being.[5] For this reason, Dionysius says, in the fourth chapter of *On the Divine Names:* "the good extends to existent beings and also to non-existent ones."[6] For, this non-existent thing—namely matter understood as subject to privation—desires a good, that is, to be. It is, consequently, evident that it is also good, for nothing except a good thing desires the good.

[6] There is still another way in which the goodness of a creature is defective in comparison with divine goodness. For, as we said, God in His very act of being holds the

---

5. This view is later modified by St. Thomas. In his *Summa Theologiae*, I, 5, 3, ad 3m, he says: "prime matter, just as it is not being except in potency, is also not good except in potency." This modification is noted in Cajetan's *Commentary,* ad loc. cit.

6. Pseudo-Dionysius, *De divinis nominibus*, IV, 7 (*PG*, 3, col. 704).

highest perfection of goodness. On the other hand, a created thing does not possess its perfection in unity, but in many items, for what is unified in the highest instance is found to be manifold in the lowest things. Consequently, God is said to be virtuous, wise, and operative with reference to the same thing, but creatures are so described with reference to a diversity of things. And so, the more multiplicity the perfect goodness of any creature requires, the more removed is it from the first goodness. If it cannot attain perfect goodness, it will keep imperfect goodness in a few items. Hence it is that, though the first and highest good is altogether simple, and the substances that are nearer to it in goodness are likewise close to it in regard to simplicity, we find some among the lowest substances to be simpler than some of their superiors, as is the case with elements in relation to animals and men; yet these lower simple beings cannot achieve the perfection of knowledge and understanding which animals and men do attain.

[7]   So, it is evident from what has been said that, though God has His own perfect and complete goodness, in accord with His simple existing being, creatures do not attain the perfection of their goodness through their being alone, but through many things. Hence, although any one of them is good in so far as it exists, it cannot be called good, without qualification, if it lack any other things required for its goodness. Thus, a man who is destitute of virtue and host to vices is indeed called good, relatively speaking; that is, to the extent that he is a being, and a man. However, in the absolute sense, he is not good, but evil. So, it is not the same thing for any creature to be and to be good without qualification, although each of them is good in so far as it exists. In God, however, to be and to be good are simply the same thing.

[8]   So, if each thing tends toward a likeness of divine goodness as its end, and if each thing becomes like the divine goodness in respect of all the things that belong to its proper goodness, then the goodness of the thing consists not only in its mere being, but in all the things needed for

its perfection, as we have shown. It is obvious, then, that things are ordered to God as an end, not merely according to their substantial act of being, but also according to those items which are added as pertinent to perfection, and even according to the proper operation which also belongs to the thing's perfection.

Chapter 21.

THAT THINGS NATURALLY TEND TO BECOME LIKE GOD INASMUCH AS HE IS A CAUSE

[1] As a result, it is evident that things also tend toward the divine likeness by the fact that they are the cause of other things.

[2] In fact, a created thing tends toward the divine likeness through its operation. Now, through its operation, one thing becomes the cause of another. Therefore, in this way, also, do things tend toward the divine likeness, in that they are the causes of other things.

[3] Again, things tend toward the divine likeness inasmuch as He is good, as we said above.[1] Now, it is as a result of the goodness of God that He confers being on all things, for a being acts by virtue of the fact that it is actually perfect. So, things generally desire to become like God in this respect, by being the causes of other things.

[4] Besides, an orderly relation toward the good has the formal character of a good thing, as is clear from what we have said.[2] Now, by the fact that it is the cause of another, a thing is ordered toward the good, for only the good is directly caused in itself; evil is merely caused accidentally, as we have shown.[3] Therefore, to be the cause of other

1. See above, ch. 20.
2. *Ibid.*
3. See above, ch. 10.

things is good. Now, a thing tends toward the divine likeness according to each good to which it inclines, since any created thing is good through participation in divine goodness. And so, things tend toward the divine likeness by the fact that they are causes of others.

[5]   Moreover, it is for the same reason that the effect tends to the likeness of the agent, and that the agent makes the effect like to itself, for the effect tends toward the end to which it is directed by the agent. The agent tends to make the patient like the agent, not only in regard to its act of being, but also in regard to causality. For instance, just as the principles by which a natural agent subsists are conferred by the agent, so are the principles by which the effect is the cause of others. Thus, an animal receives from the generating agent, at the time of its generation, the nutritive power and also the generative power. So, the effect does tend to be like the agent, not only in its species, but also in this characteristic of being the cause of others. Now, things tend to the likeness of God in the same way that effects tend to the likeness of the agent, as we have shown.[4] Therefore, things naturally tend to become like God by the fact that they are the causes of others.

[6]   Furthermore, everything is at its peak perfection when it is able to make another thing like itself; thus, a thing is a perfect source of light when it can enlighten other things. Now, everything tending to its own perfection tends toward the divine likeness. So, a thing tends to the divine likeness by tending to be the cause of other things.

[7]   And since a cause, as such, is superior to the thing caused, it is evident that to tend toward the divine likeness in the manner of something that causes others is appropriate to higher types of beings.

[8]   Again, a thing must first be perfect in itself before it can cause another thing, as we have said already. So, this final perfection comes to a thing in order that it may exist

4. See above, ch. 19.

as the cause of others. Therefore, since a created thing tends to the divine likeness in many ways, this one whereby it seeks the divine likeness by being the cause of others takes the ultimate place. Hence Dionysius says, in the third chapter of *On the Celestial Hierarchy*, that "of all things, it is more divine to become a co-worker with God";[5] in accord with the statement of the Apostle: "we are God's coadjutors" (I Cor. 3:9).

Chapter 22.

HOW THINGS ARE ORDERED TO THEIR ENDS IN VARIOUS WAYS

[1] It can be shown from the foregoing that the last thing through which any real being is ordered to its end is its operation. Yet this is done in various ways, depending on the diversity of operations.

[2] One kind of operation pertains to a thing as the mover of another, as in the actions of heating or sawing. Another is the operation of a thing that is moved by another, as in the case of being heated or being sawed. Still another operation is the perfection of an actually existing agent which does not tend to produce a change in another thing. And these last differ, first of all, from passion and motion, and secondly from action transitively productive of change in exterior matter. Examples of operations in this third sense are understanding, sensing, and willing. Hence, it is clear that the things which are moved, or passively worked on only, without actively moving or doing anything, tend to the divine likeness by being perfected within themselves; while the things that actively make and move, by virtue of their character, tend toward the divine likeness by being the causes of others. Finally, the things that move as a result of being moved tend toward the divine likeness in both ways.

5. Pseudo-Dionysius, *De caelesti hierarchia*, III, 2 (PG, 3, col. 165).

[3]   Lower bodies,[1] inasmuch as they are moved in their natural motions, are considered as moved things only, and not as movers, except in the accidental sense, for it may happen that a falling stone will put in motion a thing that gets in its way. And the same applies to alteration and the other kinds of change. Hence, the end of their motion is to achieve the divine likeness by being perfected in themselves; for instance, by possessing their proper form and being in their proper place.

[4]   On the other hand, celestial bodies move because they are moved. Hence, the end of their motion is to attain the divine likeness in both ways. In regard to the way which involves its own perfection, the celestial body comes to be in a certain place actually, to which place it was previously in potency. Nor does it achieve its perfection any less because it now stands in potency to the place in which it was previously. For, in the same way, prime matter tends toward its perfection by actually acquiring a form to which it was previously in potency, even though it then ceases to have the other form which it actually possessed before, for this is the way that matter may receive in succession all the forms to which it is potential, so that its entire potentiality may be successively reduced to act, which could not be done all at once. Hence, since a celestial body is in potency to place in the same way that prime matter is to form, it achieves its perfection through the fact that its entire

1. Here, and at many points throughout Book Three, St. Thomas will use this contrast between "lower bodies" and "celestial bodies" (*corpora inferiora et caelestia*). It was a commonplace in mediaeval science that there are these two kinds of bodies. The lower, or terrestrial, bodies were thought to include a type of prime matter subject to four kinds of change: of place, of quantitative increase or decrease, of quality, and of substance. On the other hand, higher, or celestial, bodies were considered to contain another type of prime matter, subject only to one kind of change, that of place. See A. C. Crombie, *Augustine to Galileo* (Cambridge: 1953), pp. 52–56. For an analysis of the theory in St. Thomas' teacher, St. Albert, see E. Gilson, *History of Christian Philosophy in the Middle Ages* (New York, 1955), pp. 279–282.

potency to place is successively reduced to act, which could not be done all at once.

[5] In regard to the way which involves movers that actively move, the end of their motion is to attain the divine likeness by being the causes of others. Now, they are the causes of others by the fact that they cause generation and corruption and other changes in these lower things. So, the motions of the celestial bodies, as actively moving, are ordered to the generation and corruption which take place in these lower bodies.—Nor is it unfitting that celestial bodies should move for the sake of the generation and corruption of these lower things, even though lower bodies are of less value than celestial bodies, while, of course, the end should be more important than what is for the sake of the end.

Indeed, the generating agent acts for the sake of the form of the product of generation, yet this product is not more valuable than the agent; rather, in the case of univocal agents it is of the same species as the agent. In fact, the generating agent intends as its ultimate end, not the form of the product generated, which is the end of the process of generation, but the likeness of divine being in the perpetuation of the species and in the diffusion of its goodness, through the act of handing on its specific form to others, and of being the cause of others. Similarly, then, celestial bodies, although they are of greater value than lower bodies, tend toward the generation of these latter, and through their motions to the actual eduction of the forms of the products of generation, not as an ultimate end but as thereby intending the divine likeness as an ultimate end, inasmuch as they exist as the causes of other things.

[6] Now, we should keep in mind that a thing participates in the likeness of the divine will, through which things are brought into being and preserved, to the extent that it participates in the likeness of divine goodness which is the object of His will. Higher things participate more simply and more universally in the likeness of divine good-

ness, while lower things do so more particularly and more in detail. Hence, between celestial and lower bodies the likeness is not observed according to complete equivalence, as it is in the case of things of one kind. Rather, it is like the similarity of a universal agent to a particular effect. Therefore, just as in the order of lower bodies the intention of a particular agent is focussed on the good of this species or that, so is the intention of a celestial body directed to the common good of corporeal substance which is preserved, and multiplied, and increased through generation.

[7]   As we said, since any moved thing, inasmuch as it is moved, tends to the divine likeness so that it may be perfected in itself, and since a thing is perfect in so far as it is actualized, the intention of everything existing in potency must be to tend through motion toward actuality. And so, the more posterior and more perfect an act is, the more fundamentally is the inclination of matter directed toward it. Hence, in regard to the last and most perfect act that matter can attain, the inclination of matter whereby it desires form must be inclined as toward the ultimate end of generation. Now, among the acts pertaining to forms, certain gradations are found. Thus, prime matter is in potency, first of all, to the form of an element. When it is existing under the form of an element it is in potency to the form of a mixed body;[2] that is why the elements are matter for the mixed body. Considered under the form of a mixed body, it is in potency to a vegetative soul, for this sort of soul is the act of a body. In turn, the vegetative soul is in potency to a sensitive soul, and a sensitive one to an intellectual one. This the process of generation shows: at the start of generation there is the embryo living with plant life, later with animal life, and finally with human life.[3] After this last type of form, no later and more noble form

2. The "mixed body" is composed of any combination of two or more of the four elements (earth, air, fire, water). See St. Thomas, Summa Theologiae, I, 76, 4, ad 4m (in Pegis, Basic Writings of St. Thomas, I, pp. 709–710).

3. Cf. St. Thomas, Summa Theologiae, I, 118, 2, c. and ad 2m.

is found in the order of generable and corruptible things. Therefore, the ultimate end of the whole process of generation is the human soul, and matter tends toward it as toward an ultimate form. So, elements exist for the sake of mixed bodies; these latter exist for the sake of living bodies, among which plants exist for animals, and animals for men. Therefore, man is the end of the whole order of generation.

[8] And since a thing is generated and preserved in being by the same reality, there is also an order in the preservation of things, which parallels the foregoing order of generation. Thus we see that mixed bodies are sustained by the appropriate qualities of the elements; plants, in turn, are nourished by mixed bodies; animals get their nourishment from plants: so, those that are more perfect and more powerful from those that are more imperfect and weaker. In fact, man uses all kinds of things for his own advantage: some for food, others for clothing. That is why he was created nude by nature, since he is able to make clothes for himself from other things; just as nature also provided him with no appropriate nourishment, except milk, because he can obtain food for himself from a variety of things. Other things he uses for transportation, since we find man the inferior of many animals in quickness of movement, and in the strength to do work; other animals being provided, as it were, for his assistance. And, in addition to this, man uses all sense objects for the perfection of intellectual knowledge. Hence it is said of man in the Psalms (8:8) in a statement directed to God: "Thou hast subjected all things under his feet." And Aristotle says, in the *Politics* I,[4] that man has natural dominion over all animals.

[9] So, if the motion of the heavens is ordered to generation, and if the whole of generation is ordered to man as a last end within this genus, it is clear that the end of celestial motion is ordered to man, as to an ultimate end in the genus of generable and mobile beings.

4. Aristotle, *Politics*, I, 5 (1254b 9).

[10]   Hence the statement in Deuteronomy (4:19) that God made celestial bodies, "for the service of all peoples."[5]

Chapter 23.

THAT THE MOTION OF THE HEAVENS COMES FROM AN INTELLECTUAL PRINCIPLE

[1]   From the preceding we can also show that the prime motive principle of the heavens is something intellectual.

[2]   Nothing that acts in function of its own species intends a form higher than its own form, for every agent tends toward its like. Now, a celestial body, acting under its own motion, tends toward the ultimate form, which is the human intellect; and which is, in fact, higher than any bodily form, as is clear from the foregoing.[1] Therefore, a celestial body does not act for a generation according to its own species, as a principal agent, but according to the species of a higher intellectual agent, to which the celestial body is related as an instrument to a principal agent. Now, the heavens act for the purpose of generation in accord with the way in which they are moved. So, a celestial body is moved by some intellectual substance.

[3]   Again, everything that is moved must be moved by another being, as we proved earlier.[2] Therefore, a celestial body is moved by something else. So, this other thing is either completely separated from it, or is united with it in the sense that the composite of the celestial body and the mover may be said to move itself, in so far as one of its parts is the mover and another part is the thing moved. Now, if it works this way, since everything that moves itself is alive and animated, it would follow that the heavens are animated, and by no other soul than an intellectual one:

5. Douay has "nations" for "peoples."
1. See above, ch. 22.
2. SCG, I, ch. 13.

not by a nutritive soul, for generation and corruption are not within its power; nor by a sensitive soul, for a celestial body has no diversity of organs. The conclusion is, then, that it is moved by an intellective soul.—On the other hand, if it is moved by an extrinsic mover, this latter will be either corporeal or incorporeal. Now, if it is corporeal, it will not move unless it is moved, for no body moves unless it is moved, as was evident previously.[3] Therefore, it will also have to be moved by another. And since there should be no process to infinity in the order of bodies, we will have to come to an incorporeal first mover. Now, that which is utterly separate from body must be intellectual, as is evident from earlier considerations.[4] Therefore, the motion of the heavens, that is of the first body, comes from an intellectual substance.

[4]   Besides, heavy and light bodies are moved by their generating agent, and by that which takes away any impediment to motion, as was proved in *Physics* VIII.[5] For it cannot be that the form in them is the mover, and the matter the thing moved, since nothing is moved unless it be a body. Now, just as the elemental bodies are simple and there is no composition in them, except of matter and form, so also are the celestial bodies simple. And so, if they are moved in the same way as heavy and light bodies, they must be moved directly by their generating agent, and accidentally by the agent which removes an impediment to motion. But this is impossible, for these bodies are not capable of generation: for they are not endowed with contrariety, and their motions cannot be impeded. So, these bodies must be moved by movers that function through knowing; not through sensitive knowledge, as we showed, but through intellectual knowledge.

[5]   Moreover, if the principle of celestial motion is simply a nature lacking any type of apprehension, then the prin-

3. *SCG*, II, ch. 20.
4. *SCG*, I, ch. 44.
5. Aristotle, *Physics*, VIII, 4 (256a 1).

ciple of celestial motion must be the form of a celestial body, just as is the case in the elements. For, although simple forms are not movers, they are nonetheless the principles of motions, since natural motions are resultant from them, as are all other natural properties. Now, it is impossible for celestial motion to result from the form of a celestial body, as from an active principle. A form is the principle of local motion in the same way that a certain place is proper to a body by virtue of its form; it is moved to this place by the force of its form tending to it, and, since the generating agent gives the form, it is said to be the mover. For instance, it is appropriate to fire, by virtue of its form, to be in a higher place. But one place is no more appropriate than another for a celestial body, according to its form. Therefore, the principle of celestial motion is not simply the nature of the body. So, the principle of its motion must be something that moves as a result of apprehension.

[6]   Furthermore, nature always tends toward one objective; hence, things which result from nature always occur in the same way, unless they are interfered with, and this happens to few of them. Indeed, that which has a deformity within its very definition cannot be an end to which a nature tends. Now, motion, by definition, is of this type, for whatever is moved, by virtue of that fact, is in a different condition before and after.[6] So, it is impossible for a nature to tend toward motion for the sake of motion. Therefore, it tends through motion toward rest, and the latter is related to motion as one to many. Indeed, a thing at rest is one which is in the same condition before and after.[7] If then, the motion of the heavens were simply from a nature, it would be ordered to some condition of rest. But the contrary of this is apparent, for celestial motion is continuous. Therefore, the motion of the heavens does not arise from a nature, as its active principle, but rather from an intelligent substance.

6. Aristotle, *Physics*, V, 1 (224b 1).
7. *Ibid.*, V, 6 (229b 23).

[7] Again, for every motion that is from a nature, as an active principle, if its approach to something be natural, then its removal from that objective must be unnatural and against nature. Thus, a heavy thing naturally moves downward, but for it to move in the opposite direction is against nature. Therefore, if the motion of the heavens were natural, since it tends westward naturally, it would return to the east in the manner of a thing that recedes from the west by a motion against nature. Now, this is impossible. In celestial motion there is nothing violent and against nature. So, it is impossible for the active principle of celestial motion to be a nature. Therefore, its active principle is some apprehensive power, and through understanding, as is clear from what was said earlier. So, a celestial body is moved by an intellectual substance.

[8] Yet we must not deny that celestial motion is natural. In fact, a motion is called natural, not simply because of its active principle, but also because of its passive one. This is exemplified in the generation of simple bodies. Indeed, this generation cannot be called natural by reason of the active principle, for that is moved naturally by an active principle, which has its active principle within it; "a nature is a principle of motion in that to which it belongs."[8] But the active principle in the generation of a simple body is outside. So, it is not natural by reason of the active principle, but only by reason of the passive principle, which is the matter in which the natural appetite for a natural form is present. And so, the motion of a celestial body, as far as its active principle is concerned, is not natural, but voluntary and intellectual; however, in relation to its passive principle, the motion is natural, for a celestial body has a natural aptitude for such motion.

[9] This becomes clearly evident when we consider the relation of a celestial body to its location. A thing is acted on passively, and is moved, in so far as it is in potency; while it acts and moves, in so far as it is in act. Now, a celestial

8. *Ibid.*, II, 1 (193b 23).

body, considered in its substance, is found to be indifferently related to every place, just as prime matter is to every form, as we said before.[9] Of course, it is a different situation in the case of a heavy or light body which, considered in its nature, is not indifferent to every place, but is determined by virtue of its form to a place of its own. So, the nature of a heavy or light body is the active principle of its motion, while the nature of a celestial body is the passive principle of its motion. Hence, no one should get the impression that the latter is moved violently, as is the case with heavy and light bodies that are moved by us through understanding. For there is present in heavy and light bodies a natural aptitude for motion contrary to that in which they are moved by us, and so they are moved by us through violence. However, the motion of an animated body, in which it is moved by a soul, is not violent for it as an animal, though it is violent for it as a heavy object. Celestial bodies have no aptitude for contrary motion, but only for that whereby they are moved by an intelligent substance. Consequently, it is at once voluntary, in relation to the active principle, and natural, in relation to the passive principle.

[10]   That the motion of the heavens is voluntary according to its active principle is not repugnant to the unity and uniformity of celestial motion because of the fact that the will is open to a plurality of actions and is not determined to one of them. In fact, just as a nature is determined to one objective by its power, so is the will determined to one objective by its wisdom, whereby the will is infallibly directed to one end.

[11]   It is also evident from the foregoing that in celestial motion neither the approach to a certain place, nor the regression from that place, is against nature. Such a thing does occur in the motion of heavy and light bodies for two reasons. First, because the natural tendency in heavy and light things is determined to one place; hence, just as such a body naturally tends to this place, so does it go

9. See above, ch. 22.

against nature in receding from it. Second, because two motions, one approaching a term and the other receding from it, are contrary. But, if we take into consideration in this motion of heavy and light bodies, not the final place but an intermediate one, then just as an approach may naturally be made to it, so also may a recession be naturally made from it. For the whole motion comes under one natural tendency, and these motions are not contrary but one and continuous.—So, too, is the situation in the motion of celestial bodies, for the tendency of their nature is not toward some determinate place, as has been said already. Also, the motion whereby a body moves in a circle, away from a point of reference, is not contrary to the motion whereby it approaches the point, but it is one continuous motion. Hence, each place in the motion of the heavens is like a middle point, and not like a terminal point in straight-line motion.

[12] Nor does it make any difference, as far as our present purpose is concerned, whether a heavenly body is moved by a conjoined intellectual substance which is its soul, or by a separate substance; nor whether each celestial body is moved immediately by God, or whether none is so moved, because all are moved through intermediary, created, intellectual substances; nor whether the first body alone is immediately moved by God, and the others through the mediation of created substances—provided it is granted that celestial motion comes from intellectual substance.

Chapter 24.

HOW EVEN BEINGS DEVOID OF KNOWLEDGE SEEK THE GOOD

[1] Now, if a celestial body is moved by intellectual substance, as we have shown,[1] and if the motion of a celestial

1. See above, ch. 23.

body is ordered to generation in the realm of things here below, it must be that the processes of generation and the motions of these lower things start from the intention of an intelligent substance. For the intention of the principal agent and that of the instrument are directed toward the same thing. Now, the heavens is the cause of the movements of inferior bodies, by virtue of its own motion in which it is moved by an intellectual substance. It follows, then, that the heavenly body is like an instrument for intellectual substance. Therefore, the forms and movements of lower bodies are caused by intellectual substance which intends them as a principal agent, while the celestial body is like an instrument.

[2]   It must be, then, that the species of things caused and intended by the intellectual agent exist beforehand in his intellect, as the forms of artifacts pre-exist in the intellect of the artist and are projected from there into their products. So, all the forms that are in these lower substances, and all their motions, are derived from the intellectual forms which are in the intellect of some substance, or substances. Consequently, Boethius says in his book, *The Trinity*, that "forms which are in matter have come from forms which are without matter."[2] And on this point, Plato's statement is verified, that forms separated from matter are the principles of forms that are in it.[3] Although Plato claimed that they subsist in themselves and immediately cause the forms of sensible things, we assert that they exist in an intellect and cause lower forms through the motion of the heavens.

[3]   Since everything that is moved directly and not merely accidentally by another being is directed by that being to the end of its motion, and since the celestial body is moved by an intellectual substance, and, moreover, the celestial body causes, through its own motion, all the motions in these lower things, the celestial body must be directed to

2. Boethius, *De Trinitate*, II (PL, 64, col. 1250).
3. See Aristotle, *Metaphysics*, I, 6 (987b 7).

the end of its motion by an intellectual substance, and so must all lower bodies be directed to their own ends.

[4]   So, then, it is not difficult to see how natural bodies, devoid of knowledge, are moved and perform actions for an end. They tend to the end as things directed to that end by an intellectual substance, in the way that an arrow tends toward the target when it has been aimed by the archer. Just as the arrow attains its inclination to a definite end from the archer's act of shooting it, so do natural bodies attain their inclination to natural ends, from natural movers; from which movers they also receive their forms, powers, and motions.

[5]   Consequently, it is also evident that every working of nature is the work of an intelligent substance, because an effect is more fundamentally attributed to the prime mover, which aims at the end, than to the instruments which have been directed by it. And because of this we find that the workings of nature proceed toward their end in an orderly way, as do the actions of a wise man.

[6]   Hence, it becomes obvious that even things which lack knowledge can be made to work for an end, and to seek the good by a natural appetite, and to seek the divine likeness and their own perfection. And there is no difference between saying one of these things or the other. For, by the fact that they tend to their own perfection they tend to the good, since a thing is good to the extent that it is perfect. Moreover, by virtue of tending to be good it tends to the divine likeness, for a thing is made like unto God in so far as it is good. And this or that particular good thing becomes an object of desire according as it is a likeness of prime goodness. So, too, for this reason it tends to its own good, because it tends to the divine likeness, and not conversely. Hence, it is clear that all things desire the divine likeness as an ultimate end.

[7]   Now, the good that is proper to a thing may be received in many ways. One way depends on what is appropriate to the essential character of the individual. It is

thus that an animal seeks his good, when he desires the food whereby he may be kept in existence. A second way depends on what is appropriate to the species. It is in this way that an animal desires his proper good, inasmuch as he desires the procreation of offspring and the nourishment of the same, or the performance of any other work that is for the preservation or protection of individuals belonging to his species. A third way depends on the essential character of his genus. It is in this way that an equivocal agent seeks its proper good by an act of causation, as in the case of the heavens. And a fourth way depends on the analogical likeness of things produced, in relation to their source. And it is in this way that God, Who is beyond genus, gives existing being to all, because of His own goodness.

[8] It is evident, next, that the more perfect something is in its power, and the higher it is in the scale of goodness, the more does it have an appetite for a broader common good, and the more does it seek and become involved in the doing of good for beings far removed from itself. Indeed, imperfect beings tend only to the good proper to the individual, while perfect beings tend to the good of their species. But more perfect beings tend to the good of the genus, while God, Who is most perfect in goodness, tends toward the good of being as a whole. Hence it is said by some people, and not inappropriately, that "the good, as such, is diffusive,"[4] because the better a thing is, the more does it diffuse its goodness to remote beings. And since, "in every genus, that which is most perfect is the archetype and measure of all things belonging in the genus,"[5] God, Who is most perfect in goodness and Who diffuses His goodness in the broadest way, must be in His diffusion the archetype for all diffusers of goodness. Now, inasmuch as a thing diffuses goodness to other beings, it comes to be their cause. As a result, it is also clear that a thing which tends to be-

4. See Pseudo-Dionysius, De divinis nominibus, IV, 1 (PG, 3, col. 693); also, J. Peghaire, "L'axiome Bonum est diffusivum sui dans le néo-platonisme et le thomisme," Revue de l'Université d'Ottawa, 2 (1932) 5–32.

5. Aristotle, Metaphysics, Iα, 1 (993b 24).

come the cause of others tends toward the divine likeness, and nonetheless it tends toward its own good.

[9] Therefore, it is not unfitting to say that the motions of the heavenly bodies and the actions of their movers are in some sense for the sake of these generable and corruptible bodies which are less worthy than they. They are not for the sake of these bodies, in the sense of an ultimate end; rather, by intending the generation of these bodies they intend their own good and the divine likeness as an ultimate end.

Chapter 25.

THAT TO UNDERSTAND GOD IS THE END OF EVERY INTELLECTUAL SUBSTANCE

[1] Since all creatures, even those devoid of understanding, are ordered to God as to an ultimate end, all achieve this end to the extent that they participate somewhat in His likeness. Intellectual creatures attain it in a more special way, that is, through their proper operation of understanding Him. Hence, this must be the end of the intellectual creature, namely, to understand God.

[2] The ultimate end of each thing is God, as we have shown.[1] So, each thing intends, as its ultimate end, to be united with God as closely as is possible for it. Now, a thing is more closely united with God by the fact that it attains to His very substance in some manner, and this is accomplished when one knows something of the divine substance, rather than when one acquires some likeness of Him. Therefore, an intellectual substance tends to divine knowledge as an ultimate end.

[3] Again, the proper operation of a thing is an end for it, for this is its secondary perfection. That is why whatever is fittingly related to its proper operation is said to be virtuous

2. See above, ch. 17.

and good. But the act of understanding is the proper operation of an intellectual substance. Therefore, this act is its
end. And that which is most perfect in this operation is the
ultimate end, particularly in the case of operations that are
not ordered to any products, such as the acts of understanding and sensing. Now, since operations of this type are
specified by their objects, through which they are known
also, any one of these operations must be more perfect
when its object is more perfect. And so, to understand the
most perfect intelligible object, which is God, is the most
perfect thing in the genus of this operation of understanding. Therefore, to know God by an act of understanding is
the ultimate end of every intellectual substance.

[4]   Of course, someone could say that the ultimate end of
an intellectual substance consists, in fact, in understanding
the best intelligible object—not that the best object of understanding for this or that particular intellectual substance
is absolutely the best intelligible object, but that, the higher
an intellectual substance is, the higher will its best object
of understanding be. And so, perhaps the highest created
intellectual substance may have what is absolutely best as
its best intelligible object, and, consequently, its felicity
will consist in understanding God, but the felicity of any
lower intellectual substance will lie in the understanding
of some lower intelligible object, which is, however, the
highest thing understood by it. Particularly would it seem
true of the human intellect that its function is not to understand absolutely the best intelligible object, because of
its weakness; indeed, it stands in relation to the knowing
of the greatest intelligible object, "as the owl's eye is to
the sunlight."[2]

[5]   But it seems obvious that the end of any intellectual
substance, even the lowest, is to understand God. It has
been shown above[3] that the ultimate end of all things, to
which they tend, is God. Though it is the lowest in the

2. Aristotle, *Metaphysics*, Iα, 1 (993b 9).
3. See above, ch. 17.

order of intellectual substances, the human intellect is, nevertheless, superior to all things that lack understanding. And so, since there should not be a less noble end for a more noble substance, the end for the human intellect will be God Himself. And an intelligent being attains his ultimate end by understanding Him, as was indicated. Therefore, the human intellect reaches God as its end, through an act of understanding.

[6] Again, just as things devoid of understanding tend toward God as an end, by way of assimilation, so intellectual substances do so by way of cognition, as is evident from the foregoing. Now, although things devoid of understanding tend to the likeness of their proximate agents, their natural tendency does not, however, rest there, for this tendency has as its end assimilation to the highest good, as is apparent from what we have said,[4] even though these things can only attain this likeness in a very imperfect way. Therefore, however small the amount of divine knowledge that the intellect may be able to grasp, that will be for the intellect, in regard to its ultimate end, much more than the perfect knowledge of lower objects of understanding.

[7] Besides, a thing has the greatest desire for its ultimate end. Now, the human intellect has a greater desire, and love, and pleasure, in knowing divine matters than it has in the perfect knowledge of the lowest things, even though it can grasp but little concerning divine things. So, the ultimate end of man is to understand God, in some fashion.

[8] Moreover, a thing inclines toward the divine likeness as to its own end. So, that whereby a thing chiefly becomes like God is its ultimate end. Now, an intellectual creature chiefly becomes like God by the fact that it is intellectual, for it has this sort of likeness over and above what other creatures have, and this likeness includes all others. In the genus of this sort of likeness a being becomes more like God by actually understanding than by habitually or potentially understanding, because God is always actually un-

4. See above, ch. 19.

derstanding, as we proved in Book One.[5] And, in this actual understanding, it becomes most like God by understanding God Himself, for God understands all things in the act of understanding Himself, as we proved in Book One.[6] Therefore, to understand God is the ultimate end of every intellectual substance.

[9] Furthermore, that which is capable of being loved only for the sake of some other object exists for the sake of that other thing which is lovable simply on its own account. In fact, there is no point in going on without end in the working of natural appetite, since natural desire would then be futile, because it is impossible to get to the end of an endless series. Now, all practical sciences, arts, and powers are objects of love only because they are means to something else, for their purpose is not knowledge but operation. But the speculative sciences are lovable for their own sake, since their end is knowledge itself. Nor do we find any action in human affairs, except speculative thought, that is not directed to some other end. Even sports activities, which appear to be carried on without any purpose, have a proper end, namely, so that after our minds have been somewhat relaxed through them we may be then better able to do serious jobs. Otherwise, if sport were an end in itself, the proper thing to do would be to play all the time, but that is not appropriate. So, the practical arts are ordered to the speculative ones, and likewise every human operation to intellectual speculation, as an end. Now, among all the sciences and arts which are thus subordinated, the ultimate end seems to belong to the one that is preceptive and architectonic in relation to the others. For instance, the art of navigation, to which the end, that is the use, of a ship pertains, is architectonic and preceptive in relation to the art of shipbuilding. In fact, this is the way that first philosophy is related to the other speculative sciences, for all the others depend on it, in the sense that they take their principles from it, and also the position to be assumed against

5. SCG, I, ch. 56.
6. SCG, I, ch. 49.

those who deny the principles. And this first philosophy is wholly ordered to the knowing of God, as its ultimate end; that is why it is also called *divine science*.[7] So, divine knowledge is the ultimate end of every act of human knowledge and every operation.

[10] Again, in all agents and movers that are arranged in an order, the end of the first agent and mover must be the ultimate end of all. Thus, the end of the commander of an army is the end of all who serve as soldiers under him. Now, of all the parts of man, the intellect is found to be the superior mover, for the intellect moves the appetite, by presenting it with its object; then the intellectual appetite, that is the will, moves the sensory appetites, irascible and concupiscible, and that is why we do not obey concupiscence unless there be a command from the will; and finally, the sense appetite, with the advent of consent from the will, now moves the body. Therefore, the end of the intellect is the end of all human actions. "But the end and good of the intellect are the true";[8] consequently, the first truth is the ultimate end. So, the ultimate end of the whole man, and of all his operations and desires, is to know the first truth, which is God.

[11] Besides, there is naturally present in all men the desire to know the causes of whatever things are observed. Hence, because of wondering about things that were seen but whose causes were hidden, men first began to think philosophically; when they found the cause, they were satisfied. But the search did not stop until it reached the first cause, for "then do we think that we know perfectly, when we know the first cause."[9] Therefore, man naturally desires, as his ultimate end, to know the first cause. But the first cause of all things is God. Therefore, the ultimate end of man is to know God.

7. See Aristotle, *Metaphysics*, I, 2 (983a 6).
8. Aristotle, *Nicomachean Ethics*, VI, 2 (1139a 27).
9. Aristotle, *Metaphysics*, I, 3 (983a 25).

[12]   Moreover, for each effect that he knows, man naturally desires to know the cause. Now, the human intellect knows universal being. So, he naturally desires to know its cause, which is God alone, as we proved in Book Two.[10] Now, a person has not attained his ultimate end until natural desire comes to rest. Therefore, for human happiness which is the ultimate end it is not enough to have merely any kind of intelligible knowledge; there must be divine knowledge, as an ultimate end, to terminate the natural desire. So, the ultimate end of man is the knowledge of God.

[13]   Furthermore, a body tending toward its proper place by natural appetite is moved more forcibly and swiftly as it approaches its end. Thus, Aristotle proves, in On the Heavens I, [11] that natural motion in a straight line cannot go on to infinity, for then it would be no more moved later than earlier. So, a thing that tends more forcibly later than earlier, toward an objective, is not moved toward an indefinite objective, but tends toward some determinate thing. Now, we find this situation in the desire to know. The more a person knows, the more is he moved by the desire to know. Hence, man's natural desire tends, in the process of knowing, toward some definite end. Now, this can be none other than the most noble object of knowledge, which is God. Therefore, divine knowledge is the ultimate end of man.

[14]   Now, the ultimate end of man, and of every intellectual substance, is called felicity or happiness, because this is what every intellectual substance desires as an ultimate end, and for its own sake alone. Therefore, the ultimate happiness and felicity of every intellectual substance is to know God.

[15]   And so, it is said in Matthew (5:8): "Blessed are the clean of heart, for they shall see God"; and in John (17:3):

10. SCG, II, ch. 15.
11. Aristotle, De caelo, I, 8 (272a 18).

"This is eternal life, that they may know Thee, the only true God."

[16] With this view, the judgment of Aristotle is also in agreement, in the last Book of his *Ethics*, where he says that the ultimate felicity of man is "speculative, in accord with the contemplation of the best object of speculation."[12]

Chapter 26.

WHETHER FELICITY CONSISTS
IN A WILL ACT

[1] Now, since an intellectual substance, through its own operation, attains to God, not only by understanding, but also through an act of will, by desiring and loving Him and by taking delight in Him, it may appear to someone that the ultimate end and the ultimate felicity of man do not lie in knowing, but in loving God, or in some other act of will relating to Him.[1]

[2] Especially so, since the object of the will is the good, and the good has the rational character of an end, while the true which is the object of the intellect does not have the rational character of an end, except inasmuch as it is also a good. Consequently, it does not seem that man attains his ultimate end through an act of understanding, but, rather, through an act of will.

[3] Again, the ultimate perfection of operation is delight, "which perfects activity as beauty perfects youth," as the Philosopher says in *Ethics* x.[2] So, if perfect operation is the ultimate end, it appears that the ultimate end is more in accord with an operation of the will than of the intellect.

12. Aristotle, *Nicomachean Ethics*, X, 7 (1177a 18).
1. See St. Bonaventure, *In II Sent.*, d. 38, a. 1, q. 2, resp. (editio minor, Quaracchi, 1938, t. II, pp. 917–918).
2. Aristotle, *Nicomachean Ethics*, X, 4 (1174b 31).

[4]   Besides, delight seems to be so much an object of desire for its own sake that it is never desired for the sake of something else; indeed, it is foolish to ask a person why he wishes to be delighted. Now, this is characteristic of the ultimate end: it is sought for its own sake. Therefore, the ultimate end lies in an operation of the will rather than of the intellect, it would seem.

[5]   Moreover, all men agree to the fullest extent in their appetite for the ultimate end, for it is natural. Now, more men seek delight than knowledge. So, it would seem that the end is delight rather than knowledge.

[6]   Furthermore, the will seems to be a higher power than the intellect, for the will moves the intellect to its act; indeed, the intellect actually considers, whenever it wills to, what it retains habitually.[3] Therefore, the action of the will seems to be nobler than the action of the intellect. And so, it seems that the ultimate end, which is happiness, consists rather in an act of will than in an act of intellect.

[7]   However, it can be shown that this view is quite impossible.

[8]   Since happiness is the proper good of an intellectual nature, happiness must pertain to an intellectual nature by reason of what is proper to that nature. Now, appetite is not peculiar to intellectual nature; instead, it is present in all things, though it is in different things in different ways. And this diversity arises from the fact that things are differently related to knowledge. For things lacking knowledge entirely have natural appetite only. And things endowed with sensory knowledge have, in addition, sense appetite, under which irascible and concupiscible powers are included. But things possessed of intellectual knowledge also have an appetite proportionate to this knowledge, that is, will. So, the will is not peculiar to intellectual nature by virtue of being an appetite, but only in so far as it depends on intellect. However, the intellect, in itself, is peculiar to an in-

3. See Averroes, In Aristotelis de anima, III, 18 (ed. Venetiis, 1550–1552, t. VI, 169v).

tellectual nature. Therefore, happiness, or felicity, consists substantially and principally in an act of the intellect rather than in an act of the will.

[9] Again, in the case of all powers that are moved by their objects the objects are naturally prior to the acts of these powers, just as a mover is naturally prior to the moving of its passive object. Now, the will is such a power, for the object of appetition moves the appetite. So, the will's object is naturally prior to its act. Hence, its first object precedes every one of its acts. Therefore, no act of the will can be the first thing that is willed. But that is what the ultimate end is, in the sense of happiness. So, it is impossible for happiness, or felicity, to be the very act of the will.

[10] Besides, for all the powers capable of reflection on their own acts, the act of such a power must first be brought to bear on some other object, and then directed to its own act. If the intellect is to understand itself in the act of understanding, it must first be taken that it understands something, and then, as a result, that it understands that it is understanding. For, this act of understanding which the intellect understands pertains to some object. Hence, it is necessary either to proceed through an endless series, or, if we are to come to a first object of understanding, it will not be the act of understanding but rather some intelligible thing. Likewise, the first willed object must not be the will's act but some other good thing. But, for an intellectual nature, the first thing that is willed is happiness itself, or felicity, since it is for the sake of this happiness that we will whatever we will. Therefore, it is impossible for felicity to consist essentially in an act of the will.

[11] Moreover, each thing possesses its true nature by virtue of the components which make up its substance. Thus, a real man differs from a painting of a man by virtue of the things that constitute the substance of man. Now, in their relation to the will act, true happiness does not differ from false happiness. In fact, the will, when it desires, loves or enjoys, is related in just the same way to its

object, whatever it may be that is presented to it as a highest good, whether truly or falsely. Of course, whether the object so presented is truly the highest good, or is false, this distinction is made on the part of the intellect. Therefore, happiness, or felicity, essentially consists in understanding rather than in an act of the will.

[12]   Furthermore, if any act of the will were this felicity, this act would be either one of desire, of love, or of delight. Now, it is impossible for the act of desiring to be the ultimate end. For it is by desire that the will tends toward what it does not yet possess, but this is contrary to the essential character of the ultimate end.—So, too, the act of loving cannot be the ultimate end. For a good is loved not only when possessed but also when not possessed. Indeed, it is as a result of love that what is not possessed is sought with desire, and if the love of something already possessed is more perfect, this results from the fact that the good which was loved is possessed. So, it is a different thing to possess a good which is the end, and to love it; for love, before possession, is imperfect, but after possession, perfect. —Similarly, delight is not the ultimate end. For the very possession of the good is the cause of delight: we either experience it while the good is presently possessed, or we remember it when it was formerly possessed, or we hope for it when it is to be possessed in the future. So, delight is not the ultimate end. Therefore, none of the acts of will can be this felicity substantially.

[13]   Again, if delight were the ultimate end, it would be desired for its own sake. But this is false. The value of desiring a certain delight arises from the thing which delight accompanies. For the delight that accompanies good and desirable operations is good and desirable, but that which accompanies evil deeds is evil and repulsive. So, it owes the fact that it is good and desirable to something else. Therefore, delight is not the ultimate end, in the sense of felicity.

[14]   Besides, the right order of things is in agreement with the order of nature, for natural things are ordered to

their end without error. In the order of natural things, delight is for the sake of operation, and not conversely. In fact, we see that nature has associated pleasure with those operations of animals that are clearly ordered to necessary ends; such as to the eating of food, for this is ordered to the preservation of the individual; and to the use of sexual capacities, for this is ordered to the preservation of the species. Indeed, unless pleasure were associated with them, animals would refrain from these necessary activities that we have mentioned. Therefore, it is impossible for pleasure to be the ultimate end.

[15]   Moreover, pleasure seems to be simply the repose of the will in some appropriate good, as desire is the inclination of the will toward the attainment of some good. Now, just as a man is inclined through his will to the end and reposes in it, so do physical bodies in nature possess natural inclinations to proper ends, and these inclinations come to rest when the end has already been reached. However, it is ridiculous to say that the end of a heavy body's motion is not to be in its proper place, but that the end is the resting of the inclination whereby it tends there. If nature had intended this at the beginning, that the inclination would come to rest, it would not have given such an inclination; instead, it gives it so that, by this means, the thing may tend to a proper place. When this has been reached, as an end, the repose of the inclination follows. And so, such repose is not the end, but rather a concomitant of the end. Nor, indeed, is pleasure the ultimate end; it is its concomitant. And so, by an even greater reason, no other act of the will is felicity.

[16]   If one thing has another thing as its external end, then the operation whereby the first thing primarily attains the second will be called the ultimate end of the first thing. Thus, for those to whom money is an end, we say that to possess the money is their end, but not the loving of it, nor the craving of it. Now, the ultimate end of an intellectual substance is God. So, that operation of man is substantially his happiness, or his felicity, whereby he primarily attains

to God. This is the act of understanding, for we cannot will what we do not understand. Therefore, the ultimate felicity of man lies substantially in knowing God through his intellect, and not in an act of the will.

[17]   At this point, then, the answer to the arguments against our view is clear from what we have said. For, if felicity is an object of the will because it has the rational character of a highest good, that does not make it substantially an act of the will, as the *first* argument implied.[4] On the contrary, from the fact that it is a first object, the conclusion is that felicity is not its act, as is apparent in what we have said.

[18]   Nor, indeed, is it necessary that everything whereby a thing is in any way perfected be the end of that thing, as the *second* argument claimed.[5] In fact, something may be the perfection of a thing in two ways: in one way, of a thing that already possesses its species; and in a second way, in order that the thing may acquire its species. For instance, the perfection of a house which already has its species is that to which the species of the house is ordered, namely, habitation. For a house is made for this purpose only, and so this must be included in the definition of a house if the definition is to be perfect. But the perfection for the sake of the species of the house is both that which is directed to the setting up of the species, such as its substantial principles, and also that which is ordered to the preservation of its species, such as the foundations made to hold up the house, and even those things that make the use of the house more agreeable, such as the beauty of the house. And then, that which is the perfection of the thing, in so far as it already possesses its species, is its end: as habitation is the end of the house. Likewise, the proper operation of anything, which is its use as it were, is its end. Now, the things that are perfections leading up to the species are not the end for the thing; on the contrary, the thing is their

4. See above, in this ch., ¶2.
5. *Ibid.*, ¶3.

end, matter and form are for the sake of the species. Though form is the end of the generative act, it is not the end of the thing that is already generated and possessed of its species. Rather, the form is required so that the species may be complete. Similarly, factors which preserve a thing in its species, such as health and the nutritive power, though perfectants of the animal, are not the end of the animal; rather, the opposite is true. Also, items by which a thing is improved for the perfection of its proper operations, and for the more appropriate attainment of its proper end, are not the end for the thing; rather, the opposite is so. For instance, beauty is for the man, and strength is for the body, and so for other similar things which the Philosopher talks about in *Ethics* I, saying that "they contribute to felicity instrumentally."[6]

Pleasure, however, is a perfection of operation, not in such a way that operation is ordered to it as to its species; rather, pleasure is ordered to other ends, as eating is ordered specifically to the preservation of the individual. But pleasure is like the perfection that is conducive to the species of the thing, since because of pleasure we apply ourselves more carefully and suitably to the operation in which we take pleasure. Hence the Philosopher says in *Ethics* x that "pleasure perfects operation as beauty perfects youth."[7] For, of course, beauty is for the sake of him in whom youth is found, and not the converse.

[19] Nor is the fact that men desire pleasure for its own sake, and not for the sake of something else, enough to indicate that pleasure is the ultimate end, as the *third* argument concluded.[8] For, although pleasure is not the ultimate end, it is, of course, a concomitant of this end, since pleasure arises out of the attainment of the end.

[20] Nor do more persons seek the pleasure that is associated with knowing rather than the knowledge.[9] Rather,

6. Aristotle, *Nicomachean Ethics*, I, 8–9 (1099b 2–1099b 28).
7. Aristotle, *Nicomachean Ethics*, X, 4 (1174b 31).
8. See above, in this ch., ¶4.
9. *Ibid.*, ¶5.

there are more people who seek sensual pleasures than intellectual knowledge and its accompanying pleasure, because things that are external stand out as better known, since human knowledge starts from sensible objects.

[21]   Now, what the *fifth* argument suggests,[10] that the will is higher than the intellect, in the sense of moving it, is clearly false. For, primarily and directly, the intellect moves the will; indeed, the will, as such, is moved by its object which is the known good. But the will moves the intellect rather accidentally, that is, in so far as the act of understanding is itself apprehended as good, and so is desired by the will, with the result that the intellect actually understands. Even in this act, the intellect precedes the will, for the will would never desire the act of understanding unless, first of all, the intellect were to apprehend the act of understanding as a good.—And again, the will moves the intellect actually to perform its operation, in the way that an agent is said to move; while the intellect moves the will in the way that an end moves something, since the good that is understood is the end for the will. Now, the agent comes later, in the process of moving, than does the end, since the agent does not move except for the sake of the end. Hence, it is evident that the intellect is, without qualification, higher than the will. On the other hand, the will is higher than the intellect, accidentally and in a qualified sense.

Chapter 27.

THAT HUMAN FELICITY DOES NOT CONSIST
IN PLEASURES OF THE FLESH

[1]   Now, it is clear from what we have said that it is impossible for human felicity to consist in bodily pleasures, the chief of which are those of food and sex.

10. *Ibid.,* ¶6.

[2]   In fact, we have shown[1] that in the order of nature pleasure depends on operation, and not the converse. So, if operations are not the ultimate end, the pleasures that result from them are not the ultimate end, either; nor are they concomitant with the ultimate end. It stands to reason that the operations which accompany the above-mentioned pleasures are not the ultimate end, for they are ordered to certain ends that are quite obvious: eating, for instance, to the preservation of the body, and sexual intercourse to the generation of offspring. Therefore, the aforementioned pleasures are not the ultimate end, nor are they concomitants of the ultimate end. So, felicity is not to be located in these pleasures.

[3]   Again, the will is higher than sense appetite, for it moves itself, as we said above.[2] Now, we have already shown[3] that felicity does not lie in an act of the will. Still less will it consist in the aforementioned pleasures which are located in the sense appetite.

[4]   Besides, felicity is a certain kind of good, appropriate to man. Indeed, brute animals cannot be deemed happy, unless we stretch the meaning of the term. But these pleasures that we are talking about are common to men and brutes. So, felicity should not be attributed to them.

[5]   Moreover, the ultimate end is the noblest appurtenance of a thing; in fact, the term means the best. But these pleasures are not agreeable to man by virtue of what is noblest in him, namely, his understanding, but by virtue of his sense capacity. So, felicity should not be located in pleasures of this kind.

[6]   Furthermore, the highest perfection of man cannot lie in a union with things inferior to himself, but, rather, in a union with some reality of a higher character, for the end is better than that which is for the sake of the end. Now, the aforementioned pleasures consist in this fact: that man

1. See above, ch. 26.
2. See above, ch. 25.
3. See above, ch. 26.

is, through his senses, united with some things that are his inferiors, that is, with certain sensible objects. So, felicity is not to be located in pleasures of this sort.

[7]   Again, something which is not good unless it be moderated is not good of itself; rather, it receives goodness from the source of the moderation. Now, the enjoyment of the aforementioned pleasures is not good for man unless it be moderated; otherwise, these pleasures will interfere with each other. So, these pleasures are not of themselves the good for man. But that which is the highest good is good of itself, because what is good of itself is better than what depends on something else. Therefore, such pleasures are not the highest good for man, that is, felicity.

[8]   Besides, in the case of all things that are predicated per se, an absolute variation is directly accompanied by a similar variation in the degree of intensification. Thus, if a hot thing heats, then a hotter thing heats more, and the hottest thing will heat the most. So, if the aforementioned pleasures were goods of themselves, the maximum enjoyment of them should be the best. But this is clearly false, for excessive enjoyment of them is considered vicious, and is also harmful to the body, and it prevents the enjoyment of similar pleasures. Therefore, they are not of themselves the good for man. So, human felicity does not consist in them.

[9]   Moreover, virtuous acts are praiseworthy because they are ordered to felicity.[4] So, if human felicity consisted in the aforementioned pleasures, a virtuous act would be more praiseworthy when it involved the enjoyment of these pleasures than when it required abstention from them. However, it is clear that this is false, for the act of temperance is given most praise when it involves abstaining from pleasures; as a result, it gets its name from this fact. Therefore, man's felicity does not lie in the aforesaid pleasures.

[10]   Furthermore, the ultimate end of everything is God, as is clear from what has been indicated earlier.[5] So, we

4. See Aristotle, *Nicomachean Ethics*, I, 12 (1101b 14).
5. See above, ch. 17.

should consider the ultimate end of man to be that whereby he most closely approaches God. But, through the aforesaid pleasures, man is kept away from a close approach to God, for this approach is effected through contemplation, and the aforementioned pleasures are the chief impediment to contemplation, since they plunge man very deep into sensible things, consequently distracting him from intelligible objects. Therefore, human felicity must not be located in bodily pleasures.

[11] Through this conclusion we are refuting the error of the Epicureans, who placed man's felicity in these enjoyments.[6] Acting as their spokesman, Solomon says in Ecclesiastes (5:17): "This therefore hath seemed good to me, that a man should eat and drink and enjoy the fruit of his labor . . . and this is his portion"; and again in Wisdom (2:9): "let us everywhere leave tokens of joy, for this is our portion, and this our lot."

[12] Also refuted is the error of the Cerinthians,[7] for they told a fabulous story about ultimate felicity, that after the resurrection there would be, in the reign of Christ, a thousand years of carnal pleasures of the belly. Hence, they were also called Chiliasts; that is, Millenarians.

[13] Refuted, too, are the fables of the Jews and the Saracens, who identified the rewards for just men with these pleasures, for felicity is the reward for virtue.

Chapter 28.

THAT FELICITY DOES NOT CONSIST IN HONORS

[1] It is also clear from the foregoing that the highest good for man, that is felicity, does not lie in honors.

6. See St. Augustine, *De civitate Dei*, XVIII, 41 (*PL*, 41, col. 601).
7. See St. Augustine, *De haeresibus*, 8 (*PL*, 42, 27).

[2]   Indeed, the ultimate end of man, and his felicity, is his most perfect operation, as is evident in what has preceded.[1] Now, a man's honor is not identified with his operation, but with something done by another person who shows respect for him.[2] Therefore, the felicity of man should not be identified with honors.

[3]   Again, that which is good and desirable on account of something else is not the ultimate end. But honor is of this sort. A person is not rightly honored unless it be because of some other good that is present in him. And this is why men seek to be honored, desiring, as it were, to have a witness to some good feature present in them. Hence, men take greater joy in being honored by important and wise people. So, man's felicity is not to be identified with honors.

[4]   Besides, the attainment of felicity is accomplished through virtue. Now, virtuous operations are voluntary; otherwise, they would not merit praise. So, felicity ought to be some good which man may attain by his own will. But the gaining of honor is not within the power of any man; rather, it is in the power of the one who gives the honor. Therefore, human felicity is not to be identified with honors.

[5]   Moreover, to be worthy of honor can only be an attribute of good men. But it is possible for even evil men to be honored. So, it is better to become worthy of honor than to be honored.[3] Therefore, honor is not the highest good for man.

[6]   Furthermore, the highest good is the perfect good. But the perfect good is completely exclusive of evil. Now, that in which there can be no evil cannot itself be evil. There-

1. See above, ch. 25.
2. See Aristotle, *Nicomachean Ethics*, I, 5 (1095b 25).
3. Compare the vernacular Italian sonnet, on this same subject, attributed to St. Thomas (P. Mandonnet, "Thomas d'Aquin, novice prêcheur," *Revue Thomiste*, 8 [1925], 239); there is some similarity in thought and expression.

fore, that which is in possession of the highest good cannot be evil. But it is possible for a bad man to attain honor. So, honor is not the highest good for man.

Chapter 29.

THAT MAN'S FELICITY DOES NOT CONSIST IN GLORY

[1]   From this it is also apparent that the highest good for man does not consist in glory, which means a widely recognized reputation.

[2]   Now, according to Tully, glory is "widespread repute accompanied by praise of a person."[1] And according to Ambrose, it is "an illustrious reputation accompanied by praise."[2] Now, men desire to become known in connection with some sort of praise and renown, for the purpose of being honored by those who know them. So, glory is sought for the sake of honor. Hence, if honor is not the highest good, much less is glory.

[3]   Again, praiseworthy goods are those whereby a person is shown to be well ordered to his end. Now, he who is well ordered to his end has not yet achieved the ultimate end. So, praise is not given to him who has already attained the ultimate end, but honor, as the Philosopher says in *Ethics* I.[3] Therefore, glory cannot be the highest good, because it consists principally in praise.

[4]   Besides, to know is more noble than to be known; only the more noble things know, but the lowest things are known. So, the highest good for man cannot be glory, for it consists in the fact that a person is well known.

1. Cicero, *De inventione rhetorica*, II, 55 (Teubner ed., Leipzig, 1915, p. 150b).
2. See St. Augustine, *Contra Maximinum*, II, 13 (*PL*, 42, col. 770).
3. Aristotle, *Nicomachean Ethics*, I, 12 (1101b 24).

[5]   Moreover, a person desires to be known only for good things; where bad things are concerned, he seeks concealment. So, to be known is a good and desirable thing, because of the good things that are known about a person. And so, these good things are better than being widely known. Therefore, glory is not the highest good, for it consists in a person being widely known.

[6]   Furthermore, the highest good should be perfect, for it should satisfy the appetite. Now, the knowledge associated with fame, in which human glory consists, is imperfect, for it is possessed of the greatest uncertainty and error. Therefore, such glory cannot be the highest good.

[7]   Again, the highest good for man should be what is most enduring among human affairs, for an endless duration of the good is naturally desired. Now, glory, in the sense of fame, is the least permanent of things; in fact, nothing is more variable than opinion and human praise. Therefore, such glory is not the highest good for man.

Chapter 30.

THAT MAN'S FELICITY DOES NOT CONSIST
IN RICHES

[1]   From this, moreover, it is also clear that riches are not the highest good for man.

[2]   Indeed, riches are only desired for the sake of something else; they provide no good of themselves but only when we use them, either for the maintenance of the body or some such use. Now, that which is the highest good is desired for its own sake and not for the sake of something else. Therefore, riches are not the highest good for man.

[3]   Again, man's highest good cannot lie in the possession or keeping of things that chiefly benefit man through being spent. Now, riches are chiefly valuable because they can be

expended, for this is their use. So, the possession of riches cannot be the highest good for man.

[4] Besides, an act of virtue is praiseworthy in so far as it comes closer to felicity. Now, acts of liberality and magnificence, which have to do with money, are more praiseworthy in a situation in which money is spent than in one in which it is saved. So, it is from this fact that the names of these virtues are derived. Therefore, the felicity of man does not consist in the possession of riches.

[5] Moreover, that object in whose attainment man's highest good lies must be better than man. But man is better than riches, for they are but things subordinated to man's use. Therefore, the highest good for man does not lie in riches.

[6] Furthermore, man's highest good is not subject to fortune,[1] for things subject to fortune come about independently of rational effort. But it must be through reason that man will achieve his proper end. Of course, fortune occupies an important place in the attainment of riches. Therefore, human felicity is not founded on riches.

[7] Again, this becomes evident in the fact that riches are lost in an involuntary manner, and also that they may accrue to evil men who must fail to achieve the highest good, and also that riches are unstable—and for other reasons of this kind which may be gathered from the preceding arguments.[2]

Chapter 31.

THAT FELICITY DOES NOT CONSIST IN WORLDLY POWER

[1] Similarly, neither can worldly power be man's highest good, since in its attainment, also, fortune can play a most

1. See Aristotle, *Nicomachean Ethics*, I, 9 (1099b 24).
2. See above, ch. 28ff.

important part. It is also unstable; nor is it subject to man's will; oftentimes it comes to bad men—and these characteristics are incompatible with the highest good, as was evident in the foregoing arguments.[1]

[2]   Again, man is deemed good chiefly in terms of his attainment of the highest good. Now, he is not called good, or bad, simply because he has power, for not everyone who can do good things is a good man, nor is a person bad because he is able to do evil things. Therefore, the highest good does not consist in the fact of being powerful.

[3]   Besides, all power is relative to some other thing. But the highest good is not relative to something else. Therefore, power is not man's highest good.

[4]   Moreover, a thing that one can use both for good and for evil cannot be man's highest good, for that is better which no one can use in a bad way. Now, one can use power well or badly, "for rational powers are capable of contrary effects."[2] Therefore, man's highest good does not consist in human power.

[5]   Furthermore, if any sort of power is the highest good, it ought to be the most perfect. But human power is most imperfect, since it is rooted in the wills and the opinions of men, in which there is the greatest inconstancy. And the more important the power is considered to be, the more does it depend on large numbers of people, which fact also contributes to its frailty, since what depends on many can be destroyed in many ways. Therefore, man's highest good does not lie in worldly power.

[6]   Man's felicity, then, consists in no exterior good, since all exterior goods, the ones that are called "goods of fortune," are contained under the preceding headings.

1. See above, ch. 28–30.
2. Aristotle, *Metaphysics*, VIII, 2 (1046b 4).

Chapter 32.

THAT FELICITY DOES NOT CONSIST IN GOODS OF THE BODY

[1] Moreover, that man's highest good does not lie in goods of the body, such as health, beauty, and strength, is clearly evident from similar considerations. For these things are possessed in common by both good and bad men; they are also unstable; moreover, they are not subject to the will.

[2] Again, the soul is better than the body, which is not alive, and which does not possess the aforementioned goods except by means of the soul. So, a good of the soul, like understanding and that sort of thing, is better than a good of the body. Therefore, the good of the body is not man's highest good.

[3] Besides, these goods are common to men and other animals. But felicity is the proper good of man. Therefore, man's felicity does not lie in the aforesaid goods.

[4] Moreover, many animals are better endowed than men, as far as the goods of the body go; for some are faster than man, some are stronger, and so on. If, then, man's highest good lay in these things, man would not be the most excellent of animals; which is obviously false. Therefore, human felicity does not consist in goods of the body.

Chapter 33.

THAT HUMAN FELICITY DOES NOT LIE IN THE SENSES

[1] In the same way, it is also apparent that man's highest good does not lie in the goods of his sensitive part. For these goods, too, are common to men and other animals.

[2]   Again, intellect is better than sense. So, the good of the intellect is better than the good of the senses. Therefore, man's highest good does not lie in sense.

[3]   Besides, the greatest pleasures in the sense order have to do with food and sexual activities; and so, the highest good ought to lie in these areas, if it were in sense. But it is not found in these things. Therefore, man's highest good does not lie in the senses.

[4]   Moreover, the senses are treasured because of their usefulness, and also because of their knowledge. Now, the entire utility of the senses has reference to the goods of the body. But sense cognition is subordinated to intellectual cognition; thus, animals devoid of understanding take no pleasure in sensing, except in regard to some benefit pertaining to the body, according as they obtain food or sexual satisfaction through sense knowledge. Therefore, man's highest good, his felicity, does not lie in his sensitive part.

Chapter 34.

THAT MAN'S ULTIMATE FELICITY DOES NOT LIE IN ACTS OF THE MORAL VIRTUES

[1]   It is clear, too, that the ultimate felicity of man does not consist in moral actions.

[2]   In fact, human felicity is incapable of being ordered to a further end, if it is ultimate. But all moral operations can be ordered to something else. This is evident from the most important instances of these actions. The operations of fortitude, which are concerned with warlike activities, are ordered to victory and to peace. Indeed, it would be foolish to make war merely for its own sake.[1] Likewise, the operations of justice are ordered to the preservation of peace among men, by means of each man having his own possessions undisturbed. And the same thing is evident for all

1. See Aristotle, *Nicomachean Ethics*, X, 7 (1177b 9).

the other virtues. Therefore, man's ultimate felicity does not lie in moral operations.

[3] Again, the moral virtues have this purpose: through them the mean is preserved in the internal passions and in regard to external things. Now, it is not possible for such a measuring of passions, or of external things, to be the ultimate end of human life, since these passions and exterior things are capable of being ordered to something else. Therefore, it is not possible for man's ultimate felicity to lie in acts of the moral virtues.

[4] Besides, since man is man by virtue of his possession of reason, his proper good which is felicity should be in accord with what is appropriate to reason. Now, that is more appropriate to reason which reason has within itself than which it produces in another thing. So, since the good of moral virtue is something produced by reason in things other than itself, it could not be that which is best for man; namely, felicity. Rather would felicity seem to be a good situated in reason itself.

[5] Moreover, it was shown above[2] that the ultimate end of all things is to become like unto God. So, that whereby man is made most like God will be his felicity. Now, this is not a function of moral acts, since such acts cannot be attributed to God, except metaphorically. Indeed, it does not befit God to have passions, or the like, with which moral acts are concerned. Therefore, man's ultimate felicity, that is, his ultimate end, does not consist in moral actions.

[6] Furthermore, felicity is the proper good for man. So, that which is most proper among all human goods, for man in contrast to the other animals, is the good in which his ultimate felicity is to be sought. Now, an act of moral virtue is not of this sort, for some animals share somewhat, either in liberality or in fortitude, but an animal does not participate at all in intellectual action. Therefore, man's ultimate felicity does not lie in moral acts.

2. See above, ch. 19.

Chapter 35.

THAT ULTIMATE FELICITY DOES NOT LIE IN THE ACT OF PRUDENCE

[1]   From this it is also apparent that man's ultimate felicity does not lie in an act of prudence.

[2]   For the act of prudence is only concerned with things that pertain to the moral virtues. Now, man's ultimate felicity does not lie in acts of the moral virtues,[1] nor, then, in the act of prudence.

[3]   Again, man's ultimate felicity consists in the best operation of man. Now, the best operation of man, according to what is proper to man, lies in a relationship to the most perfect object. But the operation of prudence is not concerned with the most perfect object of understanding or reason; indeed, it does not deal with necessary objects, but with contingent problems of action.[2] Therefore, man's ultimate felicity does not lie in this operation.

[4]   Besides, that which is ordered to another thing as an end is not the ultimate felicity for man. But the operation of prudence is ordered to something else as an end: both because all practical knowledge, in which category prudence is included, is ordered to action, and because prudence makes a man well disposed in regard to things that are to be chosen for the sake of the end, as is clear from Aristotle, in *Ethics* VI.[3] Therefore, man's ultimate felicity does not lie in the operation of prudence.

[5]   Moreover, irrational animals do not participate in felicity, as Aristotle proves in *Ethics* I.[4] However, some of

1. See above, ch. 34.
2. Aristotle, *Nicomachean Ethics*, VI, 6 (1140a 35).
3. *Ibid.*, VI, 13 (1145a 6).
4. *Ibid.*, I, 9 (1099b 33).

them do participate somewhat in prudence, as appears in the same writer, in *Metaphysics* 1.[5] Therefore, felicity does not consist in the operation of prudence.

Chapter 36.

THAT FELICITY DOES NOT CONSIST IN THE OPERATION OF ART

[1] It is also clear that it does not lie in the operation of art.

[2] For the knowledge that pertains to art is also practical knowledge. And so, it is ordered to an end, and is not itself the ultimate end.

[3] Again, the ends of art operations are artifacts. These cannot be the ultimate end of human life, for we ourselves are, rather, the ends for all artificial things. Indeed, they are all made for man's use. Therefore, ultimate felicity cannot lie in the operation of art.

Chapter 37.

THAT THE ULTIMATE FELICITY OF MAN CONSISTS IN THE CONTEMPLATION OF GOD

[1] So, if the ultimate felicity of man does not consist in external things which are called the goods of fortune, nor in the goods of the body, nor in the goods of the soul according to its sensitive part, nor as regards the intellective part according to the activity of the moral virtues, nor according to the intellectual virtues that are concerned with action, that is, art and prudence—we are left with the conclusion that the ultimate felicity of man lies in the contemplation of truth.

5. Aristotle, *Metaphysics*, I, 1 (980a 30).

[2] Indeed, this is the only operation of man which is proper to him, and in it he shares nothing in common with the other animals.

[3] So, too, this is ordered to nothing else as an end, for the contemplation of truth is sought for its own sake.

[4] Also, through this operation man is united by way of likeness with beings superior to him, since this alone of human operations is found also in God and in separate substances.

[5] Indeed, in this operation he gets in touch with these higher beings by knowing them in some way.

[6] Also, for this operation man is rather sufficient unto himself, in the sense that for it he needs little help from external things.

[7] In fact, all other human operations seem to be ordered to this one, as to an end. For, there is needed for the perfection of contemplation a soundness of body, to which all the products of art that are necessary for life are directed. Also required are freedom from the disturbances of the passions—this is achieved through the moral virtues and prudence—and freedom from external disorders, to which the whole program of government in civil life is directed. And so, if they are rightly considered, all human functions may be seen to subserve the contemplation of truth.

[8] However, it is not possible for man's ultimate felicity to consist in the contemplation which depends on the understanding of principles, for that is very imperfect, being most universal, including the potential cognition of things. Also, it is the beginning, not the end, of human enquiry, coming to us from nature and not because of our search for truth. Nor, indeed, does it lie in the area of the sciences which deal with lower things, because felicity should lie in the working of the intellect in relation to the noblest objects of understanding. So, the conclusion remains that

man's ultimate felicity consists in the contemplation of wisdom, based on the considering of divine matters.

[9] From this, that is also clear by way of induction, which was proved above by rational arguments,[1] namely, that man's ultimate felicity consists only in the contemplation of God.

Chapter 38.

THAT HUMAN FELICITY DOES NOT CONSIST IN THE KNOWLEDGE OF GOD WHICH IS GENERALLY POSSESSED BY MOST MEN

[1] It remains to investigate the kind of knowledge in which the ultimate felicity of an intellectual substance consists. For there is a common and confused knowledge of God which is found in practically all men; this is due either to the fact that it is self-evident that God exists, just as other principles of demonstration are—a view held by some people, as we said in Book One[1]—or, what seems indeed to be true, that man can immediately reach some sort of knowledge of God by natural reason.[2] For, when men see that things in nature run according to a definite order, and that ordering does not occur without an orderer, they perceive in most cases that there is some orderer of the things that we see. But who or what kind of being, or whether there is but one orderer of nature, is not yet grasped immediately in this general consideration, just as, when we see that a man is moved and performs other works, we perceive that there is present in him some cause of these operations which is not present in other things, and we call this cause the soul; yet we do not know at that point what the

1. See above, ch. 25. Note that ch. 26–37 contain an elaborate instance of inductive argument by exclusion.
1. *SCG*, I, ch. 10–11.
2. See J. Maritain, *Approaches to God*, trans. P. O'Reilly (New York: Harper, 1954), for a development of this theory of a "natural" but immediate knowledge of God.

soul is, whether it is a body, or how it produces these operations which have been mentioned.

[2]   Of course, it is not possible for this knowledge of God
to suffice for felicity.

[3]   In fact, the operation of the man enjoying felicity
must be without defect. But this knowledge admits of a
mixture of many errors. Some people have believed that
there is no other orderer of worldly things than the celestial
bodies, and so they said that the celestial bodies are gods.
Other people pushed it farther, to the very elements and
the things generated from them, thinking that motion and
the natural functions which these elements have are not
present in them as the effect of some other orderer, but
that other things are ordered by them. Still other people,
believing that human acts are not subject to any ordering,
other than human, have said that men who order others are
gods. And so, this knowledge of God is not enough for
felicity.

[4]   Again, felicity is the end of human acts. But human
acts are not ordered to the aforementioned knowledge, as to
an end. Rather, it is found in all men, almost at once, from
their beginning. So, felicity does not consist in this knowledge of God.

[5]   Besides, no man seems to be blameworthy because of
the fact that he lacks felicity; in point of fact, those who
lack it, but are tending toward it, are given praise. But the
fact that a person lacks the aforesaid knowledge of God
makes him appear very blameworthy. Indeed, a man's dull-
ness is chiefly indicated by this: he fails to perceive such
evident signs of God, just as a person is judged to be dull
who, while observing a man, does not grasp the fact that he
has a soul. That is why it is said in the Psalms (13:1, 52:1):
"The fool hath said in his heart: There is no God." So, this
is not the knowledge of God which suffices for felicity.

[6]   Moreover, the knowledge that one has of a thing, only
in a general way and not according to something proper to

it, is very imperfect, just like the knowledge one might have of a man when one knows simply that he is moved. For this is the kind of knowledge whereby a thing is known only in potency, since proper attributes are potentially included within common ones. But felicity is a perfect operation, and man's highest good ought to be based on what is actual and not simply on what is potential, for potency perfected by act has the essential character of the good. Therefore, the aforementioned knowledge is not enough for our felicity.

Chapter 39.

THAT HUMAN FELICITY DOES NOT CONSIST IN THE KNOWLEDGE OF GOD GAINED THROUGH DEMONSTRATION

[1]   On the other hand, there is another sort of knowledge of God, higher than the foregoing, and we may acquire it through demonstration. A closer approach to a proper knowledge of Him is effected through this kind, for many things are set apart from Him, through demonstration, whose removal enable Him to be understood in distinction from other beings. In fact, demonstration shows that God is immutable, eternal, incorporeal, altogether simple, one, and other such things which we have shown about God in Book One.[1]

Now, we reach a proper knowledge of a thing not only through affirmations but also through negations; for instance, it is proper to a man to be a rational animal, and so it is proper to him not to be inanimate or irrational. But there is this difference between these two modes of proper knowledge: through affirmations, when we have a proper knowledge of a thing, we know *what* the thing is, and how it is separated from others; but through negations, when we have a proper knowledge of a thing, we know *that* it is distinct from other things, yet what it is remains unknown.

1. SCG, I, ch. 15–38.

Now, such is the proper knowledge that we have of God through demonstrations. Of course, this is not sufficient for the ultimate felicity of man.

[2]   For, the things which pertain to a species extend to the end of that species, in most cases; in fact, things which are of natural origin are so always, or in most cases, though they may fail in a few instances because of some corruption. Now, felicity is the end of the human species, since all men naturally desire it. So, felicity is a definite common good, capable of accruing to all men, unless an impediment occurs by which some may be deprived of it.[2] Now, few men attain the knowledge of God that we have just mentioned, acquired by way of demonstration, because of the obstacles to this knowledge which we touched on in the beginning of this work.[3] Therefore, such knowledge of God is not essentially identical with human felicity.

[3]   Then, again, to be actual is the end of what is potential, as is clear from the foregoing.[4] So, felicity which is the ultimate end is an act to which no potency for further actuality is attached. But this sort of knowledge of God, acquired by way of demonstration, still remains in potency to something further to be learned about God, or to the same knowledge possessed in a higher way, for later men have endeavored to add something pertinent to divine knowledge to the things which they found in the heritage of their predecessors. Therefore, such knowledge is not identical with ultimate felicity.

[4]   Moreover, felicity excludes all unhappiness, for no man can be at once unhappy and happy. Now, deception and error constitute a great part of unhappiness; in fact, that is what all men naturally avoid. But manifold error can accompany the aforesaid knowledge that is acquired about God, and this is evident in many men who learned some truths about God by way of demonstration, and who, fol-

2. See Aristotle, *Nicomachean Ethics*, I, 9 (1099b 19).
3. *SCG*, I, ch. 4.
4. See above, ch. 20 and 22.

lowing their own opinions in cases where demonstration fails them, have fallen into many errors. In fact, if there have been any men who have discovered the truth about divine things in such a way, by means of demonstration, that no falsity attached to their judgment, it is clear that there have been few such. This is not appropriate to felicity, which is a common end. So, man's ultimate felicity does not lie in this knowledge of God.

[5] Besides, felicity consists in a perfect operation. Now, certainty is required for perfect knowledge; for this reason we are not said to know unless we learn something that cannot be otherwise, as is evident in the *Posterior Analytics.*[5] Now, the knowledge we have been talking about includes much uncertainty; the diversity of the sciences of divine matters among those who have tried to find out these things by way of demonstration shows this. Therefore, ultimate felicity is not found in such knowledge.

[6] Moreover, the will rests its desire when it has attained the ultimate end. But the ultimate end of all human knowledge is felicity. So, that knowledge of God which, when acquired, leaves no knowledge of a knowable object to be desired is essentially this felicity. But this is not the kind of knowledge about God that the philosophers were able to get through demonstrations, because, even when we acquire this knowledge, we still desire to know other things that are not known through this knowledge. Therefore, felicity is not found in such knowledge of God.

[7] Furthermore, the end of every being which is in potency is to be brought into act, for it tends toward this through the motion by which it is moved to its end. Of course, every being in potency tends to become actual, in so far as that is possible. Now, there is one kind of being in potency whose entire potency can be reduced to act; hence, its end is to be completely reduced to act. Thus, a heavy body in some unusual position is in potency to its

5. Aristotle, *Posterior Analytics*, I, 2 (72a 17).

proper place. But there is another kind of thing whose entire potency cannot be reduced to act at the same time. This is the case with prime matter, and that is why, through its change, it seeks to be actuated successively under different forms which cannot be simultaneously present in it, because of their diversity. Now, our intellect is in potency to all intelligible objects, as was explained in Book Two.[6] But two intelligible objects can exist simultaneously in the possible intellect, by way of the first act which is science, though perhaps not by way of the second act which is consideration. It is evident from this that the entire potency of the possible intellect can be reduced to act at one time. So, this is required for its ultimate end which is felicity. But the aforesaid knowledge of God which can be acquired through demonstration does not do this, since, even when we possess it, we still remain ignorant of many things. Therefore, such knowledge of God is not sufficient for ultimate felicity.

Chapter 40.

HUMAN FELICITY DOES NOT CONSIST IN THE KNOWLEDGE OF GOD WHICH IS THROUGH FAITH

[1] Now, there is still another knowledge of God, in one sense superior to the aforementioned knowledge, and by this God is known to men through faith. In comparison with the knowledge that we have of God through demonstration, this knowledge through faith surpasses it, for we know some things about God through faith which, because of their sublimity, demonstrative reason cannot attain, as we said at the beginning of this work.[1] Yet, it is not possible for man's ultimate felicity to consist in even this knowledge of God.

6. SCG, II, ch. 47.
1. SCG, I, ch. 5.

[2] Felicity, indeed, is a perfect operation of the intellect, as is clear from what we have said.[2] But, in the knowledge of faith, there is found a most imperfect operation of the intellect, having regard to what is on the side of the intellect, though the greatest perfection is discovered on the side of the object. For the intellect does not grasp the object to which it gives assent in the act of believing. Therefore, neither does man's ultimate felicity lie in this kind of knowledge of God.

[3] Again, we showed above,[3] that ultimate felicity does not consist primarily in an act of the will. But in the knowledge of faith the will takes priority; indeed, the intellect assents through faith to things presented to it, because of an act of will and not because it is necessarily moved by the very evidence of the truth. So, man's ultimate felicity does not lie in this knowledge.

[4] Besides, one who believes gives assent to things that are proposed to him by another person, and which he himself does not see. Hence, faith has a knowledge that is more like hearing than vision. Now, a man would not believe in things that are unseen but proposed to him by another man unless he thought that this other man had more perfect knowledge of these proposed things than he himself who does not see them. So, either the believer's judgment is false or else the proposer must have more perfect knowledge of the things proposed. And if the proposer only knows these things by hearing them from another man, this cannot go on indefinitely, for the assent of faith would be foolish and without certitude; indeed, we would discover no first thing certain in itself which would bring certainty to the faith of the believer. Now, it is not possible for the knowledge of faith to be false and empty, as is evident from what we have said in the opening Book.[4] Yet, if it were false and empty, felicity could not consist in such knowledge.

2. See above, ch. 25.
3. See above, ch. 26.
4. SCG, I, ch. 7.

So, there is for man some knowledge of God which is higher than the knowledge of faith: either the man who proposes the faith sees the truth immediately, as is the case when we believe in Christ; or he takes it immediately from one who does see, as when we believe the Apostles and Prophets. So, since man's felicity consists in the highest knowledge of God, it is impossible for it to consist in the knowledge of faith.

[5]   Moreover, through felicity, because it is the ultimate end, natural desire comes to rest. Now, the knowledge of faith does not bring rest to desire but rather sets it aflame, since every man desires to see what he believes. So, man's ultimate felicity does not lie in the knowledge of faith.

[6]   Furthermore, the knowledge of God has been called the end because it is joined to the ultimate end of things, that is, to God. But an item of belief is not made perfectly present to the intellect by the knowledge of faith, since faith is of things absent, not of things present. For this reason the Apostle says, in II Corinthians (5:6–7), that "while we are in the body we walk by faith and we are absent from the Lord." Yet God is brought into the presence of love through faith, since the believer assents to God voluntarily, according to what is said in Ephesians (3:17): "that Christ may dwell by faith in our hearts." Therefore, it is not possible for ultimate human felicity to consist in the knowledge of faith.

Chapter 41.

WHETHER IN THIS LIFE MAN IS ABLE TO UNDERSTAND SEPARATE SUBSTANCES THROUGH THE STUDY AND INVESTIGATION OF THE SPECULATIVE SCIENCES

[1]   An intellectual substance has still another kind of knowledge of God. Indeed, it has been stated in Book Two[1]

1. SCG, II, ch. 96ff.

that a separate substance, in knowing its own essence, knows both what is above and what is below itself, in a manner proper to its substance. This is especially necessary if what is above it is its cause, since the likeness of the cause must be found in the effects. And so, since God is the cause of all created intellectual substances, as is evident from the foregoing,[2] then separate intellectual substances, in knowing their own essence, must know God Himself by way of a vision of some kind. For a thing whose likeness exists in the intellect is known through the intellect by way of vision, just as the likeness of a thing which is seen corporeally is present in the sense of the viewer. So, whatever intellect understands a separate substance, by knowing *what* it is, sees God in a higher way than He is known by any of the previously treated types of knowledge.

[2] Hence, since some men[3] have claimed that man's ultimate end is in this life, because they know separate substances, we must consider whether man can know separate substances in this life. Now, on this point there is some dispute. For, our intellect in our present state understands nothing without a phantasm, and the phantasm is related to the possible intellect, whereby we understand, as colors are related to vision, as is evident from what we have treated in Book Two.[4] Therefore, if any of us could achieve the understanding of separate substances through the intellectual knowledge which is from phantasms, then it would be possible for a person in this life to understand separate substances themselves. Consequently, by seeing these separate substances one will participate in that mode of knowledge whereby the separate substance, while understanding itself, understands God. But, if one cannot in any way attain to the understanding of separate substances through the knowledge which depends on phantasms, then it will not be possible for man in the present state of life to achieve the aforesaid mode of divine knowledge.

2. *SCG*, II, ch. 15.
3. See Averroes, *In III De anima*, comm. 36 (VI, 175r ff.).
4. *SCG*, II, ch. 59 and 74.

[3] Now, various people have claimed in different ways that we could reach an understanding of separate substances from the knowledge which is accomplished through phantasms. For instance, Avempace claimed that, through the study of the speculative sciences, we can, on the basis of things understood through phantasms, reach an understanding of separate substances.[5] For we can by the action of the intellect abstract the quiddity of anything that has a quiddity, and which is not identical with its quiddity. Indeed, the intellect is naturally equipped to know any quiddity, in so far as it is quiddity, since the proper object of the intellect is *what a thing is*.[6] But, if what is primarily understood by the possible intellect is something having a quiddity, we can abstract through the possible intellect the quiddity of that which is primarily understood. Moreover, if that quiddity also has a quiddity, it will in turn be possible to abstract the quiddity of this quiddity. And since an infinite process is impossible, it must stop somewhere. Therefore, our intellect is able to reach, by way of resolution, the knowledge of a quiddity which has no further quiddity. Now, this is the sort of quiddity proper to a separate substance. So, our intellect can, through the knowledge of those sensible things that is received from phantasms, reach an understanding of separate substances.

[4] He proceeds, moreover, to show the same thing in another, similar way. For he maintains that the understanding of one thing, say a horse, is plurally present in me and in you, simply by means of a multiplication of spiritual species which are diversified in me and in you. So, then, it is necessary that an object of understanding, which is not based on any species of this kind, be identical in me and in you. But the quiddity of an object of understanding, which quiddity our intellect is naturally capable of abstracting, has no spiritual but individual species, as we have proved,[7] because the quiddity of a thing that is under-

5. See Averroes, *ibid.,* (VI, 177v–178r).
6. The Latin phrase is *quod quid est.*
7. *SCG,* II, ch. 75.

stood is not the quiddity of an individual, either spiritual or corporeal, for a thing that is understood, as such, is universal. So, our intellect is by nature capable of understanding a quiddity for which the understanding is one among all men. Now, such is the quiddity of a separate substance. Hence, our understanding is naturally equipped to know separate substance.

[5] However, if a careful consideration be made, these ways of arguing will be discovered to be frivolous. Since a thing that is understood, as such, is universal, the quiddity of the thing understood must be the quiddity of something universal; namely, of a genus or a species. Now, the quiddity of a genus or species pertaining to these sensible things, whose intellectual knowledge we get through phantasms, includes matter and form within itself. So, it is entirely unlike the quiddity of a separate substance, which latter is simple and immaterial. Therefore, it is not possible for the quiddity of a separate substance to be understood, simply because the quiddity of a sensible thing is understood through phantasms.

[6] Besides, the form which in actual being cannot be separated from a subject is not of the same rational character as the form which is separated in its being from such a subject, even though both of them can be taken, in an act of consideration, without such a subject. Thus, there is not the same essential character for magnitude and for a separate substance, unless we claim that magnitudes are separate things midway between specific forms and sensible things, as some of the Platonists maintained. Of course, the quiddity of a genus or species of sensible things cannot be separate in actual being from a given material individual, unless, perhaps, we maintain with the Platonists separate forms of things, but this has been disproved by Aristotle.[8] Therefore, the quiddity of the aforementioned separate substances, which in no way exist in matter, is utterly different. Therefore, separate substances cannot be understood simply by virtue of the fact that these quiddities are understood.

8. See Aristotle, *Metaphysics*, I, 9 (990b 1).

[7]   Again, if it is granted that the quiddity of a separate substance is of the same rational character as the quiddity of a genus or species of these sensible things, that does not warrant saying that it is of the same rational character *specifically*, unless we say that the species of sensible things are themselves separate substances, as the Platonists claimed. The conclusion stands, then, that they will not be of the same rational character, except according to the rational character of quiddity as quiddity. Now, this is a meaning of rational character which is common to genus and to substance. Therefore, nothing except their remote genus could be understood concerning separate substances through these sensible quiddities. Now, the fact that the genus is known does not mean that the species is known, except in potency. So, separate substances could not be understood through an understanding of the quiddities of these sensible things.

[8]   Moreover, there is a greater difference between separate substances and sensible things than between one sensible thing and another. But to understand the quiddity of one sensible thing is not enough to enable one to understand the quiddity of another sensible thing. For instance, a man who is born blind is not at all enabled to achieve understanding of the quiddity of color simply because he understands the quiddity of sound. Much less, then, is one enabled to understand the quiddity of a separate substance by the fact that he understands the quiddity of a sensible substance.

[9]   Furthermore, even if we claim that separate substances move the spheres, and that from their motions the forms of sensible things are produced, this way of knowing separate substance, from sensible things, does not suffice for a knowing of their quiddity. For a cause is known through an effect, either by reason of a likeness which exists between the effect and the cause or in so far as the effect shows the power of the cause. Now, it would not be possible to know from the effect, by reason of likeness, what the cause is unless the agent is of one species with the effect. But that is

not the way the separate substances are related to sensible things. On the other hand, on the basis of power, this cannot be done except when the effect is equal to the power of the cause. For, in that case, the whole power of the cause is known through the effect, and the power of a thing demonstrates its substance. But this cannot be asserted in the present case, for the powers of separate substances exceed all the sensible effects which we may grasp intellectually, as a universal power surpasses a particular effect. Therefore, it is not possible for us to be enabled, through an understanding of sensible things, to come to an understanding of separate substances.

[10] Again, all intelligible objects whose knowledge we reach through investigation and study belong to some one of the speculative sciences. So, if we attain the understanding of separate substances as a result of our understanding of the natures and quiddities of these sensible things, then it must be that the understanding of separate substances depends on one of the speculative sciences. Yet we do not observe this; there is no speculative science which teaches *what* any of the separate substances is, but only *that* they are. So, it is not possible for us to reach an understanding of separate substances simply because we understand sensible natures.

[11] On the other hand, if it be suggested that such a speculative science is possible, even though it has not yet been discovered, this is no argument, because it is not possible to arrive at an understanding of the aforesaid substances through any principles known to us. Indeed, all the proper principles of any science depend on first indemonstrable principles, which are self-evident, and we get our knowledge of these from the senses, as is shown at the end of the *Posterior Analytics*.[9] However, sensible things are not adequate guides to the knowledge of immaterial things, as we have proved by the arguments above. Therefore, it is not possible for there to be any science whereby one might achieve understanding of separate substances.

9. Aristotle, *Posterior Analytics*, II, 18 (99b 20).

Chapter 42.

THAT WE CANNOT IN THIS LIFE UNDERSTAND
SEPARATE SUBSTANCES IN THE WAY
THAT ALEXANDER CLAIMED

[1]   Because Alexander [of Aphrodisias] claimed that the possible intellect is capable of being generated and corrupted, in the sense that it is "a perfection of human nature resulting from a mixture of the elements," as we saw in Book Two,[1] and since it is not possible for such a power to transcend material conditions, he maintained that our possible intellect can never reach an understanding of separate substances. Yet he asserted that, in our present state of life, we are able to understand separate substances.[2]

[2]   In fact, he tried to show this in the following way. Whenever anything has reached maturity in its process of generation and has come to the full perfection of its substance, the operation proper to it will be at its peak, whether as action or as passion. For, as operation is consequent upon substance, so also is the perfection of operation a result of the perfection of substance. Hence, an animal, when it has become wholly perfect, is able to walk by itself. Now, the habitual understanding which is simply "intelligible species made to exist in the possible intellect by the agent intellect" has a twofold operation: one, to make potentially understood things to be actually understood, and it owes this to the role of the agent intellect; and the second is actually to understand the objects of understanding. These two things, then, man can do through an intellectual habit. So, whenever the generating of the habitual understanding has reached completion, both of these stated operations will be at their peak in it. Now, it always approaches the peak perfection of its gen-

1. See Averroes, *In III De anima*, comm. 5 (VI, 162r–163r).
2. See Averroes, *ibid.*

eration when it acquires new kinds of objects of understanding. And thus, its process of generation must be completed at some time, unless there be an impediment, because no process of generation tends to an indefinite termination. So, it will reach completion whenever both operations are habitually present in the intellect, by virtue of the fact that it makes all the potential objects of understanding actual, which is the completion of the first operation, and because of the fact that it understands all intelligible objects, both separate and not separate.

[3]   Now, since according to his opinion the possible intellect cannot understand separate substances, as has already been said, he thought that we will understand separate substances through the habitual understanding, in so far as the agent intellect, which he supposes to be a separate substance, becomes the form of the habitual understanding, and a form for us ourselves. Thus, we will understand through it, as we now understand through the possible intellect; and since it is the function of the power of the agent intellect to make all things which are potentially intelligible to be actually understood, and to understand the separate substances, we will understand separate substances in this life, and also all non-separate intelligible things.

[4]   So, according to this theory, we reach the knowledge of separate substances through this knowledge which comes from the phantasms, not in the sense that these phantasms and the things understood through them are means for the knowing of separate substances (as is the case with the speculative sciences, according to the position advanced in the preceding chapter), but, rather, in so far as the intelligible species are certain dispositions within us to the kind of form that the agent intellect is. And this is the first point on which these two opinions differ.

[5]   Hence, when the habitual understanding will be perfected through the production in us by the agent intellect of these intelligible species, the agent intellect will itself become a form for us, as we have said. And he calls this the

"acquired understanding," which, according to their state-ment, Aristotle says comes from outside. And so, though the ultimate human perfection is not in the speculative sciences, as the preceding opinion claimed, man is disposed through these sciences to the attainment of the ultimate perfection. And this is the *second* point on which the first and second opinions differ.

[6]   However, they differ on a *third* point, because, accord-ing to the first opinion, our actual understanding of the agent intellect is the cause of its being united with us. Whereas, according to the second opinion, the converse is the case, for, since it is united with us as a form, we under-stand it and the other separate substances.

[7]   Now, these statements are unreasonable. Indeed, the habitual understanding, as also the possible understanding, is supposed by Alexander to be generable and corruptible. Now, the eternal cannot become the form of the generable and corruptible, according to him. For this reason, he claims that the possible intellect, which is united to us as a form, is generable and corruptible, while the agent intellect which is incorruptible is a separate substance. Hence, since the agent intellect, according to Alexander, is supposed to be an eternal separate substance, it will be impossible for the agent intellect to become the form of the habitual intellect.

[8]   Moreover, the form of the intellect, as intellect, is the intelligible object, just as the form of the sense is the sen-sible object; indeed, the intellect receives nothing, strictly speaking, except in an intellectual way, just as the sense power only receives sensitively. So, if the agent intellect can-not be an intelligible object through the habitual intellect, then it will be impossible for it to be its form.

[9]   Besides, we are said to understand something in three ways. *First*, as we understand by means of the intellect which is the power from which such an operation proceeds; hence, both the intellect itself is said to understand, and also the intellect's act of understanding becomes our act of understanding. *Second*, we understand by means of an in-

telligible species; of course, we are not said to understand by it, in the sense that it understands, but because the intellective power is actually perfected by it, as the visual power is by the species of color. *Third*, we understand as by an intermediary through the knowing of which we come to the knowledge of something else.

[10]   So, if at some point man understands separate substances through the agent intellect, this must be explained by one of these ways that have been mentioned. Now, it is not explained by the third way, for Alexander did not admit that either the possible or the habitual intellect understands the agent intellect. Nor, indeed, is it in the second way, for to understand through an intelligible species is the attribute of the intellective power for which this intelligible species is the form. Now, Alexander did not grant that the possible intellect or the habitual intellect understands separate substances; hence, it is not possible for us to understand separate substances through the agent intellect in the same way that we understand other things through an intelligible species. But, if it is as through an intellective power, then the agent intellect's act of understanding must be man's act of understanding. Now, this cannot be so unless one actual being is made from the substance of the agent intellect and the substance of man; indeed, it is impossible if they are two substances with different acts of being, for the operation of the one to be the operation of the other. Therefore, the agent intellect will be one existing being with man, not one accidentally, for then the agent intellect would be not a substance but an accident, as is the case when a thing that is one being accidentally is made from color and a body. The conclusion remains, then, that the agent intellect is united with man in substantial being. It will be, then, either the human soul or a part of it, and not some separate substance as Alexander claimed. Therefore, it cannot be maintained, on the basis of Alexander's opinion, that man understands separate substances.

[11]   Furthermore, if the agent intellect at any time becomes the form of one man, so that he is enabled to under-

stand through it, by the same token it could become the form of another man similarly understanding through it. It will follow, then, that two men will understand at the same time through the agent intellect as through their own form. This is so because the agent intellect's own act of understanding is the act of understanding of the man who understands through it, as was said already. Therefore, there will be the same act of understanding for two intelligent beings; and this is impossible.

[12] As a matter of fact, his theory is entirely frivolous. First of all because, whenever the process of generation is perfected in any member of a genus its operation must be perfected, but, of course, according to the manner of its own genus and not according to the mode of a higher genus. For instance, when the generation of air is perfected it has a development and complete movement upward, but not such that it is moved to the place proper to fire. Similarly, when the development of the habitual intellect is completed its operation of understanding will be completed according to its own mode, but not according to the mode whereby separate substances understand, so that it may understand separate substances. Hence, from the generation of the habitual intellect one cannot conclude that man will understand separate substance at some time.

[13] Secondly, it is frivolous because the perfection of an operation belongs to the same power to which the operation itself belongs. So, if to understand separate substances be a perfection of the operation of the habitual intellect, it follows that the habitual intellect understands separate substances at some point in time. Now, Alexander does not claim this, for it would follow that to understand separate substances would depend on the speculative sciences which are included under the notion of habitual understanding.

[14] Thirdly, it is frivolous because the generation of things that begin to be generated is nearly always brought to completion, since all processes of generating things are due to determinate causes which achieve their effects, either

always, or in the majority of cases. If, then, the perfection of action also follows upon the completion of generation, it must also be the case that perfect operation accompanies the generated things, either always, or in the majority of cases. Now, the actual understanding of separate substances is not achieved by those who apply themselves to the development of habitual understanding, either in most cases or always; on the contrary, no man has openly declared that he had achieved this perfection. Therefore, the perfection of the operation of habitual understanding does not consist in the actual understanding of separate substances.

Chapter 43.

THAT WE CANNOT IN THIS LIFE UNDERSTAND
SEPARATE SUBSTANCES IN THE WAY
THAT AVERROES CLAIMED

[1] Because there is very great difficulty in Alexander's opinion, as a result of his supposition that the possible intellect in a condition of habituation is entirely corruptible, Averroes thought that he found an easier way to show that we sometimes understand separate substances. In fact, he asserted that the possible intellect is incorruptible and separate in being from us, as is also the agent intellect.[1]

[2] He showed, first of all, that it was necessary to hold that the agent intellect is related to principles naturally known to us, either as agent is to instrument, or as form to matter. For the habitual intellect, by which we understand, has not only this action of understanding, but also another, which is to make things actually understood; indeed, we know by experience that both actions stand within our power. Now, the action of making things actual objects of understanding is more properly indicative of the meaning of habitual intellect than is the act of understanding, for to make things actually intelligible precedes the act of under-

1. Averroes, *In III De anima*, comm. 5 (VI, 164r).

standing them. But there are some things within us which are rendered actually understood in a natural way, not as a result of our effort or of the action of our will: such are the first intelligible things. In fact, to make these actually understood does not depend on the habitual intellect, through which things that we know from study are made to be actually understood; rather, these first intelligibles are the starting point of the habitual intellect. And that is why the habit of these intelligibles is also called *understanding* by Aristotle, in *Ethics* VI.[2] Now, they are made to be actually understood by the agent intellect alone. And by means of them other things are made to be actually understood: these are the things that we know from study. So, to make these subsequent things actually understood is the work both of the habitual intellect, as regards first principles, and of the agent intellect. Now, one action is not attributed to two things unless one of them is related to the other as agent to instrument or as form to matter. So, the agent intellect is necessarily related to the first principles of the habitual intellect either as agent to instrument or as form to matter.

[3]   In fact, he indicates how this is possible in the following way. Since the possible intellect, according to his theory, is a separate substance,[3] it understands the agent intellect and the other separate substances, and also the first objects of speculative understanding. So, it is the subject for both types of objects. Now, whenever two things are united in one subject, one of them is like the form of the other. Thus, when color and light are present in a diaphanous body as their subject, one of them, namely, light, must be like the form of the other, namely, color. Now, this is necessary when they have an ordered relationship to each other, but not in the case of things accidentally associated in the same subject, like whiteness and musical ability. But speculatively understood things and the agent intellect do have an ordered relationship to each other, since

2. Aristotle, *Nicomachean Ethics*, VI, 6 (1141a 7).
3. *SCG*, II, ch. 59.

the objects of speculative understanding are rendered actually understood by means of the agent intellect. So, the agent intellect is related to the objects of speculative understanding as form is to matter.

Therefore, when the objects of speculative understanding are united with us through the phantasms, which are in a sense their subject, the agent intellect must also be connected with us, because it is the form of the objects of speculative understanding. Thus, when the objects of speculative understanding are only potentially present in us, the agent intellect is only potentially connected with us. But, when some objects of speculative understanding are actually in us, and some are potentially present, its connection with us is partly actual and partly potential. Then it is that we are said to be in motion toward the aforementioned connection, for, as more things are made to be actually understood within us, the agent intellect becomes more perfectly connected with us. This progress and movement toward the connection is accomplished through study in the speculative sciences, through which we acquire true objects of understanding, and also false opinions that are outside the orderly process of this movement are excluded, just as monstrosities are outside the order of natural operation. Hence, men may help each other in making this progress, as they are of mutual assistance in the speculative sciences.

And so, when all potential objects of understanding have been made actual within us, the agent intellect is perfectly united with us as a form, and then we will understand perfectly through it, just as we now understand perfectly through the habitual intellect. Hence, since it is the function of the agent intellect to understand separate substances, we will then understand separate substances, as we now understand the objects of speculative understanding. And this will be the ultimate felicity of man, in which man will be "like some sort of God."[4]

[4] Now, the refutation of this theory is sufficiently evident from the things that we have said earlier: in fact, it

4. Averroes, *In III De anima*, comm. 36 (VI, 1791–1801).

proceeds from the supposition of many points which are disproved in the foregoing sections.

[5]   First of all, we showed above[5] that the possible intellect is not some substance separated from us in its being. Hence, it will not be necessary for it to be the subject of separate substances, especially since Aristotle says that the intellect is possible, "in that it is able to become all things."[6] From this we see that it is the subject only of those things that are made actually understood.

[6]   Again, we have shown above,[7] concerning the agent intellect, that it is not a separate substance, but a part of the soul, to which Aristotle assigns this operation: "to make things actually understood,"[8] and this lies within our power. Hence, it will not be necessary for the act of understanding through the agent intellect to be the cause, for us, of our capacity to understand separate substances; otherwise, we would always understand them.

[7]   Furthermore, if the agent intellect is a separate substance, it cannot be joined to us except through species that have been made actually understood, according to this theory; and neither can the possible intellect, even though the possible intellect is related to these species as matter to form, while, conversely, the agent intellect is as form to matter. Now, species that have been made actually understood are joined with us, according to his theory, by means of the phantasms which are related to the possible intellect as colors to the visual power, but to the agent intellect as colors to light: as we see from the words of Aristotle in Book III of On the Soul.[9] But to the stone in which color is present, neither the action of the power of sight as it sees nor the action of the sun as it enlightens can be attributed. Therefore, according to the aforesaid theory, it would be

5. SCG, II, ch. 59.
6. Aristotle, De anima, III, 5 (430a 14).
7. SCG, II, ch. 76.
8. Aristotle, De anima, III, 5 (430a 15).
9. Ibid. (430a 16).

impossible to attribute to man either the action of the possible intellect as it understands or the action of the agent intellect as it understands separate substances or as it makes things actually understood.

[8]   Besides, according to this theory, the agent intellect is not asserted to be connected with us as a form except by the fact that it is the form of objects of speculative understanding; and it is claimed to be the form of these objects because the same action belongs to the agent intellect and to these objects of understanding, which action is to make things actually understood. So, it could not be a form for us, unless by virtue of the fact that the objects of speculative understanding share in its action. Now, these objects do not share in its operation which consists in understanding separate substances, for they are the species of sensible things, unless we go back to the opinion of Avempace that the quiddities of separate substances can be known through the things that we understand about sensible objects. Therefore, it would not be at all possible for us to understand separate substances in the aforesaid way.

[9]   Moreover, the agent intellect is related to the objects of speculative understanding, which it makes to be so, in a different way from its relation to separate substances, which it does not make, but only knows, according to this theory. So, there is no necessity for it to be joined to us in its function as knower of separate substances, even if it is joined to us in its function as maker of the objects of speculative understanding. Rather, there is clearly a *fallacy of accident* in reasoning such as his.

[10]   Again, if we know separate substances through the agent intellect, this is not accomplished because the agent intellect is the form of this or that object of speculative understanding, but because it becomes a form for us, for in this way we are enabled to understand through it. Now, it becomes a form for us even through the first objects of speculative understanding, according to his own statement.

Therefore, immediately at the start, man can know separate substances through the agent intellect.

[11]   Of course, it might be answered that the agent intellect does not become a form for us, in a perfect way, by virtue of certain objects of speculative understanding, so that we might understand separate substances through it—and the only reason for this is that these objects of speculative understanding are not sufficient for the perfecting of the agent intellect in the act of understanding separate substances. But not even all the objects of speculative understanding taken together are sufficient for that perfection of the agent intellect by which it understands separate substances. For all these objects are intelligible only in so far as they have been made to be understood, while those separate substances are intelligible by their own nature. So, not even the fact that we will know all the objects of speculative understanding will make it necessary for the agent intellect to become a form for us, in such a perfect way that we may understand separate substances through it. Or, if this is not required, then we will have to say that, in understanding any intelligible object, we understand separate substances.

Chapter 44.

THAT MAN'S ULTIMATE FELICITY DOES NOT CONSIST IN THE KIND OF KNOWLEDGE OF SEPARATE SUBSTANCES THAT THE FOREGOING OPINIONS ASSUME

[1]   Of course, it is not possible to identify human felicity with such knowledge of separate substances, as the aforementioned philosophers have maintained.[1]

[2]   Indeed, a thing is futile which exists for an end which it cannot attain. So, since the end of man is felicity, to

1. See above, ch. 41–43.

which his natural desire tends, it is not possible for the felicity of man to be placed in something that man cannot achieve. Otherwise, it would follow that man is a futile being, and his natural desire would be incapable of fulfillment, which is impossible. Now, it is clear from what has been said that man cannot understand separate substances on the basis of the foregoing opinions. So, man's felicity is not located in such knowledge of separate substances.

[3] Again, in order that the agent intellect be united to us as a form, so that we may understand separate substances through it, it is required that the generation of the habitual intellect be complete, according to Alexander;[2] or that all objects of speculative understanding be made actual within us, according to Averroes.[3] And these two views reduce to the same thing, for in this explanation the habitual intellect is generated in us, in so far as the objects of speculative understanding are made actual within us. Now, all species from sensible things are potential objects of understanding. So, in order that the agent intellect be joined with any person, he must actually understand all the natures of sensible things, and all their powers, operations, and motions, through speculative understanding. This is not possible for any man to know through the principles of the speculative sciences, by which principles we are moved to a connection with the agent intellect, as they say. For, one could not attain all these objects of knowledge from the things that come under the scope of our senses, and from which the principles of the speculative sciences are drawn. So, it is impossible for a man to achieve this connection, in the manner suggested by them. Therefore, it is not possible for man's felicity to consist in such a connection.

[4] Besides, even granting that such a connection of man with the agent intellect were possible as they describe it, it is plain that such perfection comes to very few men; so much so that not even these men, nor any other men, how-

2. See above, ch. 42.
3. See above, ch. 43.

ever diligent and expert in speculative sciences, have dared to claim such perfection for themselves. On the contrary, they all state that many things are unknown to them. Thus, Aristotle speaks of the squaring of the circle,[4] and he can give only probable arguments for his principles for the ordering of celestial bodies, as he admits himself, in Book II of *On the Heavens*,[5] and what is necessary in regard to these bodies and their movers he keeps for others to explain, in *Metaphysics* XI.[6] Now, felicity is a definite common good, which many people can attain, "unless they are defective," as Aristotle puts it, in *Ethics* I.[7] And this is also true of every natural end in any species, that the members of this species do attain it, in most cases. Therefore, it is not possible for man's ultimate felicity to consist in the aforesaid connection.

[5] However, it is clear that Aristotle, whose view the aforementioned philosophers try to follow, did not think that man's ultimate felicity is to be found in such a connection. For he proves, in *Ethics* I,[8] that man's felicity is his operation according to perfect virtue. Hence, he had to develop his teaching on the virtues, which he divided into the moral and the intellectual virtues. Now, he shows in Book x,[9] that the ultimate felicity of man lies in speculation. Hence, it clearly does not lie in the act of any moral virtue, nor of prudence or art, though these are intellectual virtues. It remains, then, that it is an operation in accord with wisdom, the chief of the three remaining intellectual virtues, which are wisdom, science, and understanding, as he points out in *Ethics* VI.[10] Hence, in *Ethics* x,[11] he gives his judgment that the wise man is happy. Now, wisdom, for

4. See Aristotle, *Categories*, 7 (7b 3).
5. See Aristotle, *De caelo*, II, 5 (288a 2).
6. See Aristotle, *Metaphysics*, XI, 8 (1073b 2).
7. Aristotle, *Nicomachean Ethics*, I, 9 (1099b 19).
8. *Ibid.*, I, 13 (1102a 5).
9. *Ibid.*, X, 7 (1177a 18).
10. *Ibid.*, VI, 6 (1141a 3).
11. *Ibid.*, X, 8 (1179a 32).

him, is one of the speculative knowledges, "the head of the others," as he says in *Ethics* VI.[12] And at the beginning of the *Metaphysics*,[13] he calls the science which he intends to treat in this work, wisdom. Therefore, it is clear that Aristotle's opinion was that the ultimate felicity which man can acquire in this life is the kind of knowledge of divine things which can be gained through the speculative sciences. But that later way of knowing divine things, not by means of the speculative sciences but by a process of generation in the natural order, was made up by some of his commentators.

Chapter 45.

THAT IN THIS LIFE WE CANNOT
UNDERSTAND SEPARATE SUBSTANCES

[1]   Hence, since separate substances cannot be known by us in this life in the preceding ways, the question remains whether we may understand these separate substances in any way during this life.

[2]   Themistius tries to show that it is possible, by an argument from a less important case.[1] Separate substances are indeed more intelligible than material ones; the latter are intelligible, in so far as they are made to be actually understood by the agent intellect, but the former are intelligible in themselves. Therefore, if our intellect comprehends these material substances, it is naturally much more capable of understanding separate substances.

[3]   Now, this argument must be judged in different ways, depending on the various opinions concerning the possible intellect. For, if the possible intellect is not a power which depends on matter, and again if it is separate in being from

12. *Ibid., loc. cit.*
13. Aristotle, *Metaphysics*, I, 1 (981b 26).
1. See Averroes, *In III De anima*, comm. 36 (VI, 176v).

body, as Averroes supposes, then it follows that it has no necessary relation to material things. Consequently, things that are more intelligible in themselves will be more intelligible to it. But then it seems to follow that, since we understand from the start by means of the possible intellect, we therefore understand separate substances from the start: which is clearly false.

[4]   But Averroes tried to avoid this difficulty by the explanation which has been mentioned above,[2] in connection with his opinion. And this is plainly false, on the basis of what we have established.

[5]   However, if the possible intellect is not separated in being from body, then by virtue of such a union in being with body it has a necessary relation to material things, so that it could not reach a knowledge of other things except by means of these material things. Hence, it does not follow that, if separate substances are more intelligible in themselves, they are for this reason more intelligible to our intellect. And the words of Aristotle in *Metaphysics* II prove this. For he says there that "the difficulty of understanding these things comes from us not from them, for our intellect is to the most evident things, as the eye of the owl is to the light of the sun."[3] Hence, since separate substances cannot be understood through material things that are understood, as was shown above,[4] it follows that our possible intellect can in no way understand separate substances.

[6]   This is also evident from the relation of the possible intellect to the agent intellect. A passive potency is only a potency in regard to those things that are within the power of its proper active principle; for, to every passive potency in nature there corresponds an active potency; otherwise, the passive potency would be useless, for it could not be reduced to act except through an active potency. Hence we see that the visual power is only receptive of colors

2. See above, ch. 43.
3. Aristotle, *Metaphysics*, Iα, 1 (993b 9).
4. See above, ch. 41.

which are illuminated by light. Now, the possible intellect, since it is a passive power in some sense, has its proper corresponding agent, namely, the agent intellect which is related to the possible intellect as light is to sight. So, the possible intellect is only in potency to those intelligible objects which are made by the agent intellect. Hence, Aristotle, describing both intellects in Book III of *On the Soul*,[5] says that the possible intellect is "the capacity to become all things," while the agent intellect is "the capacity to make all things"; so, each potency is understood to be referred to the same thing, but one is active and the other passive. Thus, since separate substances are not made to be actually intelligible by the agent intellect, but only material substances are, the possible intellect only includes the latter within its scope. Therefore, we cannot understand separate substances through it.

[7]   For this point Aristotle made use of an appropriate example, for the eye of an owl can never see the light of the sun; though Averroes tries to ruin this example[6] by saying that the similarity between our intellect in relation to separate substances and the eye of the owl in relation to the light of the sun does not extend to impossibility, but only to difficulty. He gives a proof for this, in the same place, using the following argument: If those things which are understood in themselves, namely, separate substances, were not possible for us to understand, they would be for no purpose, just as if there were a visible object which could not be seen by any visual power.

[8]   How frivolous this argument is, is quite apparent. For, though these substances might never be understood by us, they are nonetheless understood by themselves. Hence, they are not intelligible in a purposeless way, as the sun (to pursue Aristotle's example) is visible, yet not in a purposeless way, simply because the owl cannot see it. For man and other animals can see it.

5. Aristotle, *De anima*, III, 5 (430a 14).
6. Averroes, *In II Metaphysicorum*, comm. 1 (VIII, 14v).

[9]   And thus, the possible intellect, if it be granted that it is united with the body in being, cannot understand separate substances. However, it makes a difference how one thinks about its substance. For, if it is supposed to be a material power, capable of generation and corruption, as some have claimed,[7] then it follows that it is limited by its own substance to the understanding of material things. Consequently, that it could in no way understand separate substances is quite necessary, since it could not be separate in its own being.

On the other hand, if the possible intellect, though united with a body, is, however, incorruptible and not dependent on matter in its actual being, as we showed above,[8] it follows that the limitation to the understanding of material things accrues to it as a result of its union with the body. Consequently, when the soul will have been separated from this body, the possible intellect will be able to understand things that are intelligible in themselves, through the light of the agent intellect, which is the likeness in the intellectual soul of the light which is present in separate substances.

[10]   And this is the view of our faith, concerning the understanding of separate substances by us after death, and not in this life.

Chapter 46.

THAT THE SOUL DOES NOT UNDERSTAND
ITSELF THROUGH ITSELF IN THIS LIFE

[1]   Now, it seems that some objection may be offered against what we have said, on the basis of a text of Augustine which requires careful interpretation. In fact, he says in Book IX of The Trinity: "Just as the mind gathers knowledge of bodily things through the bodily senses, so does it

7. See above, ch. 42.
8. SCG, II, ch. 79ff.

obtain knowledge of incorporeal things through itself. And so, it knows itself through itself, since it is incorporeal."[1] Indeed, it does appear from these words that our mind understands itself, through itself, and by understanding itself it understands separate substances. And this is in opposition to what was shown above. Therefore, it is necessary to investigate how our soul understands itself through itself.

[2]   Now, it cannot be said that it understands *what* it is, through itself. For, a cognitive potency becomes an actual knower by the fact that there is present in it that whereby the knowing is accomplished. Of course, if it be present in a potential way in the potency, one knows potentially; but if it be there actually, one knows actually; and if it be there in an intermediate fashion, one knows habitually. But the soul is always actually present to itself, never merely potentially or habitually. So, if the soul knows itself through itself, in the sense of *what* it is, it will always actually understand what it is. And this is plainly false.

[3]   Again, if the soul understands what it is, through itself, and if every man has a soul, then every man knows what soul is. And this is plainly false.

[4]   Moreover, the knowledge which comes about through something naturally implanted in us is natural, as is the case with indemonstrable principles which are known through the light of the agent intellect. If, then, we know concerning the soul *what* it is, through the soul itself, then this will be something naturally known. Now, in the case of things that are naturally known no one can err; for instance, in the knowing of indemonstrable principles no one makes an error. So, no one would be in error concerning what the soul is, if the soul knew this through itself. And this is clearly false, for many men have held the opinion that the soul is this or that body, and some have thought it a number or a harmony.[2] Therefore, the soul

1. St. Augustine, *De Trinitate*, IX, 3 (PL, 42, col. 963).
2. *SCG*, II, ch. 63–64.

does not, through itself, know concerning itself *what* it is.

[5]   Besides, in any order, "that which exists through itself is prior to, and is the principle of, that which is through another."[3] So, that which is known through itself is known before all things that are known through another, and it is the principle of the knowing of them. Thus, the first propositions are prior to the conclusions. If, then, the soul knows through itself what it is in itself, this will be something known through itself, and, consequently, a first known thing and a principle for the knowing of other things. Now, this is clearly false. For, *what the soul is* no science takes as something known; rather, it is a topic proposed for investigation, starting from other items of knowledge. Therefore, the soul does not know concerning itself *what* it is, through itself.

[6]   Now, it appears that even Augustine himself did not intend that it does. For he says in Book x of *The Trinity* that "the soul, when seeking knowledge of itself, does not endeavor to see itself as something absent, but takes care to observe itself as present; not to learn about itself as if it were ignorant, but to distinguish itself from what it knows as another thing."[4] Thus, he makes us understand that the soul, through itself, does know itself as present, but not as distinct from other things. Consequently, he says that some people have erred on this point because they have not distinguished the soul from those things which are different from it.[5] Now, because a thing is known from the point of view of what it is, that thing is also known in distinction from others; consequently, the definition which signifies what a thing is distinguishes the thing defined from all else. Therefore, Augustine did not wish to say that, through itself, the soul knows concerning itself what it is.

[7]   But neither did Aristotle intend this. Indeed, he says in Book iii of *On the Soul* that "the possible intellect un-

3. Aristotle, *Physics*, VIII, 5 (257a 32).
4. St. Augustine, *De Trinitate*, X, 9 (*PL*, 42, col. 980).
5. *Ibid.*, X, 6 (*PL*, 42, col. 978).

derstands itself as it does other things."[6] For it understands itself through an intelligible species, by which it is made actual in the genus of intelligible objects. Considered in itself, it is merely in potency in regard to intelligible being; nothing is known according to what it is potentially, but only as it is actually. Hence, separate substances, whose substances are like something actually existing in the genus of intelligible objects, do understand, concerning themselves, *what* they are, through their own substances; while our possible intellect does so, through an intelligible species, by which it is made an actual agent which understands. Hence, also, Aristotle, in Book III of *On the Soul*, demonstrates from the very act of understanding what is the nature of the possible intellect, namely, that it is "unmixed and incorruptible,"[7] as is clear from what we have said earlier.[8]

[8] And so, according to Augustine's meaning, our mind knows itself through itself, in so far as it knows concerning itself, *that it is*. Indeed, from the fact that it perceives that it acts it perceives that it is. Of course, it acts through itself, and so, through itself, it knows concerning itself that it is.

[9] So, also, in regard to separate substances, the soul by knowing itself knows *that they are*, but not *what* they are, for to do the latter is to understand their substances. Indeed, when we know this about separate substances, either through demonstration or through faith, that there are certain intellectual substances, we would not be able to get this knowledge on either basis unless our soul knew on its own part this point: what it is to be intellectual. Consequently, the knowledge concerning the soul's understanding must be used as a starting point for all that we learn about separate substances.

[10] Nor is it a necessary conclusion that, if we succeed in knowing what the soul is through the speculative sciences,

6. Aristotle, *De anima*, III, 4 (430a 2).
7. *Ibid.* (429a 2).
8. *SCG*, II, ch. 59ff.

we must then be able to reach a knowledge of what separate substances are, through these same sciences. As a matter of fact, our act of understanding, whereby we attain to the knowledge of what our soul is, is very remote from the intelligence of a separate substance. Nevertheless, it is possible through knowing what our soul is to reach a knowledge of a remote genus for separate substances, but this does not mean an understanding of these substances.

[11] Just as we know, through itself, that the soul is, in so far as we perceive its act, and we seek to discover what it is, from a knowledge of its acts and objects, by means of the principles of the speculative sciences, so also do we know concerning the things that are within our soul, such as powers and habits, *that* they indeed are, by virtue of our perception of their acts; but we discover *what* they are, from the qualitative character of their acts.

Chapter 47.

THAT IN THIS LIFE WE CANNOT SEE GOD THROUGH HIS ESSENCE

[1] Now, if we are not able to understand other separate substances in this life, because of the natural affinity of our intellect for phantasms, still less are we able in this life to see the divine essence which transcends all separate substances.

[2] An indication of this may also be taken from the fact that the higher our mind is elevated to the contemplation of spiritual beings, the more is it withdrawn from sensible things. Now, the final limit to which contemplation can reach is the divine substance. Hence, the mind which sees the divine substance must be completely cut off from the bodily senses, either by death or by ecstasy. Thus, it is said by one who speaks for God: "Man shall not see me and live" (Exod. 33:20).

[3] But that some men are spoken of in Sacred Scripture as having seen God must be understood either in reference to an imaginary vision, or even a corporeal one: according as the presence of divine power was manifested through some corporeal species, whether appearing externally, or formed internally in the imagination; or even according as some men have perceived some intelligible knowledge of God through His spiritual effects.

[4] However, certain words of Augustine do present a difficulty; for it appears from them that we can understand God Himself in this life. He says in Book ix of *The Trinity* that "we see with the vision of the mind, in the eternal truth, from which all temporal things have been made, the form in accord with which we exist, and in accord with which we perform any action by true and right reason, either within ourselves or in bodies, and as a result of this we have with us a conception and a true knowledge of things."[1] He also says in Book xii of the *Confessions*: "Suppose both of us see that what you say is true, and both of us see that what I say is true: where, I ask, do we see it? Certainly, I do not see it in you, nor you in me, but both in that immutable truth which is above our minds."[2] Again, he says in the book *On the True Religion* that "we judge all things according to the divine truth."[3] And he says in the *Soliloquies* that "truth must be known first, and through it other things can be known."[4] And this seems to mean the divine truth. It appears, then, from his words, that we see God Himself, Who is His own truth, and thus we know other things through Him.

[5] The same writer's words seem to tend toward the same view, words which he puts in Book xii of *The Trinity*, saying the following: "It pertains to reason to judge concerning these bodily things in accord with the incorporeal and sempiternal reasons which, unless they were above the

1. St. Augustine, *De Trinitate*, IX, 7 (*PL*, 42, col. 967).
2. St. Augustine, *Confessions*, XII, 25 (*PL*, 32, col. 840).
3. St. Augustine, *De vera religione*, 31 (*PL*, 34, col. 148).
4. St. Augustine, *Soliloquia*, I, 15 (*PL*, 32, col. 883).

human mind, certainly would not be immutable."[5] Now, the immutable and sempiternal reasons cannot exist in any other location than in God, since only God, according to the teaching of our faith, is sempiternal. Therefore, it seems to follow that we are able to see God in this life, and because we see the reasons of things in Him we may judge concerning other things.

[6]   However, we must not believe that Augustine held this view, in the texts which have been quoted: that we are able in this life to understand God through His essence. So, we have to make a study of how we may see this immutable truth, or these eternal reasons, in this life, and thus judge other things in accord with this vision.

[7]   As a matter of fact, Augustine himself admits that truth is in the soul, in the Soliloquies,[6] and as a result he proves the immortality of the soul from the eternity of truth. But truth is not in the soul simply in the way that God is said to be in all things by His essence, nor as He is in all things by His likeness, in the sense that each thing is called true to the extent that it approaches the likeness of God; for it is not on this basis that the soul is set above other things. Therefore, it is present in a special way in the soul, inasmuch as it knows truth. So, just as souls and other things are indeed said to be true in their own natures, because they have a likeness to the highest nature, which is Truth Itself, since it is its own actual being as understood —so also, what is known by the soul is true in so far as some likeness exists in it of that divine truth which God knows. Hence the Gloss on Psalm 11:2: "Truths are decayed from among the children of men," says that: "as from one face there may result many reflections in a mirror, so from one first truth there may result many truths in the minds of men."[7]

5. St. Augustine, De Trinitate, XII, 2 (PL, 42, col. 999).
6. St. Augustine, Soliloquia, II, 19 (PL, 32, col. 901).
7. See St. Augustine, Enarrationes in Psalmos, in XI, 2 (PL, 36, col. 138); also Peter Lombard, In Psalm. XI, 2 (PL, 191, col. 155).

Now, although different things are known and believed to be true by different people, certain things are true on which all men agree, such as the first principles of understanding, both speculative and practical, according as an image of divine truth is reflected universally in the minds of all men. So, in so far as any mind knows anything whatever with certitude, the object is intuited in these principles, by means of which judgment is made concerning all things, by resolving them back into these principles; and so the mind is said to see all things in the divine truth, or in the eternal reasons, and is said to judge all things in accord with them. And this interpretation the words of Augustine confirm, in the *Soliloquies*,[8] for he says that the principles of the sciences are seen in the divine truth as these visible objects are seen in the light of the sun. Yet it is obvious that they are not seen in the actual body of the sun, but through its light, which is a likeness in the air of solar brilliance, transmitted to suitable bodies.

[8] Therefore, we should not gather from these words of Augustine that God can be seen in His substance in this life, but only as in a mirror. And this is what the Apostle professes concerning the knowledge of this life, for he says: "We see now through a glass in a dark manner" (I Cor. 13:12).

[9] Although this mirror, which is the human mind, reflects the likeness of God in a closer way than lower creatures do, the knowledge of God which can be taken in by the human mind does not go beyond the type of knowledge that is derived from sensible things, since even the soul itself knows what it is itself as a result of understanding the natures of sensible things, as we have said.[9] Hence, throughout this life God can be known in no higher way than that whereby a cause is known through its effect.

8. St. Augustine, *Soliloquia*, I, 8 (*PL*, 32, col. 877).
9. See above, ch. 45–46.

Chapter 48.

THAT MAN'S ULTIMATE FELICITY DOES NOT COME IN THIS LIFE

[1]   If, then, ultimate human felicity does not consist in the knowledge of God, whereby He is known in general by all, or most, men, by a sort of confused appraisal, and again, if it does not consist in the knowledge of God which is known by way of demonstration in the speculative sciences, nor in the cognition of God whereby He is known through faith, as has been shown in the foregoing;[1] and if it is not possible in this life to reach a higher knowledge of God so as to know Him through His essence, or even in such a way that, when the other separate substances are known, God might be known through the knowledge of them, as if from a closer vantage point, as we showed;[2] and if it is necessary to identify ultimate felicity with some sort of knowledge of God, as we proved above;[3] then it is not possible for man's ultimate felicity to come in this life.

[2]   Again, the ultimate end of man brings to a termination man's natural appetite, in the sense that, once the end is acquired, nothing else will be sought. For, if he is still moved onward to something else, he does not yet have the end in which he may rest. Now, this termination cannot occur in this life. For, the more a person understands, the more is the desire to understand increased in him, and this is natural to man, unless, perchance, there be someone who understands all things. But in this life this does not happen to anyone who is a mere man, nor could it happen, since we are not able to know in this life the separate substances, and they are most intelligible, as has been shown.[4] There-

1. See above, ch. 38ff.
2. See above, ch. 45.
3. See above, ch. 37.
4. See above, ch. 45.

fore, it is not possible for man's ultimate felicity to be in this life.

[3] Besides, everything that is moved toward an end naturally desires to be stationed at, and at rest in, that end; consequently, a body does not move away from the place to which it is moved naturally, unless by virtue of a violent movement which runs counter to its appetite. Now, felicity is the ultimate end which man naturally desires. So, there is a natural desire of man to be established in felicity. Therefore, unless along with felicity such an unmoving stability be attained, he is not yet happy, for his natural desire is not yet at rest. And so, when a person attains felicity he likewise attains stability and rest, and that is why this is the notion of all men concerning felicity, that it requires stability as part of its essential character. For this reason, the Philosopher says, in *Ethics* I, that "we do not regard the happy man as a sort of chameleon."[5] Now, in this life there is no certain stability, for to any man, no matter how happy he is reputed to be, illnesses and misfortunes may possibly come, and by them he may be hindered in that operation, whatever it may be, with which felicity is identified. Therefore, it is not possible for man's ultimate felicity to be in this life.

[4] Moreover, it appears inappropriate and irrational for the time of generation of a thing to be long, while the time of its maturity is short. For it would follow that a nature would be without its end, most of the time. Consequently, we see that animals which live but a short time also take but a short time to come to perfect maturity. Now, if felicity consists in perfect operation, in accord with perfect virtue,[6] whether intellectual or moral, it is impossible for it to come to man until a long time has elapsed. And this is especially evident in speculative pursuits, in which man's ultimate felicity is placed, as is clear from what we have said.[7] For man is barely able to reach perfection in scientific

5. Aristotle, *Nicomachean Ethics*, I, 10 (1100b 5).
6. *Ibid.*, X, 7 (1177a 11).
7. See above, ch. 37.

speculation in the last stage of his life. But then, in most cases, only a little part of human life remains. So, it is not possible for man's ultimate felicity to be in this life.

[5]   Furthermore, all men admit that felicity is a perfect good; otherwise, it could not satisfy desire. Now, a perfect good is one which lacks any admixture of evil, just as a perfectly white thing is completely unmixed with black. Of course, it is not possible for man in the present state of life to be entirely free from evils, not only from corporeal ones, such as hunger, thirst, heat and cold, and other things of this kind, but also from evils of the soul. For we can find no one who is not disturbed at times by unruly passions, who does not at times overstep the mean in which virtue lies,[8] either by excess or defect, who also is not mistaken in certain matters, or who at least is ignorant of things which he desires to know, or who also conceives with uncertain opinion things about which he would like to be certain. Therefore, no person is happy in this life.

[6]   Again, man naturally shrinks from death, and is sorrowful at its prospect, not only at the instant when he feels its threat and tries to avoid it, but even when he thinks back upon it. But freedom from death is something man cannot achieve in this life. Therefore, it is not possible for man in this life to be happy.

[7]   Besides, ultimate felicity does not consist in an habitual state, but in an operation, since habits are for the sake of acts. But it is impossible to perform any action continuously in this life. Therefore, it is impossible for man in this life to be entirely happy.

[8]   Furthermore, the more a thing is desired and loved, the more does its loss bring sorrow and sadness. Now, felicity is what is most desired and loved. Therefore, its loss holds the greatest prospect of sorrow. But, if ultimate felicity were possible in this life, it is certain that it would be lost, at least by death. And it is not certain whether it

8. See Aristotle, *Nicomachean Ethics*, II, 6 (1106b 24).

would last until death, since for any man in this life there is the possibility of sickness, by which he may be completely impeded from the work of virtue: such things as mental illness and the like, by which the use of reason is halted. So, such felicity always will have sorrow naturally associated with it. Therefore, it will not be perfect felicity.

[9] However, someone may say that, since felicity is a good of intellectual nature, perfect and true felicity belongs to those beings in whom a perfect intellectual nature is found, that is, to separate substances, but that in man there is found an imperfect happiness, in the manner of some sort of participation. For, in regard to the full understanding of truth, men can attain it only through enquiry, and they are utterly deficient in regard to objects which are most intelligible in their nature, as is clear from what we have said.[9] And so, felicity in its perfect character cannot be present in men, but they may participate somewhat in it, even in this life. And this seems to have been Aristotle's view on felicity. Hence, in *Ethics* I, where he asks whether misfortunes take away happiness, having shown that felicity consists in the works of virtue which seem to be most enduring in this life, he concludes that those men for whom such perfection in this life is possible are happy as men, as if they had not attained felicity absolutely, but merely in human fashion.[10]

[10] Now, we have to show that the foregoing reply does not invalidate the arguments which we have given above. Indeed, though man is by nature inferior to separate substances, he is nonetheless superior to irrational creatures. So, he attains his ultimate end in a more perfect way than they do. They achieve their ultimate end with such perfection because they seek nothing else, for the heavy thing comes to rest when it has occupied its own place; and even in the case of animals, when they enjoy sensual pleasures their natural desire is at rest. So, it is much more necessary for

9. See above, ch. 45.
10. Aristotle, *Nicomachean Ethics*, I, 10 (1101a 18).

man's natural desire to come to rest when he has reached his ultimate end. But this cannot come about in this life. Therefore, man does not attain felicity, understood as his proper end, during this life, as we have shown. Therefore, he must attain it after this life.

[11]   Again, it is impossible for natural desire to be unfulfilled, since "nature does nothing in vain."[11] Now, natural desire would be in vain if it could never be fulfilled. Therefore, man's natural desire is capable of fulfillment, but not in this life, as we have shown. So, it must be fulfilled after this life. Therefore, man's ultimate felicity comes after this life.

[12]   Besides, as long as anything is in motion toward perfection, it is not yet at the ultimate end. But all men, while learning the truth, are always disposed as beings in motion, and as tending toward perfection, because men who come later make other discoveries, over and above those found out by earlier men, as is also stated in *Metaphysics* II.[12] So, men in the process of learning the truth are not situated as if they were at the ultimate end. Thus, since man's ultimate felicity in this life seems mainly to consist in speculation, whereby the knowledge of the truth is sought, as Aristotle himself proves in *Ethics* x,[13] it is impossible to say that man achieves his ultimate end in this life.

[13]   Moreover, everything that is in potency tends to proceed into act. So, as long as it is not made wholly actual, it is not at its ultimate end. Now, our intellect is in potency in regard to all the forms of things to be known, and it is reduced to act when it knows any one of them. So, it will not be wholly in act, nor at its ultimate end, until it knows all things, at least all these material things. But man cannot achieve this through the speculative sciences, through which he knows truth in this life. Therefore, it is not possible for man's ultimate felicity to be in this life.

11. Aristotle, *De caelo*, II, 11 (291b 13).
12. Aristotle, *Metaphysics*, Ia, 1 (993a 31).
13. Aristotle, *Nicomachean Ethics*, X, 7 (1177a 18).

[14] For these and like reasons, Alexander and Averroes claimed that man's ultimate felicity does not consist in the human knowledge which comes through the speculative sciences, but through a connection with a separate substance, which they believed to be possible for man in this life.[14] But, since Aristotle saw that there is no other knowledge for man in this life than through the speculative sciences, he maintained that man does not achieve perfect felicity, but only a limited kind.

[15] On this point there is abundant evidence of how even the brilliant minds of these men suffered from the narrowness of their viewpoint. From which narrow attitudes we shall be freed if we grant in accord with the foregoing proofs that man can reach true felicity after this life, when man's soul is existing immortally; in which state the soul will understand in the way that separate substances understand, as we showed in Book Two of this work.[15]

[16] And so, man's ultimate felicity will lie in the knowledge of God that the human mind has after this life, according to the way in which separate substances know Him. For which reason our Lord promises us "a reward in heaven" and says that the saints "shall be as the angels . . . who always see God in heaven," as it is said (Matt. 5:12; 22:30; 18:10).

Chapter 49.

THAT SEPARATE SUBSTANCES DO NOT SEE GOD IN HIS ESSENCE BY KNOWING HIM THROUGH THEIR ESSENCE

[1] Moreover, we must inquire whether this knowledge whereby the separate substances and the soul after death

14. See above, ch. 42–43.
15. *SCG*, II, ch. 81.

know God, through their own essences, suffices for their ultimate felicity.

[2]   The first thing to be done, in investigating the truth of this question, is to show that the divine essence is not known through such a type of knowledge.

[3]   In fact, it is possible to know a cause from its effect, in many ways. One way is to take the effect as a means of finding out, concerning the cause, that it exists and that it is of a certain kind. This occurs in the sciences which demonstrate the cause through the effect. Another way is to see the cause in the effect itself, according as the likeness of the cause is reflected in the effect; thus a man may be seen in a mirror, by virtue of his likeness. And this way is different from the first. In fact, in the first way there are two cognitions, one of the effect and one of the cause, and one is the cause of the other; for the knowledge of the effect is the cause of the knowing of its cause. But in the second way there is one vision of both, since at the same time that the effect is seen the cause is also seen in it. A third way is such that the very likeness of the cause, in its effect, is the form by which the effect knows its own cause. For instance, suppose a box had an intellect, and so knew through its form the skilled mind from which such a form proceeded as a likeness of that mind. Now, it is not possible in any of these ways to know from the effect *what* the cause is, unless the effect be adequate to the cause, one in which the entire virtuality of the cause is expressed.

[4]   Now, separate substances know God through their substances, as a cause is known through its effect; not, of course, in the first way, for then their knowledge would be discursive; but in the second way, according as one substance sees God in another; and also in the third way, according as any one of them sees God within itself. Now, none of them is an effect adequately representing the power of God, as we showed in Book Two.[1] So, it is impossible for them to see the divine essence itself by this kind of knowledge.

1. *SCG*, II, ch. 22ff.

[5] Besides, the intelligible likeness through which a thing is understood in its substance must be of the same species or, rather, of an identical species; as the form of the house which exists in the mind of the artisan is of the same species as the form of the house which exists in matter, or, rather, the species are identical; for one is not going to understand what a donkey or a horse is through the species of a man. But the nature of a separate substance is not the same in species as the divine nature, not even the same in genus, as we showed in Book One.[2] Therefore, it is not possible for a separate substance, through its own nature, to understand the divine substance.

[6] Furthermore, every created thing is limited to some genus or species. But the divine essence is unlimited, comprehending within itself every perfection in the whole of existing being, as we showed in Book One.[3] Therefore, it is impossible for the divine substance to be seen through any created being.

[7] Moreover, every intelligible species whereby the quiddity or essence of any thing is understood comprehends that thing while representing it; consequently, we call words signifying what such a thing is *terms* and *definitions*. But it is impossible for a created likeness to represent God in this way, since every created likeness belongs to a definite genus, while God does not, as we explained in Book One.[4] Therefore, it is not possible for the divine substance to be understood through a created likeness.

[8] Furthermore, divine substance is its own existing being, as we showed in Book One.[5] But the being of a separate substance is other than its substance, as we proved in Book Two.[6] Therefore, the essence of a separate sub-

2. *SCG*, I, ch. 25.
3. *Ibid.*, ch. 28 and 43.
4. *Ibid.*, ch. 25.
5. *Ibid.*, ch. 22.
6. *SCG*, II, ch. 52.

stance is not an adequate medium whereby God could be seen essentially.

[9]   However, a separate substance does know through its own substance *that* God is, and that He is the cause of all things, that He is eminent above all and set apart from all, not only from things which exist, but also from things which can be conceived by the created mind. Even we are able to reach this knowledge of God, in some sense; for we know through His effects, that God is, and that He is the cause of other beings, that He is supereminent over other things and set apart from all. And this is the ultimate and most perfect limit of our knowledge in this life, as Dionysius says in *Mystical Theology*. "We are united with God as the Unknown."[7] Indeed, this is the situation, for, while we know of God *what He is not, what He is* remains quite unknown. Hence, to manifest his ignorance of this sublime knowledge, it is said of Moses that "he went to the dark cloud wherein God was" (Exod. 20:21).

[10]   Now, since a lower nature only touches with its highest part the lowest part of the next higher nature, this knowledge must be more eminent in separate substances than in us. This becomes evident in a detailed consideration. For, the more closely and definitely we know the effect of a cause, the more evident does it become that its cause exists. Now, separate substances, which know God through themselves, are nearer effects and more definite bearers of the likeness of God than the effects through which we know God. Therefore, the separate substances know more certainly and clearly than we that God is.

Again, since it is possible to come in some way to the proper knowledge of a thing by means of negations, as we said above,[8] the more a person can know that a large number of closely related things are set apart from an object, the more does one approach toward a proper knowledge of it. For instance, one approaches closer to a proper knowl-

7. Pseudo-Dionysius, *De mystica theologia*, I, 1 (PG, 3, 997).
8. See above, ch. 39.

edge of man when he knows that he is neither an inanimate, nor an insensitive, being than when one merely knows that he is not inanimate; even though neither of them makes it known *what* man is. Now, separate substances know more things than we do, and things that are closer to God; consequently, in their understanding, they set apart from God more things, and more intimately related things, than we do. So, they approach more closely to a proper knowledge of Him than we do, although even these substances do not see the divine substance by means of their understanding of themselves.

Also, the more one knows how a man is placed in authority over people in higher positions, the more does one know the high position of this man. Thus, though a rustic may know that the king occupies the highest office in the kingdom, since he is acquainted only with some of the lowest official positions in the kingdom with which he may have some business, he does not know the eminence of the king in the way that another man does who is acquainted with all the leading dignitaries of the kingdom and knows that the king holds authority over them; even though neither type of lower office comprehends the exalted position appropriate to the dignity of the king. Of course, we are in ignorance, except in regard to the lowest types of beings. So, although we may know that God is higher than all beings, we do not know the divine eminence as separate substances do, for the highest orders of beings are known to them, and they know that God is superior to all of them.

Finally, it is obvious that the more the large number, and great importance, of the effects of a cause become known, the more does the causality of the cause, and its power, become known. As a result, it becomes manifest that separate substances know the causality of God, and His power, better than we do; even though we know that He is the cause of all beings.

Chapter 50.

THAT THE NATURAL DESIRE OF SEPARATE SUBSTANCES DOES NOT COME TO REST IN THE NATURAL KNOWLEDGE WHICH THEY HAVE OF GOD

[1] However, it is impossible for the natural desire in separate substances to come to rest in such a knowledge of God.

[2] For everything that is an imperfect member of any species desires to attain the perfection of its species. For instance, a man who has an opinion regarding something, that is, an imperfect knowledge of the thing, is thereby aroused to desire knowledge of the thing. Now, the afore-mentioned knowledge which the separate substances have of God, without knowing His substance, is an imperfect species of knowledge. In fact, we do not think that we know a thing if we do not know its substance. Hence, it is most important, in knowing a thing, to know *what it is*. There-fore, natural desire does not come to rest as a result of this knowledge which separate substances have of God; rather, it further arouses the desire to see the divine substance.

[3] Again, as a result of knowing the effects, the desire to know their cause is aroused; thus, men began to phi-losophize when they investigated the causes of things.[1] Therefore, the desire to know, which is naturally implanted in all intellectual substances, does not rest until, after they have come to know the substances of the effects, they also know the substance of the cause. The fact, then, that sepa-rate substances know that God is the cause of all things whose substances they see, does not mean that natural de-sire comes to rest in them, unless they also see the sub-stance of God Himself.

1. Aristotle, *Metaphysics*, I, 2 (982b 12).

[4]   Besides, the problem of *why* something is so is related to the problem of *whether* it is so, in the same way that an inquiry as to *what* something is stands in regard to an inquiry as to *whether it exists*. For the question *why* looks for a means to demonstrate *that* something is so, for instance, that there is an eclipse of the moon; likewise, the question *what is it* seeks a means to demonstrate *that something exists*, according to the traditional teaching in *Posterior Analytics* II.[2] Now, we observe that those who see *that something is so* naturally desire to know *why*. So, too, those acquainted with the fact *that something exists* naturally desire to know *what this thing is*, and this is to understand its substance. Therefore, the natural desire to know does not rest in that knowledge of God whereby we know merely *that He is*.

[5]   Furthermore, nothing finite can fully satisfy intellectual desire. This is shown from the fact that, whenever a finite object is presented, the intellect extends its interest to something more, so that, given any finite line, it strives to apprehend a longer one; and the same thing takes place in regard to numbers. This is the reason for infinite series in numbers and in mathematical lines. Now, the eminence and power of any created substance are finite. Therefore, the intellect of a separate substance does not come to rest simply because it knows created substances, however lofty they may be, but it still tends by natural desire toward the understanding of substance which is of infinite eminence, as we showed concerning divine substance in Book One.[3]

[6]   Moreover, just as the natural desire to know is present in all intellectual natures, so is there present in them the natural desire to put off ignorance and lack of knowledge. Now, the separate substances know, as we have said,[4] by the aforesaid mode of knowledge, that the substance of God is above them and above everything understood by them; con-

2. Aristotle, *Posterior Analytics*, II, 1 (89b 22).
3. SCG, I, ch. 43.
4. See above, ch. 49.

sequently, they know that the divine substance is unknown to them. Therefore, their natural desire tends toward the understanding of divine substance.

[7]   Besides, the nearer a thing comes to its end, the greater is the desire by which it tends to the end; thus, we observe that the natural motion of bodies is increased toward the end. Now, the intellects of separate substances are nearer to the knowledge of God than our intellects are. So, they desire the knowledge of God more intensely than we do. But, no matter how fully we know that God exists, and the other things mentioned above,[5] we do not cease our desire, but still desire to know Him through His essence. Much more, then, do the separate substances desire this naturally. Therefore, their desire does not come to rest in the aforesaid knowledge of God.

[8]   The conclusion from these considerations is that the ultimate felicity of separate substances does not lie in the knowledge of God, in which they know Him through their substances, for their desire still leads them on toward God's substance.

[9]   Also, quite apparent in this conclusion is the fact that ultimate felicity is to be sought in nothing other than an operation of the intellect, since no desire carries on to such sublime heights as the desire to understand the truth. Indeed, all our desires for pleasure, or other things of this sort that are craved by men, can be satisfied with other things, but the aforementioned desire does not rest until it reaches God, the highest point of reference for, and the maker of, things. This is why Wisdom appropriately states: "I dwelt in the highest places, and my throne is in a pillar of a cloud" (Ecclus. 24:7). And Proverbs (9:3) says that Wisdom "by her maids invites to the tower." Let those men be ashamed, then, who seek man's felicity in the most inferior things, when it is so highly situated.

5. *Ibid.*

Chapter 51.

HOW GOD MAY BE SEEN IN HIS ESSENCE

[1] Since it is impossible for a natural desire to be incapable of fulfillment, and since it would be so, if it were not possible to reach an understanding of divine substance such as all minds naturally desire, we must say that it is possible for the substance of God to be seen intellectually, both by separate intellectual substances and by our souls.

[2] It is already sufficiently apparent from what we have said what should be the mode of this vision. For we showed above[1] that the divine substance cannot be seen intellectually by means of any created species. Consequently, if the divine essence is seen, it must be done as His intellect sees the divine essence itself through itself, and in such a vision the divine essence must be both what is seen and that whereby it is seen.

[3] Now, since the created intellect cannot understand any substance unless it becomes actual by means of some species, which is the likeness of the thing understood, informing it, a person might consider it impossible for a created intellect to be able to see, by means of the divine essence serving as a sort of intelligible species, the very substance of God. For the divine essence is a certain being subsisting through itself, and we showed in Book One[2] that God cannot be a form for any other being.

[4] In order to understand the truth of this matter, we must consider that self-subsistent substance is either a form only, or a composite of matter and form. And a thing composed of matter and form cannot be the form of another being, because the form in it is already limited to this matter in such a way that it could not be the form of another

1. See above, ch. 49.
2. *SCG*, I, ch. 26ff.

thing. But a being which subsists in such a way that it is a form only can be the form of another, provided its being is such that it could be participated by that other thing, as we showed concerning the human soul, in Book Two.[3] However, if its being could not be participated by another, it could not be the form of any other thing, for then it would be determined within itself by its own being, just as material things are by their own matter.

Now, this should be observed as obtaining in the same way in the order of intelligible being as it does in substantial or physical being. For, since the perfection of the intellect is what is true, in the order of intelligible objects, that object which is a purely formal intelligible will be truth itself. And this characteristic applies only to God, for, since the true is consequent on being,[4] that alone is its own truth which is its own being. But this is proper to God only, as we showed in Book Two.[5] So, other intelligible subsistents do not exist as pure forms in the order of intelligible beings, but as possessors of a form in some subject. In fact, each of them is a true thing but not truth, just as each is a being but not the very act of being.

So, it is manifest that the divine essence may be related to the created intellect as an intelligible species by which it understands, but this does not apply to the essence of any other separate substance. Yet, it cannot be the form of another thing in its natural being, for the result of this would be that, once joined to another thing, it would make up one nature. This could not be, since the divine essence is in itself perfect in its own nature. But an intelligible species, united with an intellect, does not make up a nature; rather, it perfects the intellect for the act of understanding, and this is not incompatible with the perfection of the divine essence.

[5] This immediate vision of God is promised us in Scripture: "We see now through a glass in a dark manner; but

3. SCG, II, ch. 68.
4. See Aristotle, Metaphysics, Ia, 1 (993b 30).
5. SCG, II, ch. 15.

then face to face" (I Cor. 13:12). It is wrong to understand this in a corporeal way, picturing in our imagination a bodily face of the Divinity, since we have shown[6] that God is incorporeal. Nor is it even possible for us to see God with our bodily face, for the power of corporeal vision, which is associated with our face, can only apply to corporeal things. Thus, then, shall we see God face to face, in the sense that we shall see Him without a medium, as is true when we see a man face to face.

[6] In this vision, of course, we become most like unto God, and we are partakers in His happiness. For God Himself understands His own substance through His own essence; and this is His felicity. Hence it is said: "When He shall appear, we shall be like to Him, because we shall see Him as He is" (I John 3:2). And the Lord says "I dispose to you, as My Father hath disposed to me . . . My table, that you may eat and drink at My table, in My kingdom" (Luke 22:29–30). Of course, this can be understood not in reference to corporeal food or drink, but to Him Who is received at the table of Wisdom, of Whom Wisdom speaks: "Eat My bread and drink the wine which I have mingled for you" (Proverbs 9:5). And so, may they who enjoy the same felicity whereby God is happy eat and drink at God's table, seeing Him in the way that He sees Himself.

Chapter 52.

THAT NO CREATED SUBSTANCE CAN, BY ITS OWN NATURAL POWER, ATTAIN THE VISION OF GOD IN HIS ESSENCE

[1] However, it is not possible for any created substance, by its own power, to be able to attain this manner of divine vision.

6. *SCG*, I, ch. 27.

[2]   Indeed, a lower nature cannot acquire that which is proper to a higher nature except through the action of the higher nature to which the property belongs. For instance, water cannot be hot except through the action of fire. Now, to see God through His divine essence is proper to the divine nature, for it is the special prerogative of any agent to perform its operation through its own form. So, no intellectual substance can see God through His divine essence unless God is the agent of this operation.

[3]   Again, the form proper to any being does not come to be in another being unless the first being is the agent of this event, for an agent makes something like itself by communicating its form to another thing. Now, it is impossible to see the substance of God unless the divine essence itself is the form whereby the intellect understands, as we have proved.[1] Therefore, it is not possible for a created substance to attain this vision, except through divine action.

[4]   Besides, if any two factors are to be mutually united, so that one of them is formal and the other material, their union must be completed through action coming from the side of the formal factor, and not through the action of the one that is material. In fact, form is the principle of action, while matter is the principle of passion. For the created intellect to see God's substance, then, the divine essence itself must be joined as an intelligible form to the intellect, as we have proved. Therefore, it is not possible for the attainment of this vision to be accomplished by a created intellect except through divine action.

[5]   Furthermore, "that which is of itself is the cause of that which is through another being."[2] But the divine intellect sees the divine substance through itself, for the divine intellect is the divine essence itself whereby the substance of God is seen, as was proved in Book One.[3] However, the created intellect sees the divine substance through

1. See above, ch. 51.
2. Aristotle, *Physics*, VIII, 5 (257a 31).
3. *SCG*, I, ch. 45.

the essence of God, as through something other than itself. Therefore, this vision cannot come to the created intellect except through God's action.

[6] Moreover, whatever exceeds the limitations of a nature cannot accrue to it except through the action of another being. For instance, water does not tend upward unless it is moved by something else. Now, seeing God's substance transcends the limitations of every created nature; indeed, it is proper for each created intellectual nature to understand according to the manner of its own substance. But divine substance cannot be understood in this way, as we showed above.[4] Therefore, the attainment by a created intellect to the vision of divine substance is not possible except through the action of God, Who transcends all creatures.

[7] Thus, it is said: "The grace of God is life everlasting" (Rom. 6:23). In fact, we have shown that man's happiness, which is called life everlasting, consists in this divine vision,[5] and we are said to attain it by God's grace alone, because such a vision exceeds all the capacity of a creature and it is not possible to reach it without divine assistance. Now, when such things happen to a creature, they are attributed to God's grace. And the Lord says: "I will manifest Myself to him" (John 14:21).

Chapter 53.

THAT THE CREATED INTELLECT NEEDS AN INFLUX OF DIVINE LIGHT IN ORDER TO SEE GOD THROUGH HIS ESSENCE

[1] For such a noble vision, the created intellect must be elevated by means of an influx of divine goodness.

4. See above, ch. 49.
5. See above, ch. 50.

[2]   Indeed, it is not possible for what is the proper form of one thing to become the form of another unless the latter thing participates some likeness of the thing to which the form belongs. For instance, light can only become the act of a body if the body participates somewhat in the diaphanous. But the divine essence is the proper intelligible form for the divine intellect and is proportioned to it; in fact, these three are one in God: the intellect, that whereby understanding is accomplished, and the object which is understood. So, it is impossible for this essence to become the intelligible form of a created intellect unless by virtue of the fact that the created intellect participates in the divine likeness. Therefore, this participation in the divine likeness is necessary so that the substance of God may be seen.

[3]   Again, nothing is receptive of a more sublime form unless it be elevated by means of a disposition to the capacity for this form, for a proper act is produced in a proper potency. Now, the divine essence is a higher form than any created intellect. So, in order that the divine essence may become the intelligible species for a created intellect, which is needed in order that the divine substance may be seen, it is necessary for the created intellect to be elevated for this purpose by a more sublime disposition.

[4]   Besides, suppose that two things are not united at first, and then later they are united; this must be done by changing both of them, or at least one. Now, suppose that a created intellect starts for the first time to see God's substance; then, necessarily, according to the preceding arguments,[1] the divine essence must be united with it for the first time as an intelligible species. Of course, it is not possible for the divine essence to be changed, as we showed above.[2] So, this union must start to exist by means of a change in the created intellect. In fact, this change can only come about by means of the created intellect acquiring some new disposition.

1. See above, ch. 51.
2. SCG, I, ch. 13.

Indeed, the same conclusion follows if it be granted that a created intellect is endowed with such a vision from the start of its creation. For, if this vision exceeds the capacity of a created nature, as we have proved,[3] then any created intellect may be understood to enjoy complete existence in the species proper to its nature, without seeing the substance of God. Hence, whether it begins to see God at the start of its existence, or later, something must be added to its nature.

[5] Furthermore, nothing can be elevated to a higher operation unless because its power is strengthened. But there are two possible ways in which a thing's power may be strengthened. One way is by a simple intensification of the power itself; thus, the active power of a hot thing is increased by an intensification of the heat, so that it is able to perform a stronger action of the same species. A second way is by the imposition of a new form; thus, the power of a diaphanous object is increased so that it can shine with light, by virtue of its becoming actually luminous, through the form of light received for the first time within it. And in fact, this latter kind of increase of power is needed for the acquisition of an operation of another species. Now, the power of a created intellect is not sufficient to see the divine substance, as is clear from what we have said.[4] So, its power must be increased in order that it may attain such a vision. But the increase through the intensification of a natural power does not suffice, since this vision is not of the same essential type as the vision proper to a natural created intellect. This is evident from the difference between the objects of these visions. Therefore, an increase of the intellectual power by means of the acquisition of a new disposition must be accomplished.

[6] However, since we reach the knowledge of intelligible things from sensible things, we also take over the names proper to sense knowledge for intellectual knowledge, espe-

3. See above, ch. 52.
4. *Ibid.*

cially the ones which apply to sight, which, compared to the other senses, is more noble and more spiritual, and so more closely related to the intellect. Thus it is that this intellectual knowledge is called *vision*. And since corporeal vision is not accomplished without light, those things whereby intellectual vision is perfected take on the name *light*. Hence, even Aristotle, in Book III of *On the Soul*,[5] likens the agent intellect to light, because of the fact that the agent intellect makes things actually intelligible, just as light in a way makes things actually visible. Therefore, this disposition whereby the created intellect is raised to the intellectual vision of divine substance is fittingly called the light of glory;[6] not because it makes some object actually intelligible, as does the light of the agent intellect, but because it makes the intellect actually powerful enough to understand.

[7]   Now, this is the light of which it is said in the Psalms (35:10): "In Thy light we shall see the light," that is, of the divine substance. And it is said in the Apocalypse (22:5; see also 21:23): "The city," that is, of the Blessed, "hath no need of the sun, nor of the moon . . . for the glory of God hath enlightened it." And it is said in Isaias (60:19): "Thou shalt no more have the sun for thy light by day, neither shall the brightness of the moon enlighten thee; but the Lord shall be unto thee for an everlasting light, and thy God for thy glory."—It is also so, because in God to be and to understand is the same thing; and because He is for all the cause of understanding, He is said to be the *light* (John 1:9): "That was the true light which enlightened every man that cometh into this world" (John 1:9); and: "God is light" (I John 1:5); and in the Psalms (103:2): "Thou . . . art clothed with light as with a garment."— And for this reason also, both God and the angels are described in Sacred Scripture in figures of fire (Exod. 24:17; Acts 2:3; Ps. 103:4), because of the brilliance of fire.

5. Aristotle, *De anima*, III, 5 (430a 15).
6. See St. Thomas, *Quaestiones Quodlibetales*, VII, q. 1, a. 1, c.

Chapter 54.

ARGUMENTS BY WHICH IT SEEMS TO BE PROVED THAT GOD CANNOT BE SEEN IN HIS ESSENCE, AND THE ANSWERS TO THEM

[1] Now, someone will object against the preceding statements. No light that is added to the power of vision can elevate this power to a vision of things which exceed the capacity of bodily sight, for the power of sight is able to see colored objects only. But divine substance exceeds all the capacity of a created intellect, even more than understanding exceeds the capacity of sense. Therefore, the created intellect could not be elevated by any adventitious light so as to see the divine substance.

[2] Again, the light which is received in a created intellect is something created. And so, it is infinitely removed from God. Therefore, the created intellect cannot be elevated to the vision of the divine substance by this kind of light.

[3] Besides, if the aforesaid light can in fact do this because it is a likeness of the divine substance, then since every intellectual substance, by the fact of being intellectual, bears the divine likeness, the very nature of any intellectual substance whatever is adequate to the divine vision.

[4] Furthermore, if this light is created, then nothing prevents it from being created connatural with some creature; hence, there could be a created intellect which, by its own connatural light, would see the divine substance. The contrary of this has been proved.[1]

[5] Moreover, "the infinite as such is unknown."[2] Now, we have shown in Book One[3] that God is infinite. There-

1. See above, ch. 52.
2. Aristotle, *Physics*, I, 4 (187b 7).
3. *SCG*, I, ch. 43.

fore, the divine substance cannot be seen by means of the aforesaid light.

[6]   Again, there must be a proportion between the understander and the thing understood. But there is no proportion between the created intellect, even when perfected by this light, and the divine substance, because their distance apart still remains infinite. Therefore, the created intellect cannot be elevated to the vision of the divine substance by any light.

[7]   For these and similar reasons some men have been moved to assert that the divine substance is never seen by any created intellect. Of course, this position both takes away true happiness from the rational creature, for it can consist in nothing other than a vision of divine substance, as we have shown;[4] and it also contradicts the text of Sacred Scripture, as is evident from the preceding texts.[5] Consequently, it is to be spurned as false and heretical.

[8]   Indeed, it is not difficult to answer these arguments. The divine substance is not beyond the capacity of the created intellect in such a way that it is altogether foreign to it, as sound is from the object of vision, or as immaterial substance is from sense power; in fact, the divine substance is the first intelligible object and the principle of all intellectual cognition. But it is beyond the capacity of the created intellect, in the sense that it exceeds its power; just as sensible objects of extreme character are beyond the capacity of sense power. Hence, the Philosopher says that "our intellect is to the most evident things, as the eye of the owl is to the light of the sun."[6] So, a created intellect needs to be strengthened by a divine light in order that it may be able to see the divine essence. By this, the first argument is answered.[7]

4. See above, ch. 50.
5. See above, ch. 51.
6. Aristotle, *Metaphysics*, Ia, 1 (993b 9).
7. See ¶1, above; successive arguments bear the same numbers as their respective paragraphs.

[9] Moreover, this sort of light raises the created intellect to the vision of God, not on the basis of a diminution of its distance from the divine substance, but by virtue of a power which it receives from God in relation to such an effect; even though it remains far away from God in its being, as the *second* argument suggested. In fact, this light does not unite the created intellect with God in the act of being but only in the act of understanding.

[10] Since, however, it is proper to God Himself to know His own substance perfectly, the aforesaid light is a likeness of God, inasmuch as it conduces to the seeing of God's substance. But no intellectual substance can be a likeness of God in this sense. For, since the divine simplicity is not equaled by any created substance, it is not possible for a created substance to have its entire perfection in the same identity; indeed, this is proper to God, as we showed in Book One,[8] for He is being, understanding and blessed, identically. So, in a created intellectual substance, the light whereby it is beatified in the divine vision is one thing, while the light whereby it is in any sense perfected within its natural species, and whereby it understands in a manner proportioned to its substance, is quite a different thing. From this the answer to the *third* argument is evident.

[11] Now, the *fourth* is answered by the fact that the vision of the divine substance exceeds every natural power, as we have shown. Hence, the light whereby the created intellect is perfected for the vision of the divine substance must be supernatural.

[12] Nor does the fact that God is called infinite hinder the vision of the divine substance, as the *fifth* argument suggested. For, He is not called infinite in the privative sense, as quantity is. This latter kind of infinity is rationally unknown, because it is like matter devoid of form, which is the principle of knowledge. Rather, He is called infinite in the negative sense, like a self-subsistent form, not limited by

8. *SCG*, I, ch. 28.

matter receiving it. Hence, a being which is infinite in this sense is most knowable in itself.

[13]   Now, the proportion of the created intellect to the understanding of God is not, in fact, based on a commensuration in an existing proportion, but on the fact that proportion means any relation of one thing to another, as of matter to form, or of cause to effect. In this sense, then, nothing prevents there being a proportion of creature to God on the basis of a relation of one who understands to the thing understood, just as on the basis of the relation of effect to cause. Hence the answer to the *sixth* objection is clear.

Chapter 55.

THAT THE CREATED INTELLECT DOES NOT COMPREHEND THE DIVINE SUBSTANCE

[1]   However, since the type of action appropriate to any agent depends on the efficacy of its active principle, and thus a thing whose heat is stronger performs the act of heating more intensely, then it must be that the manner of knowing depends on the efficacy of the principle of the act of knowing.

[2]   Now, the aforementioned light[1] is a certain principle of divine knowledge, because the created intellect is elevated by it to the seeing of the divine substance. Therefore, the mode of the divine vision must be commensurate with the power of this light. Of course, the aforementioned light, in its power, falls far short of the clarity of the divine intellect. So, it is impossible for the divine substance to be seen as perfectly by means of this kind of light, as it is seen by the divine intellect itself. Indeed, the divine intellect sees its substance as perfectly as its perfect capacity to be seen permits. In fact, the truth of the divine substance and

1. See above, ch. 53.

the clarity of the divine intellect are equal, or, better, they are but one. So, it is impossible for a created intellect, by means of the aforesaid light, to see the divine substance as perfectly as its perfect capacity to be seen permits. Now, everything that is comprehended by a knower is known by him in as perfect a way as the knowable object permits. For instance, a person who knows that a triangle has three angles equal to two right angles, but merely as a matter of opinion on the basis of probable reasoning, since it is said to be so by wise men, does not yet comprehend it; but only the man who knows this as a definite knowable object, by means of whatever is its cause. It is impossible, then, for the created intellect to comprehend the divine substance.

[3] Again, a finite power in its operation cannot be on a par with an infinite object. But the divine substance is something infinite in relation to every created intellect, since every created intellect is limited under a definite species. So, it is impossible for any created intellect's vision to be equal to the seeing of the divine substance; that is to say, to seeing it as perfectly as its capacity to be seen permits. Therefore, no created intellect may comprehend it.

[4] Besides, every agent acts perfectly to the extent that it participates in the form which is the principle of its operation. Now, the intelligible form, by which the divine substance is seen, is the divine essence itself, and, though it becomes the intelligible form of the created intellect, the created intellect does not grasp it according to its entire capacity. So, it does not see it as perfectly as its capacity to be seen permits. Therefore, it is not comprehended by the created intellect.

[5] Furthermore, no object of comprehension exceeds the limitations of the one who comprehends. Thus, if the created intellect were to comprehend the divine substance, the divine substance would not exceed the limits of the created intellect. But this is impossible. Therefore, it is not possible for a created intellect to comprehend the divine substance.

[6]   Now, this statement that the divine substance is seen by the created intellect, yet not comprehended, does not mean that part of it is seen and part not seen, because the divine substance is entirely simple. Rather, it means that it is not seen as perfectly by the created intellect as its visibility would permit. In the same way, a man who has an opinion regarding a demonstrative conclusion is said to know it but not to comprehend it, since he does not know it perfectly, that is, in a scientific way, though there is no part of it that he does not know.

Chapter 56.

THAT NO CREATED INTELLECT WHILE SEEING GOD SEES ALL THAT CAN BE SEEN IN HIM

[1]   It is evident from this that, though the created intellect may see the divine substance, it does not know all that can be known through the divine substance.

[2]   For it is only in the case of the principle being comprehended by the intellect that, once the principle is known, all its effects are of necessity known through it. Indeed, in that case, when all its effects are known from itself, a principle is known in its entire capacity. Now, other things are known through the divine essence, as the effect is known from its cause. But, since the created intellect cannot know the divine substance in such a way that it comprehends it, the intellect does not have to see all things that can be known through this substance, when it sees it.

[3]   Again, the higher the nature of an intellect, the more does it know: either in the sense of a multitude of things, or even in the sense of a greater number of reasons for the same things. But the divine intellect surpasses every created intellect. So, it knows more than any created intellect does, and it does not know anything without seeing its essence, as we showed in Book One.[1] Therefore, more things are

1. SCG, I, ch. 49.

knowable through the divine essence than any created intellect can see, through the aforesaid essence.

[4] Besides, the quantity of a power depends on the things that it can do. So, it is the same to know all the things that a power can do and to comprehend the power itself. But, since the divine power is infinite, no created intellect can comprehend it, just as its essence cannot be comprehended, as we have proved.[2] Nor can the created intellect know all that the divine power can do. But all things that the divine power can do are knowable through the divine essence, for God knows all and in no other way than through His essence. Therefore, the created intellect, seeing the divine substance, does not see all that can be seen in God's substance.

[5] Moreover, no cognoscitive power knows a thing except under the rational character of its proper object. For instance, we do not know anything by sight except according as it is colored. Now, the proper object of the intellect is *that which is*, that is, the substance of a thing, as is stated in Book III of *On the Soul*.[3] Therefore, whatever the intellect knows about any thing, it knows through knowing the substance of the thing. Consequently, in any demonstration through which the proper accidents become known to us, we take as our principle *that which is*, as is stated in *Posterior Analytics* I.[4] Now, if the intellect knows the substance of a thing through its accidents, in accordance with what is said in Book I of *On the Soul*,[5] that "the accidents contribute a good deal to the knowing of that which is," this is accidental, inasmuch as the intellect must attain to substance through the knowledge of sensible accidents. For this reason, this procedure has no place in mathematics, but only in the area of physical things. Therefore, whatever is in a thing and cannot be known through a knowledge of its substance must be unknown to the intellect.

2. See above, ch. 55.
3. Aristotle, *De anima*, III, 4 (429b 10).
4. Aristotle, *Posterior Analytics*, I, 4 (73a 37).
5. Aristotle, *De anima*, I, 1 (402b 21).

However, what a volitional agent wills cannot be known through a knowledge of his substance, for the will does not incline to its object in a purely natural way; this is why the will and nature are said to be two active principles. So, an intellect cannot know what a volitional agent wills except, perhaps, through certain effects. For instance, when we see someone acting voluntarily we may know what he wishes: either through their cause, as God knows our will acts, just as He does His other effects, because He is for us a cause of our willing; or by means of one person indicating his wish to another, as when a man expresses his feeling in speech. And so, since many things are dependent on the simple will of God, as is partly clear from earlier considerations,[6] and will later be more evident,[7] though the created intellect may see God's substance, it does not know all that God sees through His substance.

[6] Of course, someone can object against the foregoing that God's substance is something greater than all the things which He can make, or understand, or will, apart from Himself; hence, if the created intellect can see God's substance, it is much more possible for it to know all things which God understands, or wills, or makes, except for Himself.

[7] But, if it is carefully considered, the fact that something is known in itself does not have the same meaning as that it is known in its cause. For some things easily known in themselves are not, however, easily known in their causes. So, it is true that it is a greater thing to understand the divine substance than anything whatever other than that substance which might be known in itself. However, to know the divine substance and to see its effects in it is a more perfect knowledge than to know the divine substance without seeing the effects in it. And this seeing of the divine substance can be done without comprehension of it. But for all things which can be understood through it

6. SCG, I, ch. 81.
7. SCG, III, ch. 64ff.

to be known is something which cannot happen without comprehending this substance, as is evident from what we have said.[8]

Chapter 57.

THAT EVERY INTELLECT, WHATEVER ITS LEVEL, CAN BE A PARTICIPANT IN THE DIVINE VISION

[1] Since the created intellect is exalted to the vision of the divine substance by a certain supernatural light, as is evident from what has been said,[1] there is no created intellect so low in its nature that it cannot be elevated to this vision.

[2] It has been shown,[2] in fact, that this light cannot be connatural with any creature, but that it surpasses every created nature in its power. But what is done by supernatural power is not hindered by a diversity of nature, since divine power is infinite. And so, in the case of the healing of an afflicted person, accomplished miraculously, it makes no difference whether the person is much or little afflicted. Therefore, the varying level of the intellectual nature does not hinder the lowest member of such a nature from being able to be brought to this vision by the aforementioned light.

[3] Again, the gap between the intellect, at its highest natural level, and God is infinite in perfection and goodness. But the distance from the highest to the lowest intellect is finite, for there cannot be an infinite distance between one finite being and another. So, the distance which lies between the lowest created intellect and the highest one is like nothing in comparison to the gap which lies

8. For a qualification of this point, see SCG, III, 59, ¶6.
1. See above, ch. 53.
2. *Ibid.*

between the highest created intellect and God. Now, that which is practically nothing cannot make a noticeable difference; thus, the distance between the center of the earth and our level of vision is like nothing in comparison with the distance that lies between our eye level and the eighth sphere, in regard to which sphere the whole earth takes the place of a point; this is why no noticeable variation results from the fact that astronomers in their demonstrations use our eye level of sight as the center of the earth.[3] Therefore, it makes no difference what level of intellect it is that is elevated to the vision of God by the aforementioned light: it may be the highest, the lowest, or one in the middle.

[4]   Besides, it was proved above[4] that every intellect naturally desires the vision of the divine substance, but natural desire cannot be incapable of fulfillment. Therefore, any created intellect whatever can attain to the vision of the divine substance, and the inferiority of its nature is no impediment.

[5]   Hence it is that the Lord promises men the glory of the angels: "They shall be," He says, speaking of men, "like the angels of God in heaven" (Matt. 22:30). And also it is said that there is "the same measure for man and for angel" (Apoc. 21:17). For this reason, too, almost everywhere in Sacred Scripture angels are described in the shape of men: either wholly, as is evident of the angels who appeared to Abraham in the likeness of men (Gen. 18:2); or partially, as is the case of the animals of whom it is said that "they had the hands of a man under their wings" (Ezech. 1:8).

[6]   By this conclusion we refute the error of those who have said that the human soul, no matter how much it be elevated, cannot attain equality with the higher intellects.

3. This would seem to indicate that St. Thomas had some technical knowledge of the use of the astrolabe. See A. C. Crombie, *Augustine to Galileo* (Cambridge: 1953), p. 66, for a diagram illustrating the point.
4. See above, ch. 50.

Chapter 58.

THAT ONE BEING IS ABLE TO SEE GOD MORE PERFECTLY THAN ANOTHER

[1] Since the mode of operation results from the form which is the principle of operation, and since the principle of the vision in which the created intellect sees the divine substance is the aforementioned light, as is clear from what we have said,[1] the mode of the divine vision must be in accord with the mode of this light. Now, it is possible for there to be different degrees of participation in this light, and so one intellect may be more perfectly illuminated than another. Therefore, it is possible that one of those who see God may see Him more perfectly than another, even though both see His substance.

[2] Again, whenever there is a highest member which surpasses others in a genus, we also find that there are degrees of more and less, depending on the greater proximity to, or distance from, this highest member. For instance, certain things are more or less hot depending on whether they are more or less near to fire, which is the highest type of hot thing. But God sees His own substance most perfectly, being the only One Who comprehends it, as we showed above.[2] And so, of those who see Him, one may see His substance more or less than another, depending on whether one is more or less near to Him.

[3] Besides, the light of glory elevates to the divine vision due to the fact that it is a certain likeness of the divine intellect, as we have already stated.[3] Now, it is possible for a thing to become more or less like God. Therefore, it is pos-

1. See above, ch. 53.
2. See above, ch. 55.
3. See above, ch. 53.

sible for one to see the divine substance more or less perfectly.

[4]   Furthermore, because the end is related in a proportional way to the things which are directed to the end, these things must participate in the end differently, depending on the different ways in which they are disposed toward the end. But the vision of the divine substance is the ultimate end of every intellectual substance, as is clear from what we have said.⁴ Now, not all intellectual substances are disposed with equal perfection to the end; some, in fact, are more virtuous and others less, and virtue is the road to felicity. So, there must be diversity within the divine vision: some seeing the divine substance more perfectly; others, less perfectly.

[5]   Thus it is that, in order to indicate the variation in this felicity, the Lord says: "In My Father's house there are many mansions" (John 14:2).

[6]   On this basis, then, the error of those who say that all rewards are equal is refuted.

[7]   Moreover, just as the different degrees of glory among the blessed are evident from the mode of this vision, so from the side of the object that is seen the glory appears to be the same, for the felicity of each person is due to his seeing God's substance, as we proved. Therefore, it is the same being that makes all blessed; yet they do not all grasp happiness therefrom in equal degree.

[8]   Hence, there is no contradiction between the foregoing and what our Lord teaches (Matt. 20:10), that to all who labor in the vineyard, though they may not do equal work, there is paid nevertheless the same reward, namely, a penny, because it is the same reward that is given to all, to be seen and enjoyed, namely, God.

[9]   On this point we must also take into consideration the fact that the order of corporeal movements is some-

4. See above, ch. 50.

what contrary to that of spiritual movements. For there is numerically the same first subject for all corporeal motions, but the ends are different. While there are, on the other hand, different first subjects for spiritual movements, that is to say, for acts of intellectual apprehension and of willing, their end is, however, numerically the same.

Chapter 59.

HOW THOSE WHO SEE THE DIVINE SUBSTANCE
MAY SEE ALL THINGS

[1] Since the vision of the divine substance is the ultimate end of every intellectual substance, as is evident from what we have said,[1] and since the natural appetite of everything comes to rest when the thing reaches its ultimate end, the natural appetite of an intellectual substance must come to rest completely when it sees the divine substance. Now, the natural appetite of the intellect is to know the genera and species and powers of all things, and the whole order of the universe; human investigation of each of the aforementioned items indicates this. Therefore, each one who sees the dvine substance knows all the things mentioned above.

[2] Again, the intellect and the senses differ on this point, as is clear from Book III of *On the Soul*:[2] the power to sense is destroyed, or weakened, by the more striking sense objects, so that later it is unable to perceive weaker objects; but the intellect, not being corrupted or hindered by its object but only perfected, after understanding a greater object of the intellect, is not less able to understand other intelligibles but more able. Now, the highest object in the genus of intelligible objects is the divine substance. So, the intellect which is elevated by divine light in order to see God's substance is much more perfected by this same light,

1. See above, ch. 50.
2. Aristotle, *De anima*, III, 4 (429a 14).

so that it may understand all other objects which exist in the nature of things.

[3]   Besides, intelligible being is not of lesser scope than natural being, but perhaps it is more extensive; indeed, intellect is from its origin capable of understanding all things existing in reality, and it also understands things that have no natural being, such as negations and privations. So, whatever things are needed for the perfection of natural being are also needed for the perfection of intelligible being, and even more. But the perfection of intelligible being is present when the intellect reaches its ultimate end, just as the perfection of natural being consists in the very establishment of things in actual being. Therefore, God shows the intellect that is seeing Him all the things which He has produced for the perfection of the universe.

[4]   Moreover, although one of the intellects seeing God may see Him more perfectly than another, as we have shown,[3] each one sees Him so perfectly that its whole natural capacity is fulfilled. Or, rather, this vision exceeds all natural capacity, as we have shown.[4] So, each one seeing the divine substance knows in this divine substance all the things to which its natural capacity extends. But the natural capacity of every intellect extends to the knowing of all genera and species and orders of things. Therefore, each one who sees God will know these things in the divine substance.

[5]   Hence it is that the Lord replies to Moses, when he asks for the vision of the divine substance: "I will show thee all good" (Exod. 33:19). And Gregory says: "What do they not know, who know Him Who knows all things?"[5]

[6]   Moreover, if the foregoing statements are carefully considered, it becomes clear that, in a way, those who see

3. See above, ch. 58.
4. See above, ch. 52.
5. St. Gregory, *Dialogus* II, 33 (*PL*, 77, col. 194).

the divine substance do see all things; whereas, in another way, they do not. Indeed, if the word *all* means whatever things pertain to the perfection of the universe, it is obvious from what has been said that those who see the divine substance do see all things, as the arguments that have just been advanced show. For, since the intellect is in some way all things,[6] whatever things belong to the perfection of nature belong also in their entirety to the perfection of intelligible being. For this reason, according to Augustine's *Literal Commentary on Genesis*, whatever things have been made by the Word of God to subsist in their proper nature have also come to be in the angelic understanding, so that they might be understood by the angels.[7] Now, within the perfection of natural being belong the nature of species and their properties and powers, for the inclination of nature is drawn to the natures of species, since individuals are for the sake of the species. So, it is pertinent to the perfection of intellectual substance to know the natures of all species and their powers and proper accidents. Therefore, this will be obtained in the final beatitude through the vision of the divine essence. Moreover, through the cognition of natural species the individuals existing under these species are known by the intellect that sees God, as can be made evident from what has been said above on the knowledge appropriate to God and the angels.[8]

[7]   However, if the term *all* means all the things that God knows in seeing His own essence, then no created intellect sees all things in God's substance, as we have showed above.[9]

[8]   But this can be considered under several points. First, in regard to those things which God can make but has not made, nor will ever make. Indeed, all things of this kind cannot be known unless His power is comprehended, and

6. See Aristotle, *De anima*, III, 5 (430a 14).
7. St. Augustine, *De Genesi ad litteram*, II, 8 (*PL*, 34, col. 269).
8. *SCG*, I, ch. 69; II, ch. 96ff.
9. See above, ch. 56.

this is not possible for any intellectual creature, as we showed above.[10] Hence, the statement in Job 11 [7ff.]: "Peradventure thou wilt understand the steps of God, and wilt find out the Almighty perfectly? He is higher than heaven, and what wilt thou do? He is deeper than hell, and how wilt thou know? The measure of Him is longer than the earth, and broader than the sea." Indeed, these things are not said as though God were great in quantitative dimensions, but because His power is not limited to all things which are seen to be great, for, on the contrary, He can make even greater things.

[9] Secondly, let us consider it in regard to the reasons for the things that have been made: the intellect cannot know all of these unless it comprehend the divine goodness. For, the reason for everything that has been made is derived from the end which its maker intended. But the end of all things made by God is divine goodness. Therefore, the reason for the things that have been made is so that the divine goodness might be diffused among things. And so, one would know all the reasons for things created if he knew all the goods which could come about in created things in accord with the order of divine wisdom. This would be to comprehend divine goodness and wisdom, something no created intellect can do. Hence it is said: "I understand that man can find no reason of all those works of God" (Eccle. 8:17).

[10] Thirdly, we may consider the point in regard to those things which depend on the will of God alone: for instance, predestination, election, justification, and other similar things which pertain to the sanctification of the creature. On this matter, it is said: "No man knoweth the things of a man, but the spirit of man that is in him. So the things also that are of God, no man knoweth, but the Spirit of God" (I Cor. 2:11; Douay modified).

10. See above, ch. 55.

Chapter 60.

THAT THOSE WHO SEE GOD SEE ALL THINGS IN HIM AT ONCE

[1]   Now that we have shown[1] that the created intellect, seeing the divine substance, understands all the species of things in God's very substance, and that whatever things are seen by one species must be seen at once and by one vision, since a vision corresponds to the principle of the vision, it necessarily follows that the intellect which sees the divine substance contemplates all things at once and not in succession.

[2]   Again, the highest and perfect felicity of intellectual nature consists in the vision of God, as we showed above.[2] But felicity is not a matter of habit but of act, since it is the ultimate perfection and the ultimate end. So, of the things that are seen through the vision of the divine substance, whereby we are made blessed, all are seen actually. Therefore, one is not first and then another later.

[3]   Besides, when each thing reaches its ultimate end it rests, for all motion is in order to attain an end. Now, the ultimate end of the intellect is the vision of the divine substance, as we showed above. So, the intellect seeing the divine substance is not moved from one intelligible object to another. Therefore, it considers actually at once all the things that it knows through this vision.

[4]   Moreover, the intellect knows all the species of things in the divine substance, as is clear from what has been said.[3] Now in some genera there are infinite species, for example, of numbers, figures, and proportions. So, the in-

1. See above, ch. 59.
2. See above, ch. 50.
3. See above, ch. 59.

tellect sees an infinity of things in the divine substance. But it could not see all of these unless it saw them at once, for it is impossible to pass through an infinity of things. Therefore, all that the intellect sees in the divine substance must be seen at once.

[5] Hence, what Augustine says, in *Book* xv of *The Trinity:* "Our thoughts will not then be fleeting, going to and fro from some things to others, but we shall see all our knowledge in one single glance."[4]

Chapter 61.

THAT THROUGH THE VISION OF GOD ONE BECOMES A PARTAKER OF ETERNAL LIFE

[1] From this consideration it is apparent that the created intellect becomes a partaker in the eternal life through this vision.

[2] For, eternity differs from time in this way: time has its being in a sort of succession, whereas the being of eternity is entirely simultaneous.[1] But we have shown that there is no succession in the aforesaid vision; instead, all things that are seen through it are seen at once, and in one view. So, this vision is perfected in a sort of participation in eternity. Moreover, this vision is a kind of life, for the action of the intellect is a kind of life.[2] Therefore, the created intellect becomes a partaker in eternal life through this vision.

[3] Again, acts are specified by their objects. But the object of the aforementioned vision is the divine substance in itself, and not in a created likeness of it, as we showed

---

4. St. Augustine, *De Trinitate,* XV, 16 (*PL,* 42, col. 1079).
1. See Boethius, *De consolatione philosophiae,* V, prose 6 (*PL,* 63, col. 858).
2. See Aristotle, *Nicomachean Ethics,* IX, 9 (1170a 18).

above.[3] Now, the being of the divine substance is in eternity, or, rather, is eternity itself. Therefore, this vision also consists in a participation in eternity.

[4] Besides, if a given action is done in time, this will be either because the principle of the action is in time—in this sense the actions of temporal things are temporal; or because of the terminus of the operation, as in the case of spiritual substances which are above time but perform their actions on things subject to time. Now, the aforementioned vision is not in time by virtue of what is seen, for this is the eternal substance; nor by virtue of that whereby the seeing is accomplished, for this also is the eternal substance; nor even by virtue of the agent who sees, that is the intellect, whose being does not come under time, since it is incorruptible, as we proved above.[4] Therefore, this vision consists in a participation in eternity, as completely transcending time.

[5] Furthermore, the intellective soul is created "on the border line between eternity and time," as is stated in the *Book on Causes,*[5] and as can be shown from our earlier statements.[6] In fact, it is the lowest in the order of intellects, yet its substance is raised above corporeal matter, not depending on it. But its action, as joined to lower things which exist in time, is temporal. Therefore, its action, as joined to higher things which exist above time, participates in eternity. Especially so is the vision by which it sees the divine substance. And so, by this kind of vision it comes into the participation of eternity; and for the same reason, so does any other created intellect that sees God.

[6] Hence, the Lord says: "This is eternal life, that they may know Thee, the only true God" (John 17:3).

3. See above, ch. 50.
4. *SCG,* II, ch. 55 and 79.
5. *Liber de causis,* II (ed. Bardenhewer [Freiburg: 1882], p. 162); on this anonymous work, see E. Gilson, *History of Christian Philosophy,* pp. 235–237.
6. *SCG,* II, ch. 68.

Chapter 62.

THAT THOSE WHO SEE GOD WILL SEE HIM PERPETUALLY

[1]   Now, it is clear from this that those who obtain ultimate felicity as a result of the divine vision never depart from it.

[2]   For, "everything which at one time exists, and at another does not, is measured by time," as is clear in *Physics* iv.[1] But the aforementioned vision, which makes intellectual creatures happy, is not in time but in eternity.[2] So, it is impossible for a person to lose it, once he has become a partaker in it.

[3]   Again, the intellectual creature does not reach his ultimate end until his natural desire comes to rest. But, just as one naturally desires felicity, so also does he naturally desire everlasting felicity; for, since he is everlasting in his substance, he desires to possess forever that object which is desired for its own sake and not because of something else. Therefore, his felicity would not be the ultimate end unless it endured perpetually.

[4]   Besides, everything that is possessed with love may cause sorrow, provided it be recognized that such a thing may be lost. But the aforesaid vision which makes men happy is especially loved by its possessors, since it is the most lovable and desirable of objects. Therefore, it would not be possible for them to avoid sorrow if they knew that they would lose it at some time. Now, if it were not perpetual, they would know this, for we have shown already,[3] that, while seeing the divine substance, they also know

1. Aristotle, *Physics*, IV, 12 (221b 28).
2. See above, ch. 61.
3. See above, ch. 59.

other things that are naturally so. Hence, they certainly know what kind of vision it is, whether perpetual or to stop at some future time. So, this vision would not be theirs without sorrow. And thus it will not be true felicity which should be made free from all evil, as we showed above.[4]

[5] Moreover, that which is naturally moved toward something, as to the end of its motion, may not be removed from it without violence, as in the case of a weight when it is thrown upward. But from what we have said,[5] it is obvious that every intellectual substance tends by natural desire toward that vision. So, it cannot fail to continue that vision, unless because of violence. But nothing is taken away from a thing by violence unless the power removing it is greater than the power which causes it. Now, the cause of the divine vision is God, as we proved above.[6] Therefore, since no power surpasses the divine power, it is impossible for this vision to be taken away by violence. Hence, it will endure forever.

[6] Furthermore, if a person ceases to see what he formerly saw, this cessation will be either because the power of sight fails him, as when one dies or goes blind, or because he is impeded in some other way, or it will be because he does not wish to see any longer, as when a man turns away his glance from a thing that he formerly saw, or because the object is taken away. And this is true in general whether we are talking about sensory or intellectual vision. Now, in regard to the intellectual substance that sees God there cannot be a failure of the ability to see God: either because it might cease to exist, for it exists in perpetuity, as we showed above,[7] or because of a failure of the light whereby it sees God, since the light is received incorruptibly both in regard to the condition of the receiver and of the giver. Nor can it lack the will to enjoy such a vision, because

4. See above, ch. 48.
5. See above, ch. 50.
6. See above, ch. 53.
7. *SCG*, II, ch. 55.

it perceives that its ultimate felicity lies in this vision, just as it cannot fail to will to be happy. Nor, indeed, may it cease to see because of a removal of the object, for the object, which is God, is always existing in the same way; nor is He far removed from us, unless by virtue of our removal from Him. So, it is impossible for the vision of God, which makes men happy, ever to fail.

[7]   Again, it is impossible for a person to will to abandon a good which he is enjoying, unless because of some evil which he perceives in the enjoyment of that good; even if it be simply that it is thought to stand in the way of a greater good. For, just as the appetite desires nothing except under the rational character of a good, so does it shun nothing except under the character of an evil. But there can be no evil in the enjoyment of this vision, because it is the best to which the intellectual creature can attain. Nor, in fact, can it be that he who is enjoying this vision might think that there is some evil in it, or that there is something better than it. For the vision of the highest Truth excludes all falsity. Therefore, it is impossible for the intellectual substance that sees God ever to will to be without that vision.

[8]   Besides, dislike of an object which one formerly enjoyed with delight occurs because this thing produces some kind of real change, destroying or weakening one's power. And this is why the sense powers, subject to fatigue in their actions because of the changing of the bodily organs by sense objects, are corrupted, even by the best of such objects. Indeed, after a period of enjoyment, they grow to dislike what they formerly perceived with delight. And for this reason we even suffer boredom in the use of our intellect, after a long or strenuous meditation, because our powers that make use of the bodily organs become tired, and intellectual thinking cannot be accomplished without these. But the divine substance does not corrupt; rather, it greatly perfects the intellect. Nor does any act exercised through bodily organs accompany this vision. Therefore, it is impossible for anyone who at one time took joy in the delight of this vision to grow weary of it.

[9] Furthermore, nothing that is contemplated with wonder can be tiresome, since as long as the thing remains in wonder it continues to stimulate desire. But the divine substance is always viewed with wonder by any created intellect, since no created intellect comprehends it. So, it is impossible for an intellectual substance to become tired of this vision. And thus, it cannot, of its own will, desist from this vision.

[10] Moreover, if any two things were formerly united and later come to be separated, this must be due to a change in one of them. For, just as a relation does not come into being for the first time without a change in one of the things related, so also it does not cease to be without a new change in one of them. Now, the created intellect sees God by virtue of being united to Him in some way, as is clear from what we have said.[8] So, if this vision were to cease, bringing this union to an end, it would have to be done by a change in the divine substance, or in the intellect of the one who sees it. Both of these changes are impossible: for the divine substance is immutable, as we showed in Book One,[9] and, also, the intellectual substance is raised above all change when it sees God's substance. Therefore, it is impossible for anyone to depart from the felicity in which he sees God's substance.

[11] Besides, the nearer a thing is to God, Who is entirely immutable, the less mutable is it and the more lasting. Consequently, certain bodies, because "they are far removed from God," as is stated in *On Generation* II,[10] cannot endure forever. But no creature can come closer to God than the one who sees His substance. So, the intellectual creature that sees God's substance attains the highest immutability. Therefore, it is not possible for it ever to lapse from this vision.

8. See above, ch. 51.
9. *SCG*, I, ch. 13.
10. Aristotle, *De generatione et corruptione*, II, 10 (336b 30).

[12]   Hence it is said in the Psalm (83:5): "Blessed are they that dwell in Thy house, O Lord: they shall praise Thee for ever and ever." And in another text: "He shall not be moved for ever that dwelleth in Jerusalem" (Ps. 124:1). And again: "Thy eyes shall see Jerusalem, a rich habitation, a tabernacle that cannot be removed; neither shall the nails thereof be taken away for ever; neither shall any of the cords thereof be broken, because only there our Lord is magnificent" (Isa. 33:20-21). And again: "He that shall overcome, I will make him a pillar in the temple of My God: and he shall go out no more" (Apoc. 3:12).

[13]   By these considerations, then, the error of the Platonists is refuted, for they said that separated souls, after having attained ultimate felicity, would begin to desire to return to their bodies, and having brought to an end the felicity of that life they would again become enmeshed in the troubles of this life; and also the error of Origen, who said that souls and angels, after beatitude, could again return to unhappiness.[11]

Chapter 63.

HOW MAN'S EVERY DESIRE IS FULFILLED IN THAT ULTIMATE FELICITY

[1]   From the foregoing it is quite apparent that, in the felicity that comes from the divine vision,[1] every human desire is fulfilled, according to the text of the Psalm (102:5): "Who satisfieth thy desire with good things." And every human effort attains its completion in it. This, in fact, becomes clear to anyone who thinks over particular instances.

[2]   For there is in man, in so far as he is intellectual, one type of desire, concerned with the knowledge of truth; indeed, men seek to fulfill this desire by the effort of the

11. Origen, Peri Archon, II, 3 (PG, 11, col. 242-243).
1. SCG, IV, ch. 54.

contemplative life. And this will clearly be fulfilled in that vision, when, through the vision of the First Truth, all that the intellect naturally desires to know becomes known to it, as is evident from what was said above.[2]

[3] There is also a certain desire in man, based on his possession of reason, whereby he is enabled to manage lower things; this, men seek to fulfill by the work of the active and civic life. Indeed, this desire is chiefly for this end, that the entire life of man may be arranged in accord with reason, for this is *to live in accord with virtue*. For the end of the activity of every virtuous man is the good appropriate to his virtue, just as, for the brave man, it is to act bravely. Now, this desire will then be completely fulfilled, since reason will be at its peak strength, having been enlightened by the divine light, so that it cannot swerve away from what is right.

[4] Going along, then, with the civic life are certain goods which man needs for civic activities. For instance, there is a *high position of honor*, which makes men proud and ambitious, if they desire it inordinately. But men are raised through this vision to the highest peak of honor, because they are in a sense united with God, as we pointed out above.[3] For this reason, just as God Himself is the "King of ages" (I Tim. 1:17), so are the blessed united with Him called *kings*: "They shall reign with Christ" (Apoc. 20:6).

[5] Another object of desire associated with civic life is *popular renown*; by an inordinate desire for this men are deemed lovers of vainglory. Now, the blessed are made men of renown by this vision, not according to the opinion of men, who can deceive and be deceived, but in accord with the truest knowledge, both of God and of all the blessed. Therefore, this blessedness is frequently termed *glory* in Sacred Scripture; for instance, it is said in the Psalm (149:5): "The saints shall rejoice in glory."

2. See above, ch. 59.
3. See above, ch. 51.

[6]   There is, indeed, another object of desire in civic life; namely, *wealth*. By the inordinate desire and love of this, men become illiberal and unjust. But in this beatitude there is a plenitude of all goods, inasmuch as the blessed come to enjoy Him Who contains the perfection of all good things. For this reason it is said in Wisdom (7:11): "All good things came to me together with her." Hence it is also said in the Psalm (111:3): "Glory and wealth shall be in His house."

[7]   There is even a third desire of man, which is common to him and the other animals, *to enjoy pleasures*. Men chiefly seek after this in the voluptuous life, and they become intemperate and incontinent through immoderation in regard to it. However, the most perfect delight is found in this felicity: as much more perfect than the delight of the sense, which even brute animals can enjoy, as the intellect is superior to sense power; and also as that good in which we shall take delight is greater than any sensible good, and more intimate, and more continually delightful;[4] and also as that delight is freer from all admixture of sorrow, or concern about trouble. Of this it is said in the Psalm (35:9): "They shall be inebriated with the plenty of Thy house, and Thou shalt make them drink of the torrent of Thy pleasure."

[8]   There is, moreover, a natural desire common to all things by which they desire *their own preservation*, to the extent that this is possible: men are made fearful and excessively chary of work that is hard for them by immoderation in this desire. But this desire will then be completely satisfied when the blessed attain perfect sempiternity and are safe from all harm; according to the text of Isaias (49:10) and Apocalypse (21 [see 7:16]): "They shall no more hunger or thirst, neither shall the sun fall on them, nor any heat."

[9]   And so, it is evident that through the divine vision intellectual substances obtain true felicity, in which their

4. Compare the strange parallel in Algazel, *Metaphysics*, II, 5 (ed. Muckle, p. 186).

desires are completely brought to rest and in which is the full sufficiency of all the goods which, according to Aristotle,[5] are required for happiness. Hence, Boethius also says that "happiness is a state of life made perfect by the accumulation of all goods."[6]

[10] Now, there is nothing in this life so like this ultimate and perfect felicity as the life of those who contemplate truth, to the extent that it is possible in this life. And so, the philosophers who were not able to get full knowledge of this ultimate happiness identified man's ultimate happiness with the contemplation which is possible in this life.[7] On this account, too, of all other lives the contemplative is more approved in divine Scripture, when our Lord says: "Mary hath chosen the better part," namely, the contemplation of truth, "which shall not be taken from her" (Luke 10:42). In fact, the contemplation of truth begins in this life, but reaches its climax in the future; whereas the active and civic life does not go beyond the limits of this life.

Chapter 64.

THAT GOD GOVERNS THINGS BY HIS PROVIDENCE

[1] From the points that have been set forth we have adequately established that God is the end of all things. The next possible conclusion from this is that He governs, or rules, the whole of things by His providence.[1]

[2] Whenever certain things are ordered to a definite end they all come under the control of the one to whom the

5. Aristotle, *Nicomachean Ethics*, X, 7 (1177a 24).
6. Boethius, *De consolatione philosophiae*, III, prose 2 (PL, 63, col. 724).
7. Aristotle, *Nicomachean Ethics*, X, 7 (1177a 18).
1. This is the start of the second major topic in Book Three; the consideration of "Providence in general" runs to ch. 110.

end primarily belongs. This is evident in an army: all divisions of an army and their functions are ordered to the commander's good as an ultimate end, and this is victory. And for this reason it is the function of the commander to govern the whole army. Likewise, an art which is concerned with the end commands and makes the laws for an art concerned with means to the end. Thus, the art of civil government commands that of the military; the military commands the equestrian; and the art of navigation commands that of shipbuilding. So, since all things are ordered to divine goodness as an end, as we showed,[2] it follows that God, to Whom this goodness primarily belongs, as something substantially possessed and known and loved, must be the governor of all things.

[3]   Again, whoever makes a thing for the sake of an end may use the thing for that end. Now, we showed above that all things possessing being in any way whatever are God's products,[3] and also that God makes all things for an end which is Himself.[4] Therefore, He uses all things by directing them to their end. Now, this is to govern. So, God is the governor of all things through His providence.

[4]   Besides, we have shown[5] that God is the first unmoved mover. The first mover does not move fewer things, but more, than the secondary movers, for the latter do not move other things without the first. Now, all things that are moved are so moved because of the end, as we showed above.[6] So, God moves all things to their ends, and He does so through His understanding, for we have shown above[7] that He does not act through a necessity of His nature, but through understanding and will. Now, to rule or govern by providence is simply *to move things toward an*

2. See above, ch. 7.
3. *SCG*, II, ch. 15.
4. *SCG*, I, ch. 75.
5. *SCG*, I, ch. 13.
6. See above, ch. 2.
7. *SCG*, I, ch. 81; II, ch. 23ff.

end through understanding. Therefore, God by His providence governs and rules all things that are moved toward their end, whether they be moved corporeally, or spiritually as one who desires is moved by an object of desire.

[5] Moreover, that natural bodies are moved and made to operate for an end, even though they do not know their end, was proved[8] by the fact that what happens to them is always, or often, for the best; and, if their workings resulted from art, they would not be done differently. But it is impossible for things that do not know their end to work for that end, and to reach that end in an orderly way, unless they are moved by someone possessing knowledge of the end, as in the case of the arrow directed to the target by the archer. So, the whole working of nature must be ordered by some sort of knowledge. And this, in fact, must lead back to God, either mediately or immediately, since every lower art and type of knowledge must get its principles from a higher one, as we also see in the speculative and operative sciences. Therefore, God governs the world by His providence.

[6] Furthermore, things that are different in their natures do not come together into one order unless they are gathered into a unit by one ordering agent. But in the whole of reality things are distinct and possessed of contrary natures; yet all come together in one order, and while some things make use of the actions of others, some are also helped or commanded by others. Therefore, there must be one orderer and governor of the whole of things.

[7] Moreover, it is not possible to give an explanation, based on natural necessity, for the apparent motions of celestial bodies, since some of them have more motions than others, and altogether incompatible ones. So, there must be an ordering of their motions by some providence, and, consequently, of the motions and workings of all lower things that are controlled by their motions.

8. See above, ch. 3.

[8]   Besides, the nearer a thing is to its cause, the more does it participate in its influence. Hence, if some perfection is more perfectly participated by a group of things the more they approach a certain object, then this is an indication that this object is the cause of the perfection which is participated in various degrees. For instance, if certain things become hotter as they come nearer to fire, this is an indication that fire is the cause of heat. Now, things are found to be more perfectly ordered the nearer they are to God. For, in the lower types of bodies, which are very far away from God in the dissimilarity of their natures, there is sometimes found to be a falling away from the regular course of nature, as in the case of monstrosities and other chance events; but this never happens in the case of the celestial bodies, though they are somewhat mutable, and it does not occur among separate intellectual substances. Therefore, it is plain that God is the cause of the whole order of things. So, He is the governor of the whole universe of reality through His providence.

[9]   Furthermore, as we proved above,[9] God brings all things into being, not from the necessity of His nature, but by understanding and will. Now, there can be no other ultimate end for His understanding and will than His goodness, that is, to communicate it to things, as is clear from what has been established.[10] But things participate in the divine goodness to the extent that they are good, by way of likeness. Now, that which is the greatest good in caused things is the good of the order of the universe; for it is most perfect, as the Philosopher says.[11] With this, divine Scripture is also in agreement, for it is said in Genesis (1:31): "God saw all the things He had made, and they were very good," while He simply said of the individual works, that "they were good." So, the good of the order of things caused by God is what is chiefly willed and caused by God. Now, to govern things is nothing but to impose order on them.

9. SCG, I, ch. 81; II, ch. 23ff.
10. SCG, I, ch. 75ff.
11. Aristotle, Metaphysics, XI, 10 (1075a 12).

Therefore, God Himself governs all things by His understanding and will.

[10] Moreover, any agent intending an end is more concerned about what is nearer to the ultimate end, because this nearer thing is also an end for other things. Now, the ultimate end of the divine will is His goodness, and the nearest thing to this latter, among created things, is the good of the order of the whole universe, since every particular good of this or that thing is ordered to it as to an end (just as the less perfect is ordered to what is more perfect); and so, each part is found to be for the sake of its whole. Thus, among created things, what God cares for most is the order of the universe. Therefore, He is its governor.

[11] Again, every created thing attains its ultimate perfection through its proper operation, for the ultimate end and the perfection of a thing must be either its operation or the term or product of its operation. Of course, the form, by virtue of which the thing exists, is its first perfection, as is evident from Book II of *On the Soul*.[12] But the order of caused things, according to the distinction of their natures and levels, proceeds from divine Wisdom, as we showed in Book Two.[13] So also does the order of their operations, whereby caused things draw nearer to their ultimate end. Now, to order the actions of certain things toward their end is to govern them. Therefore, God provides governance and regulation for things by the providence of His wisdom.

[12] Hence it is that Sacred Scripture proclaims God as Lord and King, according to the text of the Psalm (99:2): "The Lord, He is God"; and again: "God is the King of all the earth" (Ps. 46:8); for it is the function of the king and lord to rule and govern those subject to their command. And so, Sacred Scripture attributes the course of things to divine decree: "Who commandeth the sun, and it riseth

12. Aristotle, *De anima*, II, 1 (412a 28).
13. *SCG*, II, ch. 45.

not, and shutteth up the stars, as it were under a seal" (Job 9:7); and also in the Psalm (148:6): "He hath made a decree and it shall not pass away."

[13] Now, by this conclusion the error of the ancient philosophers of nature[14] is refuted, for they said that all things come about as a result of material necessity, the consequence of which would be that all things happen by chance and not from the order of providence.

Chapter 65.

THAT GOD PRESERVES THINGS IN BEING

[1] Now, from the fact that God rules things by His providence it follows that He preserves them in being.

[2] Indeed, everything whereby things attain their end pertains to the governance of these things. For things are said to be ruled or governed by virtue of their being ordered to their end. Now, things are ordered to the ultimate end which God intends, that is, divine goodness, not only by the fact that they perform their operations, but also by the fact that they exist, since, to the extent that they exist, they bear the likeness of divine goodness which is the end for things, as we showed above.[1] Therefore, it pertains to divine providence that things are preserved in being.

[3] Again, the same principle must be the cause of a thing and of its preservation, for the preservation of a thing is nothing but the continuation of its being. Now, we showed above[2] that God, through His understanding and will, is the cause of being for all things. Therefore, He preserves all things in being through His intellect and will.

14. See Aristotle, *Physics*, II, 8 (198b 12).
1. See above, ch. 19.
2. *SCG*, II, ch. 23ff.

[4] Besides, no particular univocal agent can be the un-qualified cause of its species; for instance, this individual man cannot be the cause of the human species, for he would then be the cause of every man, and, consequently, of himself—which is impossible. But this individual man is the cause, properly speaking, of that individual man. Now, this man exists because human nature is present in this matter, which is the principle of individuation. So, this man is not the cause of a man, except in the sense that he is the cause of a human form coming to be in this matter. This is to be the principle of the generation of an individual man. So, it is apparent that neither this man, nor any other univocal agent in nature, is the cause of anything except the generation of this or that individual thing. Now, there must be some proper agent cause of the human species itself; its composition shows this, and also the ordering of its parts, which is uniform in all cases unless it be accidentally im-peded. And the same reasoning applies to all the other species of natural things.

Now, this cause is God, either mediately or immediately. For we have shown[3] that He is the first cause of all things. So, He must stand in regard to the species of things as the individual generating agent in nature does to generation, of which he is the direct cause. But generation ceases as soon as the operation of the generative agent ceases. Therefore, all the species of things would also cease as soon as the divine operation ceased. So, He preserves things in being through His operation.

[5] Moreover, though motion may occur for any existing thing, motion is apart from the being of the thing. Now, nothing corporeal, unless it be moved, is the cause of any-thing, for no body acts unless by motion, as Aristotle proves.[4] Therefore, no body is the cause of the being of anything, in so far as it is being, but it is the cause of its being moved toward being, that is, of the thing's becom-ing. Now, the being of any thing is participated being,

3. *SCG*, I, ch. 13; II, ch. 15.
4. Aristotle, *Physics*, VII, 2 (243a 3).

since no thing is its own act of being, except God, as we proved above.[5] And thus, God Himself, Who is His own act of being, must be primarily and essentially the cause of every being. So, divine operation is related to the being of things as the motion of a corporeal mover is to the becoming and passive movement of the things that are made or moved. Now, it is impossible for the becoming and passive movement of a thing to continue if the motion of the mover cease. Therefore, it is impossible for the being of a thing to continue except through divine operation.

[6] Furthermore, just as art work presupposes a work of nature, so does a work of nature presuppose the work of God the creator. In fact, the material for art products comes from nature, while that of natural products comes through creation by God. Moreover, art objects are preserved in being by the power of natural things; a home, for instance, by the solidity of its stones. Therefore, all natural things are preserved in being by nothing other than the power of God.

[7] Again, the impression of an agent does not continue in the product, if the agent's action ceases, unless the impression be converted into the nature of the product. Indeed, the forms of things generated, and their properties, remain in them after generation until the end, since they become natural to them. And likewise, habits are difficult to change because they are turned into a nature. But dispositions and passions, whether of the body or soul, endure for a little while after the action of the agent, but not forever, since they are present in a state transitional to nature. Now, whatever belongs to the nature of a higher type of being does not last at all after the action of the agent; light, for instance, does not continue in a diaphanous body when the source of light has gone away. Now, to be is not the nature or essence of any created thing, but only of God, as we showed in Book One.[6] Therefore, no thing can remain in being if divine operation cease.

5. SCG, I, ch. 22; II, ch. 15.
6. SCG, I, ch. 22.

[8]   Furthermore, there are two positions regarding the origin of things: one, from faith, holding that things have been brought into being by God, at the beginning; and the position of certain philosophers, that things have emanated from God eternally.[7] Now, in either position one has to say that things are preserved in being by God. For, if things are brought into being by God, after they were not existing, then the being of things, and similarly their non-being, must result from the divine will; for He has permitted things not to be, when He so willed; and He made things to be, when He so willed. Hence, they exist just as long as He wills them to be. Therefore, His will is the preserver of things.

But, if things have eternally emanated from God, we cannot give a time or instant at which they first flowed forth from God. So, either they never were produced by God, or their being is always flowing forth from God as long as they exist. Therefore, He preserves things in being by His operation.

[9]   Hence it is said: "Upholding all things by the word of His power" (Heb. 1:3). And Augustine says: "The power of the Creator, and the strength of the Omnipotent and All-sustaining is the cause of the subsistence of every creature. And, if this power were ever to cease its ruling of the things which have been created, their species would at once come to an end, and all nature would collapse. For the situation is not like that of a man who has built a house and has then gone away, and, while he is not working and is absent, his work stands. For, if God were to withdraw His rule from it, the world could not stand, even for the flick of an eye."[8]

[10]   Now, by this conclusion the position of the exponents of the Law of the Moors[9] is refuted, for, in order to

7. SCG, II, ch. 31ff.

8. St. Augustine, *De Genesi ad litteram*, IV, 12 (PL, 34, col. 304).

9. On these Mohammedan theologians (*Mutakallimin*) see Maimonides, *Guide for the Perplexed*, I, 73 (trans. M. Fried-

be able to maintain that the world needs God's preservation, they took the view that all forms are accidents, and
that no accident endures through two instants. So that, in
this view, the informing of things would be in continuous
process, as if a thing would not need an agent cause except while in the process of becoming. Hence, also, some
of these people are said to claim that indivisible bodies
(out of which, they say, all substances are composed and
which alone, according to them, possess stability) could last
for about an hour if God were to withdraw His governance
from things. Also, some of them say that a thing could
not even cease to be unless God caused in it the accident
of "cessation."—Now, all these views are clearly absurd.

Chapter 66.

THAT NOTHING GIVES BEING EXCEPT IN SO
FAR AS IT ACTS BY DIVINE POWER

[1]   From this it is manifest that no lower agents give
being except in so far as they act by divine power.

[2]   Indeed, a thing does not give being except in so far
as it is an actual being. But God preserves things in being
by His providence, as we showed.[1] Therefore, it is as a
result of divine power that a thing gives being.

[3]   Again, when several different agents are subordinated
to one agent, the effect that is produced by their common
action must be attributed to them as they are united in
their participation in the motion and power of this agent.
For several agents do not produce one result unless they are
as one. It is clear, for example, that all the men in an army
work to bring about victory, and they do this by virtue of
being subordinated to the leader, whose proper product is

---

länder [London: 1936], p. 124); also E. Gilson, *History of
Christian Philosophy*, pp. 182–183.

1. See above, ch. 65.

victory. Now, we showed in Book One[2] that the first agent is God. So, since being is the common product of all agents, because every agent produces actual being, they must produce this effect because they are subordinated to the first agent and act through His power.

[4] Besides, in the case of all agent causes that are ordered, that which is last in the process of generation and first in intention is the proper product of the primary agent. For instance, the form of a house, which is the proper product of the builder, appears later than the preparation of the cement, stones, and timbers, which are made by the lower workmen who come under the builder. Now, in every action, actual being is primarily intended, but is last in the process of generation. In fact, as soon as it is achieved, the agent's action and the patient's motion come to rest. Therefore, being is the proper product of the primary agent, that is, of God; and all things that give being do so because they act by God's power.

[5] Moreover, the ultimate in goodness and perfection among the things to which the power of a secondary agent extends is that which it can do by the power of the primary agent, for the perfection of the power of the secondary agent is due to the primary agent. Now, that which is most perfect of all effects is the act of being, for every nature or form is perfected by the fact that it is actual, and it is related to actual being as potency is to act. Therefore, the act of being is what secondary agents produce through the power of the primary agent.

[6] Besides, the order of the effects follows the order of the causes. But the first among all effects is the act of being, since all other things are certain determinations of it. Therefore, being is the proper effect of the primary agent, and all other things produce being because they act through the power of the primary agent. Now, secondary agents, which are like particularizers and determinants of the

2. *SCG*, I, ch. 13.

primary agent's action, produce as their proper effects other perfections which determine being.

[7]   Furthermore, that which is of a certain kind through its essence is the proper cause of what is of such a kind by participation. Thus, fire is the cause of all things that are afire. Now, God alone is actual being through His own essence, while other beings are actual beings through participation, since in God alone is actual being identical with His essence. Therefore, the being of every existing thing is His proper effect. And so, everything that brings something into actual being does so because it acts through God's power.

[8]   Hence it is said: "God created, that all things might be" (Wis. 1:14). And in several texts of Scripture it is stated that God makes all things. Moreover, it is said in the *Book on Causes*[3] that not even an intelligence gives being "unless in so far as it is divine," that is, in so far as it acts through divine power.

Chapter 67.

THAT GOD IS THE CAUSE OF OPERATION
FOR ALL THINGS THAT OPERATE

[1]   It is evident, next, that God is the cause enabling all operating agents to operate. In fact, every operating agent is a cause of being in some way, either of substantial or of accidental being. Now, nothing is a cause of being unless by virtue of its acting through the power of God, as we showed.[1] Therefore, every operating agent acts through God's power.

[2]   Again, every operation that results from a certain power is attributed causally to the thing which has given

3. *Liber de causis*, I (ed. Bardenhewer [Freiburg: 1882], p. 162).
1. See above, ch. 66.

the power. For instance, the natural motion of heavy and light things results from their form, depending on whether they are heavy or light, and so the cause of their motion is said to be the generating agent that has given them the form. Now, every power in any agent is from God, as from a first principle of all perfection. Therefore, since every operation results from a power, the cause of every operation must be God.

[3] Besides, it is obvious that every action which cannot continue after the influence of a certain agent has ceased results from that agent. For instance, the manifestation of colors could not continue if the sun's action of illuminating the air were to cease, so there is no doubt that the sun is the cause of the manifestation of colors. And the same thing appears in connection with violent motion, for it stops with the cessation of violence on the part of the impelling agent. But just as God has not only given being to things when they first began to exist, and also causes being in them as long as they exist, conserving things in being, as we have shown,[2] so also has He not merely granted operative powers to them when they were originally created, but He always causes these powers in things. Hence, if this divine influence were to cease, every operation would cease. Therefore, every operation of a thing is traced back to Him as to its cause.

[4] Moreover, whatever agent applies active power to the doing of something, it is said to be the cause of that action. Thus, an artisan who applies the power of a natural thing to some action is said to be the cause of the action; for instance, a cook of the cooking which is done by means of fire. But every application of power to operation is originally and primarily made by God. For operative powers are applied to their proper operations by some movement of body or of soul. Now, the first principle of both types of movement is God. Indeed, He is the first mover and is altogether incapable of being moved, as we showed above.[3]

2. See above, ch. 65.
3. SCG, I, ch. 13.

Similarly, also, every movement of a will whereby powers are applied to operation is reduced to God, as a first object of appetite and a first agent of willing. Therefore, every operation should be attributed to God, as to a first and principal agent.

[5]   Furthermore, in all agent causes arranged in an orderly way the subsequent causes must act through the power of the first cause. For instance, in the natural order of things, lower bodies act through the power of the celestial bodies; and, again, in the order of voluntary things, all lower artisans work in accord with the direction of the top craftsman. Now, in the order of agent causes, God is the first cause, as we showed in Book One.[4] And so, all lower agent causes act through His power. But the cause of an action is the one by whose power the action is done rather than the one who acts: the principal agent, for instance, rather than the instrument. Therefore, God is more especially the cause of every action than are the secondary agent causes.

[6]   Again, every agent is ordered through his operation to an ultimate end, for either the operation itself is the end, or the thing that is made, that is, the product of the operation. Now, to order things to their end is the prerogative of God Himself, as we showed above.[5] So, we have to say that every agent acts by the divine power. Therefore, He is the One Who is the cause of action for all things.

[7]   Hence it is said: "Lord, Thou hast wrought all our works in us" (Isa. 26:12); and: "Without Me, you can do nothing" (John 15:5); and: "It is God Who worketh in us both to will and to accomplish according to His good will" (Phil. 2:13). And for this reason, the products of nature are often attributed, in Scripture, to divine working, because it is He Who works in every agent operating naturally or voluntarily, as the text has it: "Hast Thou not milked me as milk, and curdled me like cheese? Thou hast clothed me

4. *Ibid.*
5. See above, ch. 64.

with skin; Thou hast put me together with bones and sinews" (Job 10:10–11); and in the Psalm (17:14): "The Lord thundered from heaven, and the Highest gave His voice: hail and coals of fire."

Chapter 68.

THAT GOD IS EVERYWHERE

[1] As a consequence, it is clear that God must be everywhere and in all things.

[2] For, the mover and the thing moved must be simultaneous, as the Philosopher proves.[1] But God moves all things to their operations, as we have shown.[2] Therefore, He is in all things.

[3] Again, everything that is in a place, or in something, is in some way in contact with it. For instance, a bodily thing is in place in something according to the contact of dimensive quantity; while an incorporeal thing is said to be in something according to the contact of power, since it lacks dimensive quantity. And so, an incorporeal thing is related to its presence in something by its power, in the same way that a corporeal thing is related to its presence in something by dimensive quantity. Now, if there were any body possessed of infinite dimensive quantity, it would have to be everywhere. So, if there be an incorporeal being possessed of infinite power, it must be everywhere. But we showed in Book One[3] that God is of infinite power. Therefore, He is everywhere.

[4] Besides, as a particular cause is to a particular effect, so is a universal cause to a universal effect. Now, a particular cause must be simultaneous with its proper particular

1. Aristotle, *Physics*, VII, 2 (243a 3).
2. See above, ch. 67.
3. *SCG*, I, ch. 43.

effect. Thus, fire heats through its essence, and the soul confers life on the body through its essence. Therefore, since God is the universal cause of the whole of being, as we showed in Book Two,[4] it must be that wherever being is found, the divine presence is also there.

[5] Moreover, whenever an agent is present only to one of its effects, its action cannot be transferred to another, unless by using the first effect as an intermediary, because the agent and the patient must be simultaneous. For instance, the organic motive power does not move a member of the body except through the heart as an intermediary. So, if God were present to but one of His effects—for instance, to the first moved sphere which would be moved immediately by Him—it would follow that His action could not be transferred to another thing except through the mediation of this sphere. Now, this is not appropriate. Indeed, if the action of any agent cannot be transferred to other things except through the mediation of a first effect, then this effect must correspond proportionally with the agent according to its entire power; otherwise, the agent could not use his entire power. We see an instance of this in the fact that all the motions that the motive power can cause can be carried out through the heart. But there is no creature that can serve as a medium for the carrying out of whatever the divine power can do, for divine power infinitely surpasses every created thing, as is evident from the things shown in Book One.[5] Therefore, it is not appropriate to say that divine action does not extend to other effects except through the mediation of a first one. So, He is not merely present in one of His effects, but in all of them. The same reasoning will be used if a person says that He is present in some and not in others, because, no matter how many divine effects are taken, they could not be sufficient to carry out the execution of the divine power.

[6] Furthermore, an agent cause must be simultaneous with its proximate and immediate effect. But there is in

4. SCG, II, ch. 15.
5. SCG, I, ch. 43.

everything a proximate and immediate effect of God Himself. For we showed in Book Two[6] that God alone can create. Now, there is in everything something caused by creation: prime matter in the case of corporeal things, in incorporeal things their simple essences, as is evident from the things that we determined in Book Two.[7] Therefore, God must be simultaneously present in all things, particularly since He continually and always preserves in being those things which He has brought into being from non-being, as has been shown.[8]

[7] Hence it is said: "I fill heaven and earth" (Jer. 23:24); and in the Psalm (138:8): "If I ascend into heaven, Thou art there; if I descend into hell, Thou art present."

[8] Through this conclusion, moreover, the error is set aside of those who say that God is in some definite part of the world (for instance, in the first heaven and in the eastern section) and that He is consequently the principle of heavenly motion.—Of course, this statement of theirs could be supported, if soundly interpreted: not, for instance, that we may understand God as being confined to some determinate part of the world, but that the source of all corporeal motions, according to the order of nature, takes its start from a determinate part, being moved by God. Because of this He is spoken of in Sacred Scripture also as being in the heavens in a particular way; in the text of Isaias toward the end (66:1): "Heaven is My throne," and in the Psalm (113:16): "The heaven of heaven is the Lord's," and so on.—But from the fact that, apart from the order of nature, God performs some operation in even the lowest of bodies which cannot be caused by the power of a celestial body it is clearly shown that God is immediately present, not only in the celestial body, but also in the lowest things.

6. *SCG*, II, ch. 21.
7. *SCG*, II, ch. 15ff.
8. See above, ch. 65.

[9]   But we must not think that God is everywhere in such a way that He is divided in various areas of place, as if one part of Him were here and another part there. Rather, His entire being is everywhere. For God, as a completely simple being, has no parts.

[10]   Nor is His simplicity something like that of a point, which is the terminus of a continuous line and thus has a definite position on this line, with the consequence that one point is impossible unless it be at one, indivisible place. In fact, God is indivisible, in the sense of existing entirely outside the genus of continuous things. And so, He is not determined in regard to place, either large or small, by any necessity of His essence requiring Him to be in a certain place, for He has been from eternity prior to all place. But by the immensity of His power He touches upon all things that are in place, for He is the universal cause of being, as we said.[9] Thus, He is present in His entirety wherever He is, since He touches upon all things by His simple power.

[11]   Yet, we must not think that He is present in things, in the sense of being combined with them as one of their parts. For it was shown in Book One[10] that He is neither the matter nor the form of anything. Instead, He is in all things in the fashion of an agent cause.

Chapter 69.

ON THE OPINION OF THOSE WHO TAKE
AWAY PROPER ACTIONS FROM
NATURAL THINGS

[1]   From this conclusion some men have taken the opportunity to fall into error, thinking that no creature has an active role in the production of natural effects.[1] So, for

9. See above, ¶4.

10. SCG, I, ch. 17 and 27.

1. On this teaching of the *Mutakallimin*, see E. Gilson, "Pourquoi saint Thomas a critiqué saint Augustin," *Archives d'his-*

instance, fire does not give heat, but God causes heat in the presence of fire, and they said like things about all other natural effects.[2]

[2] Now, they tried to support this error by arguments pointing out that no form, substantial or accidental, can be brought into being except by way of creation. Indeed, forms and accidents cannot come into being from matter, since they do not have matter as one of their parts. Hence, if they are made, they must be made from nothing, and this is to be created. And because creation is an act of God alone, as we showed in Book Two,[3] it would seem to follow that God alone produces both substantial and accidental forms in nature.

[3] Of course, the opinion of some philosophers is partly in agreement with this position. In fact, since everything that does not exist through itself is found to be derived from that which does exist through itself, it appears that the forms of things, which are not existing through themselves but in matter, come from forms which are existent through themselves without matter. It is as if forms existing in matter were certain participations in those forms which exist without matter. And because of this, Plato claimed that the species of sensible things are certain forms separate from matter, which are the causes of being for these sensible things, according as these things participate in them.[4]

[4] On the other hand, Avicenna maintained that all substantial forms flow forth from the agent Intelligence.[5] But he claimed that accidental forms are dispositions of matter

toire littéraire et doctrinale du moyen âge, 1 (1926–1927), 8–35; and also Gilson, *History of Christian Philosophy*, pp. 182–216.

2. See Averroes, *In Metaphysicam*, IX, comm. 7 (VIII, 109r); XII, comm. 18 (VIII, 143v).

3. *SCG*, II, ch. 21.

4. See Aristotle, *Metaphysics*, I, 9 (990a 34).

5. Avicenna, *Metaphysica*, IX, 5 (fol. 105rv).

which have arisen from the action of lower agents disposing matter. In this way he avoided the foolish aspects of the preceding erroneous view.

[5]   Now, an indication of this seemed to lie in the fact that no active power is found to exist in these bodies, except accidental form; for instance, the active and passive qualities, which do not appear to be adequate in their power to cause substantial forms.

[6]   Moreover, certain things are found, among things here below, which are not generated as like from like; for instance, animals generated as a result of putrefaction. Hence, it seems that the forms of these beings come from higher principles; by the same reasoning, so do other forms, some of which are much more noble.

[7]   In fact, some people derive an argument for this from the weakness of natural bodies in regard to acting. For every bodily form is combined with quantity, but quantity hinders action and motion. As an indication of this, they assert that the more that is added to the quantity of a body, the heavier it becomes and the more its motion is slowed down. So, from this they conclude that no body is active but only passive.

[8]   They also try to show this by the fact that every patient is a subject for an agent, and every agent, apart from the first which creates, needs a subject lower than itself. But no substance is lower than corporeal substance. Hence, it appears that no body is active.

[9]   They also add, in regard to this point, that corporeal substance is at the greatest distance from the first agent; hence, it does not seem to them that active power could reach the whole way to corporeal substance. Instead, just as God is an agent only, so is corporeal substance passive only, for it is the lowest in the genus of things.

[10]   So, because of these arguments, Avicebron maintained in the book, *The Source of Life*,[6] that no body is

6. Avicebron, *Fons vitae*, II, 9 (ed. C. Baeumker, BGPM, I, 41).

active, but that the power of spiritual substance, passing through bodies, does the actions which seem to be done by bodies.

[11] Moreover, certain exponents of the Law of the Moors are reported[7] to adduce in support of this argument the point that even accidents do not come from the action of bodies, because an accident does not pass from subject to subject. Hence, they regard it as impossible for heat to pass over from a hot body into another body heated by it. They say, rather, that all accidents like this are created by God.

[12] Now, many inappropriate conclusions follow from the foregoing theories. For, if no lower cause, and especially no bodily one, performs any operation, but, instead, God operates alone in all things, and if God is not changed by the fact that He operates in different things, then different effects would not follow from the diversity of things in which God operates. Now, this appears false to the senses, for cooling does not result from putting something near a hot object, but only heating; nor does the generation of anything except a man result from the semen of man. Therefore, the causality of the lower type of effects is not to be attributed to divine power in such a way as to take away the causality of lower agents.

[13] Again, it is contrary to the rational character of wisdom for there to be anything useless in the activities of the possessor of wisdom. But, if created things could in no way operate to produce their effects, and if God alone worked all operations immediately, these other things would be employed in a useless way by Him, for the production of these effects. Therefore, the preceding position is incompatible with divine wisdom.

[14] Besides, the giver of some principal part to a thing gives the thing all the items that result from that part. For

7. See Maimonides, *Guide for the Perplexed*, I, 73 (ed. Friedländer, p. 125); and above, ch. 65, ¶10.

instance, the cause that gives weight to an elemental body also gives it downward motion. But the ability to make an actual thing results from being actually existent, as is evident in the case of God, for He is pure act and is also the first cause of being for all things, as we showed above.[8] Therefore, if He has communicated His likeness, as far as actual being is concerned, to other things, by virtue of the fact that He has brought things into being, it follows that He has communicated to them His likeness, as far as acting is concerned, so that created things may also have their own actions.

[15] Furthermore, the perfection of the effect demonstrates the perfection of the cause, for a greater power brings about a more perfect effect. But God is the most perfect agent. Therefore, things created by Him obtain perfection from Him. So, to detract from the perfection of creatures is to detract from the perfection of divine power. But, if no creature has any active role in the production of any effect, much is detracted from the perfection of the creature. Indeed, it is part of the fullness of perfection to be able to comunicate to another being the perfection which one possesses. Therefore, this position detracts from the divine power.

[16] Moreover, as it is the function of the good to make what is good, so it is the prerogative of the highest good to make what is best. But God is the highest good, as we showed in Book One.[9] So, it is His function to make all things best. Now, it is better for a good that is conferred on a thing to be common to many than for it to be exclusive, for "the common good is always found to be more divine than the good of one alone."[10] But the good of one being becomes common to many if it can pass from one

8. *SCG*, II, ch. 15.

9. *SCG*, I, ch. 41.

10. Aristotle, *Nicomachean Ethics*, I, 2 (1094b 9); see also I. Th. Eschmann, O. P., "Bonum commune . . . Eine Studie ueber den Wertvorrang des Personalen bei Thomas von Aquin," *Mediaeval Studies*, 6 (1944), 62–120.

to the other; this cannot occur unless it can diffuse this good to others through its own action. On the other hand, if it lacks the power to transfer this good to others, it continues to keep it exclusively. Therefore, God so communicates His goodness to created beings that one thing which receives it can transfer it to another. Therefore, to take away their proper actions from things is to disparage the divine goodness.

[17] Again, to take away order from created things is to deprive them of their best possession, for individual things are good in themselves, but all things together are best because of the order of the whole. Indeed, the whole is always better than its parts, and is their end. Now, if actions be taken away from things, the mutual order among things is removed, for, in regard to things that are different in their natures, there can be no gathering together into a unity of order unless by the fact that some of them act and others undergo action. Therefore, it is inappropriate to say that things do not have their own actions.

[18] Besides, if effects are not produced by the action of created things, but only by the action of God, it is impossible for the power of any created cause to be manifested through its effects. Of course, an effect does not show the power of a cause unless by virtue of the action which proceeding from the power terminates in the effect. Now, the nature of a cause is not known through the effect unless its power is known through this effect, for the power results from the nature. So, if created things have no actions productive of effects, it follows that no nature of anything would ever be known through the effect. And thus, all the knowledge of natural science is taken away from us, for the demonstrations in it are chiefly derived from the effect.

[19] Furthermore, it is inductively evident in all cases that like produces like. But what is generated in lower things is not merely the form, but the thing composed of matter and form, since every process of generation is from something, namely from matter, and to something, namely

form. Therefore, the generating agent cannot be merely a form, but is, rather, the composite of matter and form. Therefore, it is not the separate species of things, as the Platonists claimed, nor the agent Intelligence, as Avicenna held, that is, the cause of the forms which exist in matter; rather, it is the individual composed of matter and form.

[20]   Moreover, if to act is the result of a being which is in act, it is inappropriate for a more perfect act to be deprived of action. But the substantial form is a more perfect act than accidental form. So, if accidental forms in corporeal things have their proper actions, by all the greater reason the substantial form has its proper action. But to dispose matter is not a proper action for it, since this is done by alteration, for which accidental forms are sufficient. Therefore, the substantial form of the generating agent is the source of the action, as a substantial form is put into the product of generation.

[21]   Now, it is easy to break down the arguments which they bring forward. In fact, since a thing is made so that it will exist, and since a form is not called a being in the sense that it possesses being but because the composite exists by means of it, so also the form is not made, in the proper sense, but it begins to be by the fact that the composite is reduced from potency to act, which is the form.

[22]   Nor, indeed, is it necessary that everything which has a form by participation should receive it immediately from that which is form essentially; rather, it may receive it immediately from another being that has a similar form, participated in the same way, and, of course, this being may act by the power of the separate form, if there be any such. So, it is in this way that an agent produces an effect like itself.

[23]   Likewise, it is not necessary, because every action of lower bodies is done by active and passive qualities which are accidents, that only an accident be produced by their actions. For, just as they are caused by the substantial form

which, together with matter, is the cause of all the proper accidents, these accidental forms also act by the power of the substantial form. Now, that which acts by the power of another produces an effect similar not only to itself but more especially to that by whose power it acts. For instance, from the action of an instrument there is produced in the artifact a likeness of the form in the mind of the artist. Consequently, it follows that substantial forms are produced from the action of accidental forms, as they act instrumentally through the power of the substantial forms.

[24] In the case of animals generated from putrefaction, the substantial form is caused by a corporeal agent, namely, the celestial body which is the first agent of alteration; and so all things that produce a change of form in these lower bodies do so by its power. And for this reason the celestial power is enough, without a univocal agent, to produce some imperfect forms. But to produce perfect forms, like the souls of perfect animals, there is also required a univocal agent together with the celestial agent. In fact, such animals are not generated except from semen. And that is why Aristotle says that "man and the sun generate man."[11]

[25] Moreover, it is not true that quantity impedes the action of a form, except accidentally; that is to say, in so far as all continuous quantity is in matter, and form existing in matter, having lesser actuality, is consequently less powerful in acting. Hence, a body that has less matter and more form, for instance, fire, is more active. But, if we consider a kind of action which a form existing in matter may have, then quantity helps to increase rather than to diminish the action. For instance, the larger a hot body is, granting equal intensity of heat, the more is it able to give off heat; and granting equal degree of weight, the bigger a heavy body is, the more rapidly will it be moved by natural motion; that is why it is moved more slowly by unnatural motion. Therefore, the fact that heavy bodies have slower unnatural motion when they have larger quantity does not

11. Aristotle, *Physics*, II, 2 (194b 14).

show that quantity impedes action, but that it helps to increase it.

[26]   Nor, indeed, is it necessary for every body to lack action because bodily substance is generically the lowest in the order of things. For, even among bodies, one is higher than another, and more formal, and more active: as fire is in regard to lower bodies. Nor, in fact, is even the lowest body prevented from acting. For it is clear that a body cannot act in its entirety, since it is composed of matter which is potential being, and of form which is act. Indeed, each thing acts according as it is in act. And because of this, every body acts in accord with its form; and related to it is another body, namely, the patient, which is a subject by virtue of its matter, because its matter is in potency to the form of the agent. But, conversely, if the matter of the agent's body be in potency to the form of the patient's body, they will be mutually related as agent to patient. This happens, for instance, between two elemental bodies. But, on the other hand, one may be only an agent and the other only a patient in relation to the first, as is the relation between a celestial body and an elemental body. And so, a body that is an agent acts on a subject, not by virtue of its entire body, but of the form through which it acts.

[27]   Nor is it even true that bodies are at the greatest distance from God. For, since God is pure act, things are more or less distant from Him on this basis: that they are more or less in act or in potency. So, among beings that is most distant from God which is merely potential; namely, prime matter. Hence, its function is solely to undergo, and not to perform, action. But bodies, as composed of matter and form, approach the divine likeness because they possess form, which Aristotle calls a divine thing.[12] And because of this, they act in so far as they possess form, but they undergo action in so far as they possess matter.

[28]   Again, it is laughable to say that a body does not act because an accident does not pass from subject to subject.

12. *Ibid.*, I, 9 (192a 16).

For a hot body is not said to give off heat in this sense, that numerically the same heat which is in the heating body passes over into the heated body. Rather, by the power of the heat which is in the heating body, a numerically different heat is made actual in the heated body, a heat which was previously in it in potency. For a natural agent does not hand over its own form to another subject, but it reduces the passive subject from potency to act.

[29] Therefore, we do not take away their proper actions from created things, though we attribute all the effects of created things to God, as an agent working in all things.

Chapter 70.

HOW THE SAME EFFECT IS FROM GOD
AND FROM A NATURAL AGENT

[1] Now, it seems difficult for some people to understand how natural effects are attributed to God and to a natural agent.

[2] For it does not seem possible for one action to proceed from two agents. So, if the action whereby a natural effect is produced proceeds from a natural body, it does not proceed from God.

[3] Again, when a thing can be done adequately by one agent, it is superfluous for it to be done by many; in fact, we see that nature does not do with two instruments what it can do with one. So, since the divine power is sufficient to produce natural effects, it is superfluous to use natural powers, too, for the production of the same effects. Or, if the natural power adequately produces the proper effect, it is superfluous for the divine power to act for the same effect.

[4] Besides, if God produces the entire natural effect, then nothing is left of the effect for the natural agent to produce.

So, it does not seem to be possible to say that God produces the same effects that natural agents produce.

[5]   However, these points present no difficulty, provided the things previously established be considered. In every agent, in fact, there are two things to consider: namely, the thing itself that acts, and the power by which it acts. Fire, for instance, heats by means of heat. But the power of a lower agent depends on the power of the superior agent, according as the superior agent gives this power to the lower agent whereby it may act; or preserves it; or even applies it to the action, as the artisan applies an instrument to its proper effect, though he neither gives the form whereby the instrument works, nor preserves it, but simply gives it motion. So, it is necessary for the action of a lower agent to result not only from the agent by its own power, but also from the power of all higher agents; it acts, then, through the power of all. And just as the lowest agent is found immediately active, so also is the power of the primary agent found immediate in the production of the effect. For the power of the lower agent is not adequate to produce this effect of itself, but from the power of the next higher agent; and the power of the next one gets this ability from the power of the next higher one; and thus the power of the highest agent is discovered to be of itself productive of the effect, as an immediate cause. This is evident in the case of the principles of demonstration, the first of which is immediate. So, just as it is not unfitting for one action to be produced by an agent and its power, so it is not inappropriate for the same effect to be produced by a lower agent and God: by both immediately, though in different ways.

[6]   It is also evident that, though a natural thing produces its proper effect, it is not superfluous for God to produce it, since the natural thing does not produce it except by divine power.

[7]   Nor is it superfluous, even if God can by Himself produce all natural effects, for them to be produced by cer-

tain other causes. For this is not a result of the inadequacy of divine power, but of the immensity of His goodness, whereby He has willed to communicate His likeness to things, not only so that they might exist, but also that they might be causes for other things. Indeed, all creatures generally attain the divine likeness in these two ways, as we showed above.[1] By this, in fact, the beauty of order in created things is evident.

[8] It is also apparent that the same effect is not attributed to a natural cause and to divine power in such a way that it is partly done by God, and partly by the natural agent; rather, it is wholly done by both, according to a different way, just as the same effect is wholly attributed to the instrument and also wholly to the principal agent.

Chapter 71.

THAT DIVINE PROVIDENCE DOES NOT ENTIRELY EXCLUDE EVIL FROM THINGS

[1] Now, from these conclusions it becomes evident that divine providence, whereby He governs things, does not prevent corruption, deficiency, and evil from being found in things.

[2] Indeed, divine governance, whereby God works in things, does not exclude the working of secondary causes, as we have already shown.[1] Now, it is possible for a defect to happen in an effect, because of a defect in the secondary agent cause, without there being a defect in the primary agent. For example, in the case of the product of a perfectly skilled artisan, some defect may occur because of a defect in his instrument. And again, in the case of a man whose motive power is strong, he may limp as a result of no defect in his bodily power to move, but because of a

1. See above, ch. 20–21.
1. See above, ch. 69–70.

twist in his leg bone. So, it is possible, in the case of things made and governed by God, for some defect and evil to be found, because of a defect of the secondary agents, even though there be no defect in God Himself.

[3]   Moreover, perfect goodness would not be found in created things unless there were an order of goodness in them, in the sense that some of them are better than others. Otherwise, all possible grades of goodness would not be realized, nor would any creature be like God by virtue of holding a higher place than another. The highest beauty would be taken away from things, too, if the order of distinct and unequal things were removed. And what is more, multiplicity would be taken away from things if inequality of goodness were removed, since through the differences by which things are distinguished from each other one thing stands out as better than another; for instance, the animate in relation to the inanimate, and the rational in regard to the irrational. And so, if complete equality were present in things, there would be but one created good, which clearly disparages the perfection of the creature. Now, it is a higher grade of goodness for a thing to be good because it cannot fall from goodness; lower than that is the thing which can fall from goodness. So, the perfection of the universe requires both grades of goodness. But it pertains to the providence of the governor to preserve perfection in the things governed, and not to decrease it. Therefore, it does not pertain to divine goodness, entirely to exclude from things the power of falling from the good. But evil is the consequence of this power, because what is able to fall does fall at times. And this defection of the good is evil, as we showed above.[2] Therefore, it does not pertain to divine providence to prohibit evil entirely from things.

[4]   Again, the best thing in any government is to provide for the things governed according to their own mode, for the justice of a regime consists in this. Therefore, as it would be contrary to the rational character of a human

2. See above, ch. 7.

regime for men to be prevented by the governor from acting in accord with their own duties—except, perhaps, on occasion, due to the need of the moment—so, too, would it be contrary to the rational character of the divine regime to refuse permission for created things to act according to the mode of their nature. Now, as a result of this fact, that creatures do act in this way, corruption and evil result in things, because, due to the contrariety and incompatibility present in things, one may be a source of corruption for another. Therefore, it does not pertain to divine providence to exclude evil entirely from the things that are governed.

[5] Besides, it is impossible for an agent to do something evil, unless by virtue of the fact that the agent intends something good, as is evident from the foregoing.[3] But, to prohibit universally the intending of the good for the individual on the part of created things is not the function of the providence of Him Who is the cause of every good thing. For, in that way, many goods would be taken away from the whole of things. For example, if the inclination to generate its like were taken away from fire (from which inclination there results this particular evil which is the burning up of combustible things), there would also be taken away this particular good which is the generation of fire and the preservation of the same according to its species. Therefore, it is not the function of divine providence totally to exclude evil from things.

[6] Furthermore, many goods are present in things which would not occur unless there were evils. For instance, there would not be the patience of the just if there were not the malice of their persecutors; there would not be a place for the justice of vindication if there were no offenses; and in the order of nature, there would not be the generation of one thing unless there were the corruption of another. So, if evil were totally excluded from the whole of things by divine providence, a multitude of good things would have to be sacrificed. And this is as it should be, for the good is

3. See above, ch. 3–4.

stronger in its goodness than evil is in its malice, as is clear from earlier sections.[4] Therefore, evil should not be totally excluded from things by divine providence.

[7]   Moreover, the good of the whole takes precedence over the good of a part. It is proper for a governor with foresight to neglect some lack of goodness in a part, so that there may be an increase of goodness in the whole. Thus, an artisan hides the foundations beneath earth, so that the whole house may have stability. But, if evil were removed from some parts of the universe, much perfection would perish from the universe, whose beauty arises from an ordered unification of evil and good things. In fact, while evil things originate from good things that are defective, still, certain good things also result from them, as a consequence of the providence of the governor. Thus, even a silent pause makes a hymn appealing. Therefore, evil should not have been excluded from things by divine providence.

[8]   Again, other things, particularly lower ones, are ordered to man's good as an end. Now, if no evils were present in things, much of man's good would be diminished, both in regard to knowledge and in regard to the desire or love of the good. In fact, the good is better known from its comparison with evil, and while we continue to suffer certain evils our desire for goods grows more ardent. For instance, how great a good health is, is best known by the sick; and they also crave it more than do the healthy. Therefore, it is not the function of divine providence totally to exclude evils from things.

[9]   For this reason, it is said: "I make peace and create evil" (Isa. 45:7; Douay modified); and again: "There is no evil in a city which God will not do" (Amos 3:6).

[10]   Now, with these considerations we dispose of the error of those who, because they noticed that evils occur in the world, said that there is no God. Thus, Boethius introduces a certain philosopher who asks: "If God exists,

4. See above, ch. 11–12.

whence comes evil?"[5] But it could be argued to the contrary: "If evil exists, God exists." For, there would be no evil if the order of good were taken away, since its privation is evil. But this order would not exist if there were no God.

[11] Moreover, by the foregoing arguments, even the occasion of error is removed from those who denied that divine providence is extended to these corruptible things, because they saw that many evils occur in them; they said, moreover, that only incorruptible things are subject to divine providence, things in which no defect or evil part is found.[6]

[12] By these considerations, the occasion of erring is also taken away from the Manicheans who maintained two first agent principles, good and evil, as though evil could have no place under the providence of a good God.[7]

[13] So, too, the difficulty of some people is solved; namely, whether evil actions are from God. Indeed, since it has been shown[8] that every agent produces its action by acting through the divine power, and, consequently that God is the cause both of all effects and all actions, and since it was also shown[9] that evil and defects occur in things ruled by divine providence as a result of the establishment of secondary causes in which there can be deficiency, it is evident that bad actions, according as they are defective, are not from God but from defective proximate causes; but, in so far as they possess something of action and entity, they must be from God. Thus limping arises from the motive power, in so far as it possesses something of mo-

5. Boethius, *De consolatione philosophiae*, I, prose 4 (*PL*, 63, col. 625).

6. See Maimonides, *Guide for the Perplexed*, III, 17 (ed. Friedländer, p. 282) who gives this as Aristotle's view; see also Averroes, *In Metaphysicam*, XII, comm. 52 (VIII, 337). Compare St. Thomas, *Summa Theologiae*, I, 22, 2 c.

7. See St. Augustine, *De haeresibus*, 46 (*PL*, 42, col. 34).

8. See above, ch. 66ff.

9. See above, ¶2.

tion, but in regard to what it has by way of defect it is due to the crookedness of the leg.

Chapter 72.

THAT DIVINE PROVIDENCE DOES NOT EXCLUDE CONTINGENCY FROM THINGS

[1]   Just as divine providence does not wholly exclude evil from things, so also it does not exclude contingency,[1] or impose necessity on things.

[2]   It has already been shown[2] that the operation of providence, whereby God works in things, does not exclude secondary causes, but, rather, is fulfilled by them, in so far as they act by God's power. Now, certain effects are called necessary or contingent in regard to proximate causes, but not in regard to remote causes. Indeed, the fact that a plant bears fruit is a fact contingent on a proximate cause, which is the germinative power which can be impeded and can fail, even though the remote cause, the sun, be a cause acting from necessity. So, since there are many things among proximate causes that may be defective, not all effects subject to providence will be necessary, but a good many are contingent.

[3]   Again, it pertains to divine providence that the grades of being which are possible be fulfilled, as is evident from what was said above.[3] But being is divided into the contingent and the necessary, and this is an essential division of being. So, if divine providence excluded all contingency, not all grades of beings would be preserved.

[4]   Besides, the nearer certain things are to God, the more they participate in His likeness; and the farther they are

1. See Aristotle, *Physics*, VIII, 5 (256a 4–258b 9).
2. See above, ch. 69ff.
3. See above, ch. 71.

away, the more defective are they in regard to His likeness. Now, those that are nearest to God are quite immobile; namely, the separate substances which most closely approach the likeness of God, Who is completely immutable. But the ones which are next to these, and which are moved immediately by those which always exist in the same way, retain a certain type of immobility by the fact that they are always moved in the same way, which is true of the celestial bodies. It follows, then, that those things which come after them and are moved by them are far distant from the immutability of God, so that they are not always moved in the same way. And beauty is evident in this order. Now, every necessary thing, as such, always exists in the same way. It would be incompatible, then, with divine providence, to which the establishment and preservation of order in things belongs, if all things came about as a result of necessity.

[5] Furthermore, that which is necessary is always. Now, no corruptible thing always exists. So, if divine providence required this, that all things be necessary, it would follow that nothing corruptible exists among things, and, consequently, nothing generable. Thus, the whole area of generable and corruptible things would be removed from reality. This detracts from the perfection of the universe.

[6] Moreover, in every motion there is some generation and corruption, for, in a thing that is moved, something begins and something ceases to be. So, if all generation and corruption were removed as a result of taking away the contingency of things, as we showed, the consequence would be that even motion would be taken away from things, and so would all movable things.

[7] Besides, the weakening of the power of any substance, and the hindering of it by a contrary agent, are due to some change in it. So, if divine providence does not prevent motion from going on in things, neither will the weakening of their power be prevented, nor the blocking of their power by the resistance of another thing. Now, the result of the weakness in power, and the impeding of it, is that a thing

in nature does not always work uniformly, but sometimes fails in regard to what is appropriate for it naturally; and so, natural effects do not occur by necessity. Therefore, it is not the function of divine providence to impose necessity on things ruled by it.

[8]   Furthermore, among things that are properly regulated by providence there should be none incapable of fulfillment. So, if it be manifest that some causes are contingent, because they can be prevented from producing their effects, it would evidently be against the character of providence for all things to happen out of necessity. Therefore, divine providence does not impose necessity on things by entirely excluding contingency from things.

Chapter 73.

THAT DIVINE PROVIDENCE DOES NOT EXCLUDE FREEDOM OF CHOICE

[1]   From this it is also evident that providence is not incompatible with freedom of will.

[2]   Indeed, the governance of every provident ruler is ordered either to the attainment, or the increase, or the preservation of the perfection of the things governed. Therefore, whatever pertains to perfection is to be preserved by providence rather than what pertains to imperfection and deficiency. Now, among inanimate things the contingency of causes is due to imperfection and deficiency, for by their nature they are determined to one result which they always achieve, unless there be some impediment arising either from a weakness of their power, or on the part of an external agent, or because of the unsuitability of the matter. And for this reason, natural agent causes are not capable of varied results; rather, in most cases, they produce their effect in the same way, failing to do so but rarely. Now, the fact that the will is a contingent cause arises

from its perfection, for it does not have power limited to one outcome but rather has the ability to produce this effect or that; for which reason it is contingent in regard to either one or the other. Therefore, it is more pertinent to divine providence to preserve liberty of will than contingency in natural causes.

[3] Moreover, it is proper to divine providence to use things according to their own mode. Now, the mode of acting peculiar to each thing results from its form, which is the source of action. Now, the form whereby an agent acts voluntarily is not determined, for the will acts through a form apprehended by the intellect, since the apprehended good moves the will as its object. Now, the intellect does not have one form determined to an effect; rather, it is characteristic of it to comprehend a multitude of forms. And because of this the will can produce effects according to many forms. Therefore, it does not pertain to the character of providence to exclude liberty of will.

[4] Besides, by the governance of every provident agent the things governed are led to a suitable end; hence, Gregory of Nyssa says of divine providence that it is the "will of God through which all things that exist receive a suitable end."[1] But the ultimate end of every creature is to attain the divine likeness, as we showed above.[2] Therefore, it would be incompatible with providence for that whereby a thing attains the divine likeness to be taken away from it. Now, the voluntary agent attains the divine likeness because it acts freely, for we showed in Book One[3] that there is free choice in God. Therefore, freedom of will is not taken away by divine providence.

[5] Again, providence tends to multiply goods among the things that are governed. So, that whereby many goods are removed from things does not pertain to providence. But, if freedom of will were taken away, many goods would be

1. See Nemesius, *De natura hominis*, 43 (PG, 40, col. 792).
2. See above, ch. 19.
3. *SCG*, I, ch. 88.

removed. Taken away, indeed, would be the praise of human virtue which is nothing, if man does not act freely. Taken away, also, would be justice which rewards and punishes, if man could not freely do good or evil. Even the careful consideration of circumstances in processes of deliberation would cease, for it is useless to dwell upon things that are done of necessity. Therefore, it would be against the very character of providence if liberty of will were removed.

[6]   Hence it is said: "God made man from the beginning and left him in the hand of his own counsel"; and again: "Before man is life and death, good and evil, that which he shall choose shall be given him" (Ecclus. 15:14, 18).

[7]   Now, by these considerations the opinion of the Stoics is set aside, for they said that all things come about by necessity, according to an irrevocable order of causes, which the Greeks called εἱμαρμένη.[4]

Chapter 74.

THAT DIVINE PROVIDENCE DOES NOT EXCLUDE FORTUNE AND CHANCE

[1]   It is also apparent from the foregoing that divine providence does not take away fortune and chance from things.

[2]   For it is in the case of things that happen rarely that fortune and chance are said to be present. Now, if some things did not occur in rare instances, all things would happen by necessity. Indeed, things that are contingent in most cases differ from necessary things only in this: they can fail to happen, in a few cases. But it would be contrary to the essential character of divine providence if all things occurred by necessity, as we showed.[1] Therefore, it would

4. See Nemesius, De natura hominis, 37 (PG, 40, col. 752).
1. See above, ch. 72.

also be contrary to the character of divine providence if nothing were to be fortuitous and a matter of chance in things.

[3] Again, it would be contrary to the very meaning of providence if things subject to providence did not act for an end, since it is the function of providence to order all things to their end. Moreover, it would be against the perfection of the universe if no corruptible thing existed, and no power could fail, as is evident from what was said above.[2] Now, due to the fact that an agent fails in regard to an end that is intended, it follows that some things occur by chance. So, it would be contrary to the meaning of providence, and to the perfection of things, if there were no chance events.

[4] Besides, the large number and variety of causes stem from the order of divine providence and control. But, granted this variety of causes, one of them must at times run into another cause and be impeded, or assisted, by it in the production of its effect. Now, from the concurrence of two or more causes it is possible for some chance event to occur, and thus an unintended end comes about due to this causal concurrence. For example, the discovery of a debtor, by a man who has gone to market to sell something, happens because the debtor also went to market. Therefore, it is not contrary to divine providence that there are some fortuitous and chance events among things.

[5] Moreover, what does not exist cannot be the cause of anything. Hence, each thing must stand in the same relation to the fact that it is a cause, as it does to the fact that it is a being. So, depending on the diversity of order in beings, there must also be a diversity of order among causes. Now, it is necessary for the perfection of things that there be among things not only substantial beings but also accidental beings. Indeed, things that do not possess ultimate perfection in their substance must obtain such perfection through accidents, and the more of these there are, the farther are they from the simplicity of God. From the fact,

2. See above, ch. 71.

then, that a certain subject has many accidents it follows
that it is a being accidentally, because a subject and an accident, and even two accidents of one substance, are a unit
and a being accidentally; as in the example of a white man,
and of a musical, white being. So, it is necessary to the
perfection of things that there should also be some accidental causes. Now, things which result accidentally from
any causes are said to happen by chance or fortune. Therefore, it is not contrary to the rational character of providence, which preserves the perfection of things, for certain
things to come about as a result of chance or fortune.

[6]   Furthermore, that there be order and a gradation of
causes is important to the order of divine providence. But
the higher a cause is, the greater is its power; and so, its
causality applies to a greater number of things. Now, the
natural intention of a cause cannot extend beyond its
power, for that would be useless. So, the particular intention of a cause cannot extend to all things that can happen.
Now, it is due to the fact that some things happen apart
from the intention of their agents that there is a possibility
of chance or fortuitous occurrence. Therefore, the order of
divine providence requires that there be chance and fortune in reality.

[7]   Hence it is said: "I saw that the race is not to the
swift . . . but time and chance in all" (Ecclus. 9:11; Douay
modified), that is, among things here below.

Chapter 75.

THAT GOD'S PROVIDENCE APPLIES TO
CONTINGENT SINGULARS

[1]   It is obvious from what we have shown that divine
providence reaches out to singulars that are generable and
corruptible.

[2]   Except for the fact of their contingency, and the fact that many of them come about by chance and fortune, it does not seem that providence is inapplicable to them. For it is only on this basis that they differ from incorruptible things, and the universal natures of corruptible things, to which providence does apply, as people say. But contingency is not incompatible with providence, nor are chance or fortune or voluntary action, as we have shown.[1] Therefore, nothing prohibits providence from also applying to these things, just as it does to incorruptible and universal things.

[3]   Again, if God does not exercise providence over these singulars, this is either because He does not know them, or because He is not able to do so, or because He does not wish to take care of them. Now, it cannot be said that God does not know singulars; we showed above[2] that God does possess knowledge of them. Nor can it be said that God is unable to take care of them, for His power is infinite, as we proved above.[3] Nor, indeed, are these singulars incapable of being governed, since we see them governed by the use of reason in the case of men, and by means of natural instinct in the case of bees and many brute animals that are governed by some sort of natural instinct. Nor, in fact, can it be said that God does not wish to govern them, since His will is universally concerned with every good thing,[4] and the good of things that are governed lies chiefly in the order of governance. Therefore, it cannot be said that God takes no care of these singulars.

[4]   Besides, all secondary causes, by the fact of being causes, attain the divine likeness, as is evident from what we said above.[5] Now, we find one thing in common among causes that produce something: they take care of their

1. See above, ch. 72ff.
2. *SCG*, I, ch. 65.
3. *SCG*, II, ch. 22.
4. *SCG*, I, ch. 75ff.
5. See above, ch. 21.

products. Thus, animals naturally nourish their young. So, God takes care of the things of which He is the cause. Now, He is the cause even of these particular things, as is obvious from our previous statements.[6] So, He does take care of them.

[5] Moreover, we showed above[7] that God does not act in regard to created things by a necessity of His nature, but through His will and intellect. Now, things done by intellect and will are subject to the care of a provident agent, for that is what such care seems to consist in: the fact that certain things are managed through understanding. And so, the things that result from His action are subject to divine providence. But we showed before[8] that God works through all secondary causes, and that all their products may be traced back to God as their cause; so it must be that the things that are done among singulars are His works. Therefore, these singulars, and also their motions and operations, come under the scope of divine providence.

[6] Furthermore, foolish is the providence of a person who does not take care of the things needed by the things for which he does care. But it is obvious that, if all particular things vanished, their universals could not endure. So, if God be only concerned with universals, and if He be entirely negligent of these singulars, then His providence will be foolish and imperfect.

[7] However, suppose someone says that God takes care of these singulars to the extent of preserving them in being, but not in regard to anything else; this is utterly impossible. In fact, all other events that occur in connection with singulars are related to their preservation or corruption. So, if God takes care of singulars as far as their preservation is concerned, He takes care of every contingent event connected with them.

6. SCG, II, ch. 15.
7. SCG, II, ch. 23ff.
8. See above, ch. 67.

[8]   Of course, a person could say that the mere care of the universals is enough for the preservation of particulars in being, for in each species there are provided the means whereby any individual of the species may be preserved in being. For example, organs for the taking in and digestion of food have been given to animals, and also horns with which to protect themselves. Moreover, good uses of these cannot fail to be made, except in rare instances, because things that are from nature produce their effects in all cases, or frequently. Thus, it is not possible for all individuals to fail, even though a particular one may do so.

[9]   But according to this argument all events that occur in connection with individuals will be subject to providence, in the same way that their preservation in being is, because nothing can happen in connection with the singular members of any species that cannot be reduced in some way to the sources of that species. And so, singulars come no more under the scope of divine providence in regard to their preservation in being than they do in regard to their other aspects.

[10]   Furthermore, in the relation of things to their end, an order appears, such that accidents exist for the sake of substances, in order that substances may be perfected by them; on the other hand, within substances matter is for the sake of form, for it participates in divine goodness through form, and that is why all things were made, as we showed above.[9] Consequently, it is clear that singulars exist for the sake of the universal nature. The sign of this is the fact that, in the case of beings whose universal nature can be preserved by one individual, there are not plural individuals of one species, as is instanced by the sun and the moon. But, since providence has the function of ordering things to their end, both the ends and the things that are related to an end must be a matter of concern to providence. Therefore, not only universals, but also singulars, come under the scope of providence.

9. See above, ch. 17.

[11]   Again, this is the difference between speculative and practical knowledge: speculative knowledge and the functions that pertain to it reach their perfection in the universal, while the things that belong to practical knowledge reach their perfection in the particular. In fact, the end of speculative cognition is truth, which consists primarily and essentially in immaterial and universal things; but the end of practical cognition is operation, which is concerned with singulars. So, the physician does not heal man as a universal, but, rather, this individual man, and the whole science of medicine is ordered to this result. Now, it is obvious that providence belongs to the area of practical knowledge, for its function is to order things to their end. Therefore, God's providence would be most imperfect if it were to confine itself to universals and not extend as far as singulars.

[12]   Besides, speculative knowledge is perfected in the universal rather than in the particular, because universals are better known than particulars. Because of this, the knowledge of the most universal principles is common. However, that man who has not only universal, but also a proper, knowledge of things is more perfect in speculative science, for, the man who knows only universally merely knows a thing potentially. This is why a student is led from a universal knowledge of principles to a proper knowledge of conclusions, by his teacher who possesses knowledge of both —just as a thing is brought from potency to act by an actual being. So, in practical science, he is much more perfect who directs things to act, not only universally, but also in the particular case. Therefore, divine providence, being most perfect, extends to singulars.

[13]   Moreover, since God is the cause of actual being because He is being, as was shown above,[10] He must be the agent of providence for being, because He is being. Indeed, He does provide for things, because He is their cause. So, whatever a thing is, and whatever its mode of existing, it falls under His providence. Now, singulars are beings, and

10. SCG, II, ch. 15.

more so than universals, for universals do not subsist of themselves, but are only in singulars. Therefore, divine providence also applies to singulars.

[14] Furthermore, created things are subject to divine providence inasmuch as they are ordered by it to their ultimate end, which is divine goodness. Therefore, the participation of divine goodness by created things is accomplished by divine providence. But even contingent singulars participate in divine goodness. So, divine providence must extend even to them.

[15] Hence it is said: "Are not two sparrows sold for a farthing: and not one of them shall fall on the ground without My Father" (Matt. 10:29; see 6:26; Douay modified). And again: "She reacheth from end to end mightily" (Wis. 8:1), that is, from the noblest creatures down to the lowest of them. So, also, we oppose the view of those who said: "The Lord hath forsaken the earth, and the Lord seeth not" (Ezech. 9:9); and again: "He walketh about the poles of heaven, and He doth not consider our things" (Job 22:14; Douay recast).

[16] By this conclusion we set aside the opinion of those who said that divine providence does not extend as far as these singular things. In fact, some attribute this opinion to Aristotle, even though it cannot be gathered from his own words.

Chapter 76.

THAT GOD'S PROVIDENCE APPLIES IMMEDIATELY TO ALL SINGULARS

[1] Now, some have conceded that divine providence extends to singulars, but through certain intermediary causes. Indeed, Plato asserted a threefold providence, according to Gregory of Nyssa.[1] The first of these is *that of*

1. Nemesius, *De natura hominis*, 44 (PG, 40, col. 793).

the highest God, Who primarily and above all provides for
His own things, that is, for all things spiritual and intellectual, but subsequently for the whole world, as far as
genera and species go, and the universal causes which are
the celestial bodies. Then the second type of providence is
that by which provision is made for individual animals and
plants, and for other generable and corruptible individuals,
in respect to their generation and corruption, and other
changes. Now, Plato attributes this kind of providence to
the "gods that circulate about the heavens." Aristotle, on
the other hand, attributes their causality to the "oblique
circle."[2] Finally, he assigns a third kind of providence to
things that pertain to human life. So, he attributes this
function to certain "daemons living in the region of the
earth" who are caretakers for human actions, according to
him. But still, according to Plato, the second and third
types of providence depend on the first, for the highest
God has established the ones on the second and third levels
as provident agents.

[2]   Now, this theory is in agreement with the Catholic
faith, in so far as it traces the providence of all things back
to God as its first author. But it seems incompatible with
the view of the faith, in regard to this: it says that not all
particulars are immediately subject to divine providence.
Now, we can show from the foregoing that they are.

[3]   In point of fact, God has immediate knowledge of
singulars, not merely in the sense that He knows them in
their causes, but even in themselves, as we showed in Book
One of this work.[3] But it would appear inappropriate for
Him to know singulars and yet not to will their order, in
which their chief good consists, for His will is the source
of goodness in its entirety. Therefore, just as He knows
singulars immediately, He must also establish order for
them immediately.

2. Aristotle, *De generatione et corruptione*, II, 10 (336a 32).
3. SCG, I, ch. 65ff.

[4] Again, the order that is established by providence among things that are governed arises from the order which the provident agent decides on within his own mind. For example, the artistic form that is produced in matter proceeds from the form that is in the mind of the artist. Now, where there are many overseers, arranged one under the next, the order that is conceived by the higher one must be handed down to the lower one; just as a lower type of art receives its principles from a higher one. If, then, the second and third provident agents are claimed to be under the first provident agent, Who is the highest God, they must receive the order that is to be established in things from the highest God. Now, it is not possible for this order to be more perfect in them than in the highest God; on the contrary, all perfections come to other things from Him by way of descent, as appears from things said earlier.[4] The order of things must, then, be present in the secondary agents of providence, not merely universally, but also in respect to singulars; otherwise, they could not establish order in singulars by their providence. Therefore, the ordering of singulars is much more under the control of divine providence.

[5] Besides, in the case of things regulated by human providence we find that a certain higher overseer thinks out the way in which some of the big and universal matters are to be ordered, but he does not himself think out the ordering of the smallest details; rather, he leaves these to be planned by agents on a lower level. But, as a matter of fact, this is so because of his own deficiency, either because he does not know the circumstances for the individual details, or because he is not able to think out the order for all, by virtue of the effort and length of time that might be needed. Now, deficiencies of this kind are far removed from God, because He knows all singular things, and He does not make an effort to understand, or require any time for it; since, by understanding Himself He knows all other things, as we showed above.[5] Therefore, He plans even the

4. *SCG*, I, ch. 38ff.
5. *SCG*, I, ch. 46.

order for all singular things. So, His providence applies to all singulars immediately.

[6] Moreover, in human affairs the lower overseers, through their own efforts, plan the order for those things whose direction has been given them by the chief executive. Of course, they do not get this ability from the man who is in charge, or even its use. Indeed, if they did get it from him, the ordering would already be accomplished by the higher executive, and they would not be the agents responsible for this ordering, but simply the ones who carry it out. Now, it is obvious from things said above[6] that all wisdom and understanding are caused in intelligent beings by the highest God, and that no intellect can understand anything unless by divine power; just as no agent can perform any operation unless he act by this divine power. Therefore, God Himself is the disposer of all things immediately by His providence, and whatever beings are called agents of providence under Him are executors of His providence.

[7] Furthermore, a higher providence gives regulations to a lower providence, just as a statesman gives regulations and laws to the leader of an army, who gives laws and regulations to the heads of larger or smaller military units. If, then, there be other providences under the first providence of the supreme God, God must give these secondary or tertiary overseers the regulations for their commands. So, He gives them either universal regulations and laws or particular ones. But, if He gives them universal regulations for their commands, since universal regulations cannot be applied in all cases to particulars, especially in the case of variable things that do not always remain the same, these secondary or tertiary overseers would have to give orders at times that are contrary to the regulations given them for the things subject to their control. So, they would be able to pass judgment on the regulations that they have received, as to when action should accord with these regulations and

6. *SCG*, II, ch. 15; III, ch. 67.

when one should overlook them. Now, this could not be, for such judgment belongs to a superior. Indeed, it is the prerogative of the one who establishes the laws to interpret them and issue dispensations from them. So, this judgment over universally given regulations must be carried out by the supreme overseer. Of course, He could not do this if He refused to involve Himself immediately in the ordering of these singular things. So, according to this, He must be the immediate overseer of these things. On the other hand, if the secondary and tertiary overseers receive particular regulations and laws from the highest overseer, then it is quite obvious that the ordering of these singulars is done immediately by divine providence.

[8] Again, the superior overseer always holds the power of judgment over the orders issued by inferior overseers, as to whether the orders are properly given or not. If, then, the secondary or tertiary overseers are under God as the first overseer, God must hold the power of judgment over the things ordered by them. In fact, He could not do this if He did not consider the order of these singulars. Therefore, He Himself takes care by Himself of these singulars.

[9] Besides, if God does not immediately by Himself take care of these inferior singular things, this can only be either because He despises them or because His dignity might be lowered by them, as some people say.[7] But this is unreasonable. It is indeed a matter of greater dignity to oversee the planning of the order for certain things than for it to be produced in them. So, if God works in all things, as we showed above,[8] and if His dignity is not diminished thereby, and if this belongs rather to His universal and supreme power, it is in no sense something to be despised by Him, or something that might besmirch His dignity, if He exercises His providence immediately over these singulars.

7. See Averroes, *In Metaphysicam*, XII, comm. 37 and 52 (VIII, 150v and 158v).
8. See above, ch. 67ff.

[10]   Moreover, every wise being who uses his power providently sets limits on the use of his power, when he acts, by ordering the objective and the extent to which it goes; otherwise, his power would not keep pace with his wisdom in such action. But it is obvious from the foregoing[9] that the divine power, in operating, reaches to the lowest things. So, the divine wisdom is in control of ordering what, how many, and what kind of effects proceed from His power, even down to the lowest things. Therefore, He is Himself planning the order for all things immediately by His providence.

[11]   Hence it is said: "The things that are from God are well ordered" (Rom. 13:1). And again: "Thou hast done the things of old, and hast devised one thing after another; and what Thou hast willed hath been done" (Judith 9:4).

Chapter 77.

THAT THE EXECUTION OF DIVINE PROVIDENCE
IS ACCOMPLISHED BY MEANS OF
SECONDARY CAUSES

[1]   We should attend to the fact that two things are required for providence: the ordering and the execution of the order. The first of these is accomplished by the cognitive power; as a consequence, those who have more perfect knowledge are called orderers of the others. "For it is the function of the wise man to order."[1] But the second is done by the operative power. Now, the situations in these two functions are contrary to each other. For, the more perfect an ordering is, the more does it descend to small details; but the execution of small details is appropriate to a lower power, proportionate to such an effect. Now, in God the highest perfection in regard to both functions is found; in

9. *Ibid.*
1. Aristotle, *Metaphysics*, I, 2 (982a 18).

fact, there is in Him the most perfect wisdom for ordering and the most perfect power for operating. So, He Himself through His wisdom must arrange the orders for all things, even the least; on the other hand, He may execute the small details by means of other lower powers, through which He Himself works, as does a universal and higher power through a lower and particular power. It is appropriate, then, that there be inferior agents as executors of divine providence.

[2] Again, we showed above[2] that divine operation does not exclude the operations of secondary causes. But the resultants of the operations of secondary causes are within the scope of divine providence, since God orders all singulars by Himself, as we showed.[3] Therefore, secondary causes are the executors of divine providence.

[3] Besides, the stronger the power of an agent is, the farther does its operation extend to more remote effects. For instance, the bigger a fire is, the farther away are the things it heats. But this does not occur in the case of an agent that acts without a medium, for whatever it acts on is adjacent to it. Therefore, since the power of divine providence is the greatest, it must extend its operation to its most distant effects through some intermediaries.

[4] Moreover, it belongs to the dignity of a ruler to have many ministers and a variety of executors of his rule, for, the more subjects he has, on different levels, the higher and greater is his dominion shown to be. But no ruler's dignity is comparable to the dignity of the divine rule. So, it is appropriate that the execution of divine providence be carried out by diverse levels of agents.

[5] Furthermore, the propriety of its order manifests the perfection of providence, since order is the proper effect of providence. Now, it is pertinent to the propriety of order that nothing be left in disorder. So, the perfection of divine

2. See above, ch. 69ff.
3. See above, ch. 76.

providence requires that the excess of certain things over others be reduced to a suitable order. Now, this is done when one makes available some good for those that have less, from the abundance of those that have more. So, since the perfection of the universe requires that certain things participate in divine goodness more abundantly than others, as we showed above,[4] the perfection of divine providence demands that the execution of the divine rule be accomplished by those that participate more fully in divine goodness.

[6]   Besides, the order of causes is more noble than the order of effects, just as a cause is better than an effect. So, the perfection of providence is better manifested by the first order. But, if there were no intermediary causes carrying out divine providence, there would not be an order of causes in reality but only an order of effects. Therefore, the perfection of divine providence demands that there be intermediary causes as executors of it.

[7]   Hence it is said in the Psalm (102:21): "Bless the Lord, all ye His hosts; you ministers of His who do His will"; and elsewhere: "Fire, hail, snow, stormy winds, which fulfill His word" (Ps. 148:8; Douay modified).

Chapter 78.

THAT OTHER CREATURES ARE RULED BY GOD
BY MEANS OF INTELLECTUAL CREATURES

[1]   Since it is the function of divine providence to maintain order in things, and since a suitable order is such that there is a proportional descent from the highest things to the lowest, it must be that divine providence reaches the farthest things by some sort of proportion. Now, the proportion is like this: as the highest creatures are under God and are governed by Him, so the lower creatures are under the

4. SCG, II, ch. 45.

higher ones and are ruled by them. But of all creatures the highest are the intellectual ones, as is evident from what we said earlier.[1] Therefore, the rational plan of divine providence demands that the other creatures be ruled by rational creatures.

[2] Again, whatever type of creature carries out the order of divine providence, it is able to do so because it participates in something of the power of the first providential being; just as an instrument does not move unless, through being moved, it participates somewhat in the power of the principal agent. So, the beings that participate more fully in the power of the divine providence are executive agents of divine providence in regard to those that participate less. But intellectual creatures participate more than others in it, because an ability to establish order which is done by cognitive power, and an ability to execute it which is done by operative power, are both required for providence, and rational creatures share in both types of power, while the rest of creatures have operative powers only. Therefore, all other creatures are ruled by means of rational creatures under divine providence.

[3] Besides, to whomever any power is given by God, the recipient is given the power together with an ordination toward the effect of that power. For in that way all things are arranged for the best, inasmuch as each thing is ordered to all the goods that can naturally come from it. Now, the intellectual power by itself is capable of ordering and ruling; hence, we see that the operative power follows the direction of the intellective power, when they are combined in the same subject. In man, for instance, we observe that the bodily members are moved at the command of the will. The same is evident even if they are in different subjects; for instance, those men who excel in operative power must be directed by those who excel in intellectual power. Therefore, the rational plan of divine providence demands that other creatures be ruled by intellectual creatures.

1. *SCG*, II, ch. 46.

[4]   Moreover, particular powers are naturally adapted to be moved by universal powers; this is evident quite as much in the artistic as in the natural sphere. Now, it is obvious that intellectual power is more universal than any operative power, for the intellectual power contains universal forms, while each power is operative only because of some form proper to the agent. Therefore, all other creatures must be moved and regulated by means of intellectual powers.

[5]   Furthermore, in all powers arranged in an order, one is directive in relation to the next, and it knows the rational plan best. Thus, we see in the case of the arts that one art, which is concerned with the end from which the plan for the entire artistic production is derived, directs and commands another art which makes the product, as the art of navigation does in regard to shipbuilding. So, the one that introduces the form commands the one that prepares the matter. Instruments, on the other hand, which do not know the plan at all, are simply ruled. Since only intellectual creatures can know the rational plans for the ordering of creatures, it will therefore be their function to rule and govern all other creatures.

[6]   Again, that which is of itself is the cause of that which is through another. But only intellectual creatures operate by themselves, in the sense that they are masters of their operations through free choice of their will. On the other hand, other creatures are involved in operation resulting from the necessity of nature, since they are moved by something else. Therefore, intellectual creatures by their operation are motivating and regulative of other creatures.

Chapter 79.

THAT LOWER INTELLECTUAL SUBSTANCES ARE RULED BY HIGHER ONES

[1] Since certain intellectual creatures are higher than others, as is clear from the foregoing,[1] the lower ones of an intellectual nature must be governed by the higher ones.

[2] Again, more universal powers are able to move particular powers, as we said.[2] But the higher intellectual natures have more universal forms, as was shown above.[3] Therefore, they are capable of ruling the lower intellectual natures.

[3] Besides, an intellectual potency that is nearer to the principle is always capable of ruling an intellectual power that is more removed from the principle. This is evident in both speculative and active sciences; for a speculative science which derives its principles of demonstration from another science is said to be subalternated to that other; and an active science which is nearer the end, which is the principle in matters of operation, is architectonic in regard to a more distant one. Therefore, since some intellectual substances are nearer the first principle, namely God, as was shown in Book Two,[4] they will be capable of ruling others.

[4] Moreover, superior intellectual substances receive the influence of divine wisdom into themselves more perfectly, because each being receives something according to the being's own mode. Now, all things are governed by divine wisdom. And so, things that participate more in divine wisdom must be capable of governing those that participate

1. *SCG*, II, ch. 91 and 95.
2. See above, ch. 78.
3. *SCG*, II, ch. 98.
4. *SCG*, II, ch. 95.

less. Therefore, the lower intellectual substances are governed by the higher ones.

[5]   Thus, the higher spirits are also called *angels*, because they direct the lower spirits, as it were, by bringing messages to them; in fact, angels are spoken of as *messengers*. And they are also called *ministers*, because they carry out by their operation the order of divine providence even in the area of bodily things. Indeed, a minister is "like a living instrument," according to the Philosopher.[5] So this is what is said in the Psalm (103:4): "Who makest Thy angels spirits, and Thy ministers a burning fire."

Chapter 80.

ON THE ORDERING OF THE ANGELS
AMONG THEMSELVES

[1]   Since bodily things are ruled by spiritual things, as we showed,[1] and since there is an order of bodily things, the higher bodies must be ruled by the higher intellectual substances, while the lower bodies are ruled by the lower ones. Moreover, since the higher a substance is the more universal is its power, but the power of an intellectual substance is more universal than the power of a body, the higher intellectual substances, then, have powers incapable of functioning through bodily power, and so they are not united with bodies. But the lower ones have particular powers that are capable of functioning through certain bodily organs, and so they must be united with bodies.

[2]   Now, as the higher intellectual substances are more universal in their power, they are also more perfectly receptive of divine control from Him, in the sense that they know the plan of this order down to its singular details because they receive-it from God. However, this manifesting

5. Aristotle, *Politics*, I, 4 (1253b 29).
1. See above, ch. 78.

of the divine ordering stretches down by divine action to the last of the intellectual substances; as it is stated: "Is there any numbering of His soldiers? And upon whom shall not His light arise?" (Job 25:3). But the lower understandings do not receive it with such perfection that they are able to know through it the individual details which pertain to the order of providence, and which they are to execute. Rather, they know them in a general sort of way. The lower they are, the fewer details of the divine order do they receive through the first illumination which they get from the divine source. So much so, that the human understanding, which is the lowest according to natural knowledge, gets a knowledge of certain most universal items only.

[3] And thus, the higher intellectual substances obtain immediately from God a perfect knowledge of the aforementioned order; and then, other lower substances must obtain this perfect knowledge through them, just as we said above that the student's universal knowledge is brought to perfection by the knowledge of the teacher who knows in detail. Hence, Dionysius, speaking of the highest intellectual substances whom he calls the *first hierarchy*, that is, the *sacred sovereignty*, says: "they are not sanctified by other substances but they are immediately ranged about Himself by the Godhead and are conducted to the immaterial and invisible beauty, in so far as it is permitted, and to the knowable reasons for the divine workings."[2] And thus, through them, he says, "those placed below in the ranks of the celestial essences are instructed."[3] In this way, then, the higher understandings receive a perfect knowledge from a higher source of knowledge.

[4] Moreover, in every arrangement of providence this ordering of effects is derived from the form of the agent, because the effect must proceed from the cause by virtue of a certain likeness. Now, the fact that an agent communi-

2. Pseudo-Dionysius, *De coelesti hierarchia*, VII, 1 (PG, 3, col. 208).
3. *Ibid.*, col. 205.

cates a likeness of his form to his effects is due to some end. So, the first principle in providential arrangement is the end; the second is the form of the agent; and the third is the arrangement of the order of the effects. Therefore, the highest function in the order of understanding is for the rational nature of the order to be considered in relation to the end; and the second most important thing is to observe it in relation to the form; while the third thing is to know the arrangement of this order in itself, and not in a higher source. Thus, the art which considers the end is architectonic in relation to the one which considers the form, as the art of navigating a ship is to the art of making one; but the art which considers the form is architectonic in relation to the art which merely considers the orders of the motions that are ordered in terms of the form, as the art of ship-building orders the skill of the workmen.

[5]   So, there is a definite order in those understandings which grasp immediately in God Himself a perfect knowledge of the order of divine providence. For the highest and first intellects perceive the plan of the providential order in the ultimate end itself, which is the divine goodness, and some of them do so more clearly than others. These are called *Seraphim*, meaning the "ardent" or "burning" ones, because the intensity of love or desire, which are functions concerned with the end, is customarily symbolized by fire. Thus Dionysius says that, as a result of this name of theirs, there is a suggestion of "their mobility in relation to the divine, a fervent and flexible mobility, and of their leading of lower things to God,"[4] as to their end.

[6]   The second type of understandings know the plan of providence perfectly in the divine form itself. These are called *Cherubim*, which means "fullness of knowledge." Indeed, knowledge is made perfect through the form of the knowable object. Hence, Dionysius says that this way of naming them suggests that they are "capable of contemplating the first operative power of divine beauty."[5]

4. *Ibid.*
5. *Ibid.*

[7] Then, the third type of understandings consider the very arrangement of the divine judgments in themselves. These are called *Thrones*; for, by thrones the *judiciary power* is symbolized, according to this text: "Thou dost sit on the throne and judgest justice" (Ps. 9:5; Douay modified). And so Dionysius says that this designation suggests that they are "bearers of God, immediately available for all divine undertakings."[6]

[8] Now, the preceding statements are not to be understood in the sense that there is a difference between divine goodness, divine essence, and divine knowledge as it contains the arrangement of things; rather, there is a different way of considering each one.

[9] So, also, among the lower spirits who attain, through the higher spirits, a perfect knowledge of the divine order which they are to carry out there must be some order. In fact, the superior ones among them have a more universal power of knowing; hence, they obtain knowledge of the order of providence through principles and causes that are more universal, whereas the lower ones acquire it in more particular causes. For instance, the man who could consider the order of all natural things in the celestial bodies would be possessed of higher understanding than the man who is obliged, for the sake of perfect knowledge, to direct his gaze upon the lower bodies. So, those who can perfectly know the order of providence in the universal causes, which are intermediaries between God, Who is the most universal cause, and particular causes are intermediate between the ones who are able to consider the plan of this order in God Himself and the ones who must consider it in particular causes. These are placed by Dionysius in the middle hierarchy, for, just as it is directed by the highest, so also does it direct the lowest one, as he says in *On the Celestial Hierarchy* VIII.[7]

6. *Ibid.*
7. *Ibid.*, VIII, 1 (PG, 3, col. 237).

[10]   Moreover, there must be a definite order among these intellectual substances. In fact, the very arrangement in general, according to providence, is assigned first to many executors. This is accomplished through the order of *Dominations*, for it is the function of those who hold dominion to prescribe what the others execute. Hence, Dionysius says that the word *Domination* suggests "a certain freedom from control, placed above all servitude and superior to all subjection."[8]

[11]   Then, secondly, there is a distribution and multiplication in the form of diverse effects on the part of the agent and executor. In fact, this is done by the order of *Virtues*, whose name, as Dionysius says in the same place, suggests "a strong forcefulness in regard to all Godlike operations, one which does not abandon its Godlike movement because of any weakening in itself." It is evident from this that the source of universal operation belongs to this order. Hence it appears that pertinent to this order is the motion of the celestial bodies, from which bodies as universal causes, the particular effects in nature follow. So, they are called "the powers of the heavens" where it is said: "the powers of the heavens shall be moved" (Luke 21:26; Douay modified). Also pertinent to these spirits is the execution of divine works which are done outside the order of nature, for these are most sublime among the divine ministrations. For which reason, Gregory says, "those spirits are called Virtues through which miracles are frequently wrought."[9] And if there be anything else that is universal and primary in the carrying out of divine ministrations, it is proper to assign it to this order.

[12]   And, thirdly, the universal order of providence, already established in the effects, is guarded from all confusion, provided those things which might disturb this order are kept in check. Now, this pertains to the order of *Powers*. Hence, Dionysius says, in the same place, that the word

8. *Ibid.*

9. St. Gregory, *In Evangelium*, homil. 34 (*PL*, 76, col. 1251).

Powers means "a well-ordered and unconfused ordering in regard to divine undertakings." And Gregory says that pertinent to this order "is to check contrary powers."[10]

[13] Now, the lowest of the superior intellectual substances are those who receive the order of divine providence from a divine source, as it is knowable in particular causes. These are put immediately in charge of human affairs. Hence, Dionysius says of them: "this third order of spirits commands, in turn, the human hierarchies."[11] By human affairs we must understand all lower natures and particular causes which are related to man and which fall to the use of man, as is clear from the foregoing.[12]

[14] Of course, there is a certain order among these. For in human affairs there is a common good which is, in fact, the good of a state or a people,[13] and this seems to belong to the order of *Principalities*. Hence, Dionysius says, in the same chapter, that the name *Principality* suggests "a certain leadership along with sacred order." For this reason, mention is made of "Michael the Prince of the Jews," and of "a Prince of the Persians and a Prince of the Greeks" (Dan. 10:13, 20). And so, the arrangement of kingdoms and the changing of domination from one people to another ought to belong to the ministry of this order. Also, the instruction of those who occupy the position of leaders among men concerning matters pertinent to the administration of their rule seems to be the concern of this order.

[15] There is also a type of human good which does not lie in the community, but pertains to one person as such; whose profit is not confined to one but is available to many. Examples are the things to be believed and practiced by all and sundry, such as items of faith, of divine worship, and the like. This pertains to the *Archangels*, of whom Gregory

---

10. *Ibid.*

11. *Ibid.*, IX, 2 (PG, 3, col. 260).

12. See above, ch. 71.

13. See Aristotle, *Nicomachean Ethics*, I, 2 (1094b 8).

says: "they announce the most important things."[14] For instance, we call Gabriel an Archangel, because he announced the Incarnation of the Word to the Virgin, for the belief of all.

[16]   Still another human good is pertinent to each person individually. This type of good belongs to the *Angels*; of whom Gregory says: "they announce less important things."[15] So, they are said to be "guardians of men," according to the Psalm (90:11): "He hath given His angels charge over thee, to keep thee in all thy ways." Hence, Dionysius says that the Archangels are intermediate between the Principalities and the Angels, having something in common with both: with the Principalities, "in so far as they have charge of leading the lower angels," and this is as it should be, for in human affairs private goods should be allotted on the basis of the things that are common; and in common with the Angels, because "they make announcements to the Angels and through the Angels to us," and the function of the Angels is to make known to men "the things that pertain to them, in accord with what is proper to each man."[16] For this reason, too, the last order takes the common name for its own special one; that is to say, because it has the duty of making announcements immediately to us. That is also why the name Archangel is composed of both names, for Archangels are called, as it were, Principal Angels.

[17]   However, Gregory assigns a different ordering to the celestial spirits; for he numbers the Principalities among the intermediate spirits, immediately after the Dominations, while he puts the Virtues among the lowest, before the Archangels.[17] But to people who consider the matter carefully the two ways of ordering them differ but slightly. In

14. St. Gregory, *In Evangelium*, homil. 34 (*PL*, 76, col. 1250).
15. *Ibid.*
16. Pseudo-Dionysius, *De coelesti hierarchia*, IX, 2 (*PG*, 3, col. 257).
17. St. Gregory, *In Evangelium*, homil. 34 (*PL*, 76, col. 1249).

fact, according to Gregory, Principalities are called, not those put in charge of peoples, but "who are given leadership even over good spirits," as if they held first position in the execution of the divine ministrations. He says, indeed, that "to be put in the position of leader is to stand out as first among the rest." Now, we said that this characteristic, in the previously given arrangement, belongs to the order of Virtues. But, according to Gregory, the Virtues are those related to certain particular operations, when in some special case outside the general order something has to be done miraculously. On the basis of this meaning, they are quite appropriately put in the same order with the lowest ones.

[18] Moreover, both ways of ordering them can find support in the words of the Apostle. For he says: "Sitting Him," that is, Christ, "on His right hand in heavenly places, above all principality, and power, and virtue, and dominion" (Eph. 1:20–21). It is clear that in the ascending order of this list he placed Powers above Principalities, and the Virtues above these, and the Dominations over these. Now, this is the order that Dionysius kept. However, to the Colossians, in speaking of Christ, he says: "whether thrones, or dominations, or principalities, or powers, all things were created by Him and in Him" (Col. 1:16). In this text it appears that, starting with Thrones and going downward, he placed under them the Dominations, under them the Principalities, and under these the Powers. Now, this is the order that Gregory retained.

[19] Mention is made of the Seraphim in Isaias (6:2, 6); of the Cherubim in Ezechiel 1 (3ff.); of the Archangels in the canonical Epistle of Jude (9): "When Michael the archangel, disputing with the devil, etc."; and of the Angels in the Psalms, as we have said.

[20] There is also this common feature in all ordered powers, that all lower ones act by virtue of the higher power. Hence, what we explained as pertaining to the order of Seraphim all the lower orders carry out through the power

of the Seraphim. And the same conclusion should be applied to the other orders, too.

Chapter 81.

ON THE ORDERING OF MEN AMONG THEMSELVES AND TO OTHER THINGS

[1]   As a matter of fact, human souls hold the lowest rank in relation to the other intellectual substances, because, as we said above,[1] at the start of their existence they receive a knowledge of divine providence, wherein they know it only in a general sort of way. But the soul must be brought to a perfect knowledge of this order, in regard to individual details, by starting from the things themselves in which the order of divine providence has already been established in detail. So, the soul had to have bodily organs by which it might draw knowledge from corporeal things. Yet, even with such equipment, because of the feebleness of its intellectual light, man's soul is not able to acquire a perfect knowledge of the things that are important to man unless it be helped by higher spirits, for the divine disposition requires this, that lower spirits acquire perfection through the higher ones, as we showed above.[2] Nevertheless, since man does participate somewhat in intellectual light, brute animals are subject to him by the order of divine providence, for they participate in no way in understanding. Hence it is said: "Let us make man to our own image and likeness," namely, according as he has understanding, "and let him have dominion over the fishes of the sea, and the fowls of the air, and the beasts of the earth" (Gen. 1:26).

[2]   Even brute animals, though devoid of understanding, have some knowledge; and so, in accord with the order of divine providence, they are set above plants and other things

1. See above, ch. 80.
2. See above, ch. 79.

that lack knowledge. Hence it is said: "Behold I have given you every herb bearing seed upon the earth, and all trees that have in themselves seed of their own kind, to be your meat, and to all the beasts of the earth" (Gen. 1:29–30).

[3] Moreover, among things utterly devoid of knowledge one thing comes under another, depending on whether the one is more powerful in acting than the other. Indeed, they do not participate in anything of the disposition of providence, but only in its execution.

[4] Now, since man possesses intellect, sense, and bodily power, these are interrelated within him by a mutual order, according to the disposition of divine providence, in a likeness to the order which is found in the universe. In fact, corporeal power is subject to sense and intellectual power, as carrying out their command, and the sensitive power is subject to the intellectual and is included under its command.

[5] On the same basis, there is also found an order among men themselves. Indeed, those who excel in understanding naturally gain control, whereas those who have defective understanding, but a strong body, seem to be naturally fitted for service, as Aristotle says in his *Politics*.[3] The view of Solomon is also in accord with this, for he says: "The fool shall serve the wise" (Prov. 11:29); and again: "Provide out of all the people wise men such as fear God . . . who may judge the people at all times" (Exod. 18:21–22).

[6] Now, just as in the activities of one man disorder arises from the fact that understanding follows the lead of sensual power, while the sensual power is dragged down to the movement of the body by virtue of some disorder of the body, as is evident in the case of men who limp, so also does disorder arise in a human government, as a result of a man getting control, not because of the eminence of his understanding, but either because he usurps dominion for himself by bodily strength or because someone is set up as a

3. See Aristotle, *Politics*, I, 5 (1254b 25).

ruler on the basis of sensual affection. Nor is Solomon silent on this kind of disorder, for he says: "There is an evil that I have seen under the sun, as it were by an error proceeding from the face of the prince: a fool set in high dignity" (Eccles. 10:5–6). But disorder of this kind does not exclude divine providence; it comes about, indeed, with divine permission, as a result of the deficiency of lower agents, just as we explained in connection with other evils.[4] Nor is the natural order entirely perverted by such disorder, for the dominion of fools is weak unless strengthened by the counsel of the wise. Hence it is said in Proverbs (20:16): "Designs are strengthened by counsels, and wars are to be arranged by governments"; and again: "a wise man is strong, and a knowing man stout and valiant: because war is managed by due ordering, and there shall be safety when there are many counsels" (Prov. 24:5–6). And since he who gives counsel rules the man who takes counsel, and in a sense governs him, it is said in Proverbs (17:2): "a wise servant shall rule over foolish sons."

[7]   So, it is evident that divine providence imposes order on all things; thus, what the Apostle says is certainly true: "the things which are of God are well ordered" (Rom. 13:1).

Chapter 82.

THAT LOWER BODIES ARE RULED BY GOD THROUGH CELESTIAL BODIES

[1]   Now, just as there is a difference between higher and lower intellectual substances, so also is there such a difference between corporeal substances. But intellectual substances are ruled by the higher ones, since the disposition of divine providence descends proportionally to the lowest, as we have said already.[1] Therefore, on a like basis, the lower bodies are ordered through the higher ones.

4. See above, ch. 71.
1. See above, ch. 78ff.

[2]   Again, the higher a body is in place, the more formal is it found to be. And even the place of a lower body reasonably follows this rule, since it is the function of form to limit, just as it is of place. In fact, water is more formal than earth, air than water, fire than air. But the celestial bodies are superior in place to all bodies. So, they are more formal than all the others, and, therefore, more active. So, they act on the lower bodies; thus, the lower ones are disposed by them.

[3]   Besides, that which is in its nature perfected without contrariety is more universal than that which is not perfected in its nature without contrariety. Indeed, contrariety arises from the various things that determine and contract a genus; hence, in the realm of understanding, because it is universal the species of contraries are not contraries, for they may co-exist. But celestial bodies are perfected without any contrariety in their natures, for they are neither light nor heavy, neither hot nor cold. However, lower bodies are not perfected in their natures without some contrariety. Their motions also demonstrate this, for there is nothing contrary to the circular motion of the celestial bodies, and, consequently, there can be no violence in regard to them; but there are contraries to the motion of lower bodies, namely, downward motion as opposed to upward motion. So, celestial bodies are possessed of more universal power than lower bodies. But universal powers move particular ones, as is evident from what we have said.[2] Therefore, celestial bodies move and dispose lower bodies.

[4]   Moreover, it was shown above[3] that all things are ruled through intellectual substances. But celestial bodies are more like intellectual substances than are other bodies, because the former are incorruptible. They are also nearer to them, inasmuch as they are moved immediately by them, as we showed above.[4] Therefore, the lower bodies are ruled by them.

2. See above, ch. 78.
3. *Ibid.*
4. *SCG*, II, ch. 70; III, ch. 80.

[5]   Furthermore, the first source of motion must be something immutable. So, the things that are nearest to immutability should be movers of the rest. But celestial bodies
approach more closely to the immutability of the first
source than do lower bodies, for they are not moved except
by one kind of motion, namely, local motion; while other
bodies are moved by all the species of motion. Therefore,
the celestial bodies move and govern the lower bodies.

[6]   Again, the first in any genus is the cause of members
which are posterior. Now, in regard to all other motions,
the first is the motion of the heavens; first of all, of course,
because local motion is first among all motions. This is so
in regard to time, for it alone can be perpetual, as is proved
in the *Physics* VIII.[5] It is also so in regard to nature, for
without it there cannot be any other kind of motion. In
fact, a thing is not increased unless there be a preceding
alteration by which what was formerly unlike is changed
and becomes like; nor can alteration be accomplished unless there be a preceding local change, since for alteration
to be achieved the agent of alteration must now be brought
closer to the thing altered than it was before. It is also
prior in perfection, because local motion does not change
the thing in regard to any inherent factor but only according to something extrinsic; for this reason it belongs to
an already perfected thing.

Secondly, even among local motions the circular is prior.
And again, in regard to time: because it alone can be perpetual, as is proved in the *Physics*.[6] And in regard to nature:
for it is more simple and unified, since it is not divided into
beginning, middle, and end; rather, the whole motion is
like a middle. And even in perfection: because it is brought
back to its origin.

Thirdly, because only the motion of the heavens is found
always to be regular and uniform, for in the case of the
natural motions of heavy and light things there is an in-

5. Aristotle, *Physics*, VIII, 7 (260b 29).
6. *Ibid.*, 8 (261b 27); note that the point here is that *circular*
    motion is the only perpetual type.

crease in velocity toward the end; in the case of violent motion, there is an increase in retardation. So, the motion of the heavens must be the cause of all other motions.

[7] Besides, as the absolutely immobile is to unqualified motion, so is the immobile, that is qualified by a given motion, related to that motion. Now, that which is absolutely immobile is the source of all motion, as we proved above.[7] So, what is immobile in regard to alteration is the source of all alteration. Now, the celestial bodies, alone among bodily things, are inalterable; their condition shows this, for it is always the same. So, the celestial body is the cause of all alteration in things that are changed by alteration. Now, in these lower bodies alteration is the source of all motion, for through alteration a thing achieves increase and generation, whereas the agent of generation is a self-mover in the local motion of heavy and light things. Therefore, the heavens must be the cause of all motion in these lower bodies.

[8] Thus, it is evident that lower bodies are ruled by God through the celestial bodies.

Chapter 83.

EPILOGUE TO THE PRECEDING CHAPTERS

[1] Now, from all the things that have been pointed out we may gather that, as far as the planning of the order to be imposed on things is concerned, God disposes everything by Himself.[1] And so, in his commentary on the text of Job 34:13 ("What other hath He appointed over the earth?") Gregory says: "Indeed, He Who created the world by Himself rules it by Himself."[2] And Boethius says, in

---

7. *SCG,* I, ch. 13.
1. See above, ch. 77.
2. St. Gregory, *Moralia,* XXIV, 20 (*PL,* 76, col. 314).

Consolation of Philosophy III: "God disposes all things of Himself alone."[3]

[2] But, in regard to the execution, He orders the lower things through the higher ones, and the bodily things through the spiritual ones.[4] Hence, Gregory says, in his fourth *Dialogue:* "in this visible world nothing can be ordered except through an invisible creature."[5] And the lower spirits are ordered through the higher ones.[6] Hence, Dionysius says that "the heavenly intellectual essences first give divine illumination to themselves, and then bring us manifestations which are above us."[7] Also, the lower bodies are ordered by the higher ones.[8] Hence, Dionysius says that "the sun brings generation to visible bodies, and stimulates them to life itself, and nourishes, increases and perfects, cleanses and renews."[9]

[3] Moreover, Augustine speaks on all these points together, in the Book III of *The Trinity:* "As the grosser and lower bodies are ruled in a certain order by means of the subtler and more powerful ones, so are all bodies by means of the rational spirit of life, and also the sinful rational spirit of the sinner by the righteous rational spirit."[10]

3. Boethius, *De consolatione philosophiae*, III, prose 12 (PL, 63, col. 777).

4. See above, ch. 78.

5. St. Gregory, *Dialogus*, IV, 6 (PL, 77, col. 329).

6. See above, ch. 79.

7. Pseudo-Dionysius, *De coelesti hierarchia*, IV, 2 (PG, 3, col. 180).

8. See above, ch. 82.

9. Pseudo-Dionysius, *De divinis nominibus*, IV, 4 (PG, 3, col. 697–700).

10. St. Augustine, *De Trinitate*, III, 4 (PL, 42, col. 873).